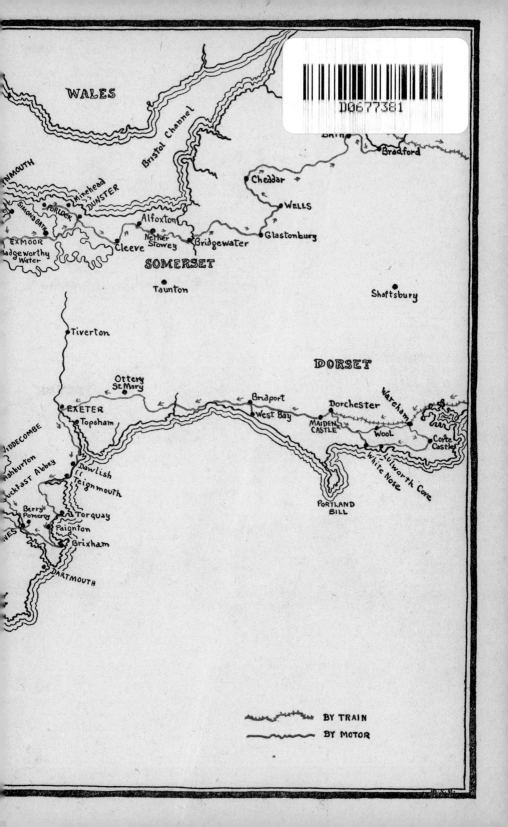

ENGLISH SPRING

BY CHARLES S. BROOKS

WITH PICTURES DRAWN IN PEN AND INK

BY MARY SEYMOUR BROOKS

Dunster Castle.

HARCOURT, BRACE AND COMPANY

NEW YORK

914.2
B79e

PRINTED IN THE UNITED STATES OF AMERICA
BY QUINN & BODEN COMPANY, INC., RAHWAY, N. J.

Typography by Robert S. Josephy

Dedicated by

CHARLES AND MARY BROOKS

to

MARY COFFINBERRY BROOKS

CONTENTS

ILLUSTRATIONS

ENGLISH SPRING

- Parliament Towers -

I. ON THE COUNTER

WE DEMAND honest dealing when we buy a book. An author must show us at the start an inventory of the merchandise he offers. He must refrain from outrageous hawking and confine himself within the decent bounds of commerce. He must apprise us of the scope and purpose of his work, before we lay our money on the counter.

With consistent candor, therefore, we confess at once that this present volume contains no more than a journey in the west of England. Our path is but a homely trail, worn by many feet, from Dorchester around to Bath by way of the rugged coast, with snug villages and open moorland, a city, and now and then a harbor by the windy sea—such sights as lie on a common course and need no scrambling into hardship. We offer you a cathedral here and there, if it can be visited without too much trouble. In fair weather we shall

3

find a seat in the open cloister where we shall hear the organ sounding through the empty vaults.

We shall discover frequent castles on our journey and be led around with a tiresome patter of fact and legend until we are too weary to care whether it was time or disaster that overthrew their walls. But the reader will at least have com-fort that we are as sleepy as himself. In such tiresome circumstance we have found it best to pay the fee at once and to escape to open air while the guide's voice goes droning on among the kings and saints of England. For there was never yet a musty Edgar or a broken Dunstan who was worth the singing of the wind on a Devon upland.

In our narrative we shall see fishing boats lying in the mud as they wait for a turn of tide, harbor lights winking in the evening mist, distant ships that smudge the horizons of the night. There will be hawthorns and laburnums, green valleys and flowering hedges such as only England offers in the springtime. From a Devon tor we shall find mist cradled in the hollows—little reservoirs of fog that await a signal from the ocean to confuse the liners from New York. We shall see a tumbled world about us in whose sterile chaos only devils raise a crop. From the cliffs of Cornwall we shall discover the stormy waters that bury the lands of Lyonesse where Tristram loved Iseult.

For two months we shall hear each night the pounding of the sea and wind; and we shall dream of Frobisher and Drake in all these harbors of the west, of their excursions towards Cathay, and of the taverns where they clinked their pewter jugs. We shall find Rome on the rim of Devon, and Saxons and Danes pillaging its coast. Phoenician vessels will lift their anchors in Mount's Bay beneath Marazion and sail eastward under colored sails.

We shall recount Celtic legends that are older than the seven hills upon the Tiber, tales that were already stale when Troy was first destroyed; but we shall be well advised that the anecdote of any local witch, however famous, must not be stretched too far. And if the devil threatens to drown all Christian churches in the sea, he must do his mischief promptly before we doze. Now and then there will be breaks in our journey at the shrine of genius, but sleepy persons may skip without offense. Like that radio in your parlor, dear reader, we also may be silenced.

As occasion prompts us, we shall urge our pen to sentimental description. Or perhaps we shall find that such labored outbursts entail too much sucking of our pencil. Wherever we discover, therefore, that better writers have gone on the journey ahead of us, we shall quote from their more vivid pages—doing this for our own ease and in the assurance that our otherwise empty platter will be reënforced to a wholesome meal.

Ours is a song of beef and cabbage in a loaf, an epic of boiled potatoes and a mess of English sweets. It is a tale of clotted cream and its tightened belt, of old inns with crumbling stairways, of an open fire when rain is splashing on the windows. Of rain we shall have much to say—of fog, also, and of wind and rattling casements. We shall write of muddy boots and draughty corridors, of aspirin and sneezing, of coal that will not burn, of an old umbrella whose ribs grew weary with incessant work. Sometimes, in mercy, even in a drizzle, we left it hooked upon our arm in order that it might have time to rest.

There are two of us, Mary and I, on this journey. Mary carries a sketching pad, for use in England's transitory gleams of sunlight. Whenever our text runs for several pages without a picture, shrewd critics will understand that the day was rainy and so cold that her stiff fingers could not hold a pencil.

These are the small wares upon our counter. It were better thrift, dear reader, to take the little lady to the *talkies* where there is noise and excitement at half our price.

A Devon Village.

II. OUR UMBRELLA RESTS

FROM A lunch cart on the platform of Waterloo Station we bought a bar of sweet chocolate and a package of what the English call biscuits; and from the train guard two bottles of Bass. We had with us, also, a jar of spicy cheese that was left from a steamer basket.

These were our lunch as we slipped past the dingy roofs of London until the parliament towers and all the city fell behind us—ten thousand dirty buildings in a row along the track, as if they waited for a public bath to open on the near-by Thames. Each building, already stripped, had hung out its shirt and socks on a backyard clothesline. If one might judge by the number of the chimney-pots of London, he would think that every room was cozy with a fire. Yet in

an excellent hotel we had shivered for a week. It must be
that they are downward vents alone, and of a one-way traffic
to admit dampness to the rooms below.

The morning had been wet and dismal; but, presently, as
we gained the green meadows of open country, the sun realized that it must do its bit in brightening the start of our
two months of holidays and, of a consequence, it pushed
out its dripping head and smiled. On the instant, as when
Midas touched dull metal, the Surrey hills were swept with
yellow light.

It was Friday, the twenty-fourth of April.

If an American shall announce to his neighbors a trip to
the British Isles in this season of the year, he will invariably
be met by Browning's phrase—"Oh, to be in England now
that April's there." And this worn quotation is always offered with an air of fresh discovery. There is no offense in
saying a trite thing if it is done modestly, but the charge is
serious when one appears to explore the deepest waters of
his brain and then pulls up only a dead fish.

The fact is that spring does frequently come to the British
Isles in April—at least to the eye and nose, when the meadows are the greenest of the year and the hedges are in blossom. And yet, taken too literally, Browning's verse will get
a tourist into trouble. Considering the poet as a reliable
almanac, he will expect the clemency of an American June
and will set out from home too jauntily in cotton. "The
chaffinch sings on the orchard bough." It sounds as if summer had already leased the valleys. We would be shirking
our responsibility did we not adhere to truth, no matter to
what vulgar domestic depth it leads us. Let us whisper in
your ear, dear reader, to save a blush. Wool undergarments
are best in an English spring. And if your ankles are thin
enough to stand the over-load, let's have them down to the
shoe tops. A hair shirt is not martyrdom northwards of the

Channel, even in August, and we are surprised that it is attacked in the King James version.

Under the persuasion of previous experience I put into my bag what I am pleased to call my fuzzies. And after the first hour of London drizzle, I found them comforting—out of doors where it was cold, and indoors where it was colder still. For in English houses there is a stale chilliness that has been collecting poisonous microbes as its hobby. Even a scratchy surface has its advantage when an anaemic fire is toying with the little lumps of a shallow grate. My only regret was that my pajamas were not, also, the product of an honest sheep. I wore my fuzzies through two months of English spring, and did not discard them until I was lodged in the steam heat of the White Star *Majestic,* sailing for New York.

As regards Browning, we announce it as a fact that, after he had written his praise of England's April, he extended the lease of his palace on the Grand Canal.

The particular April of our present travels was reputed to be the wettest and the coldest of the British annals. Rain became a jest in the London newspapers, and the *Times* quoted Browning with a tongue in its cheek. Holiday resorts canceled their advertisements of "Sunny Days for Whitsun." Merchants, accustomed to sell gauze frippery for this occasion, loaded their windows with rubber coats. He was a lucky tourist this year who stocked his bag with overshoes and wool, together with such salves and nostrums as guard him from catarrh and rheumatism. Our umbrella, like a wise old squirrel, suspected this weather from the very start; for its ribs got twisted at Brown's Hotel when we tried to lift it at the door; and now, in our railway carriage, it hung despondent from a hook and dropped its tears upon the cushions.

We had sunlight, however, as far as Winchester—white clouds drifting in a field of blue—and we were already persuading ourselves that all dirty weather was behind us, when again the windows of our compartment were splashed with rain. Was the sun's brief glance pure irony? Or did it think it but decent manners, knowing that our holidays had started, to march us out of London with a last gesture of hospitality? Certainly, just as soon as we were off its metropolitan premises, it waved good-by and left us to shift for ourselves as best we could.

The train ran through Winchester in a deep cutting with a fringe of trees on top, so we had no more than a brief glance at the cathedral's towers. A circus builds a canvas wall around its animals and clowns, and offers its entertainment only to those who have paid their dollar; and Winchester's shrewd hotels acted on this hint.

Before leaving home we had considered the best mode of traveling through western England. And we rejected at once the hiring of a motor-car.

There are persons, perhaps, who can travel by motor with sufficient restraint to see the country traversed. Such tourists will be content to nibble at the roads, to stop wherever a pretty village shows itself, to be unpersuaded by an engine that begs for speed and distance. But to most of us there is a very devil in a motor that always urges us from one village to the next. It suggests continually that another inn is more commodious than the hostelry at hand, that a far-off valley is greener than the one before our window. A motor holds a million explosions in its gas-tank and it is its business to boost us on. After a few days of this, a puncture is a relief. Out one climbs, uncertain at first whether his stiff legs will hold him—to rejoice finally at the delay. He tastes the clean air and feels the wind. He sits on a wall and swings his feet. He smokes his pipe in sunlight. If one were entirely wise he would seek a car of battered casings and find an intermittent England as each of them exploded. I know a man who discovered a certain charming vista of the Cotswold hills when his faulty ignition sputtered into silence. Another tourist of my acquaintance would have been unaware of Shere hard by the Pilgrims' Way had it not been for a few specks of dirt in the petrol. While the pipes were being cleaned he stretched his paralytic legs, and his hour was entertained by the music of a stream that flowed beneath the village bridge.

And the very purr of a motor makes a tourist lazy until, roused at last from coma, he discovers that the day has advanced to twilight and that all the lovely hamlets are behind him, only half regarded through his drowsy eyes. That largest building where he squinted upwards from his cushions was a cathedral, yet he passed it like a common distillery. The far-off Channel was seen only through his open mouth. Which of us, moreover, can afford to hold a motor idle when we spend a week at some delightful village? A motor makes travel too easy, and it is to the mishaps of a shabby inn that memory turns with sharpest pleasure.

Bicycles were an obvious suggestion. But Devon and Cornwall are too hilly for pedaling. Even the down grades offer no relief, as they are too dangerously steep for the brakes to hold. The roads, also, are crowded between walls and hedges. And they are infested with public buses that run at a mad speed and squeeze the hedges on a turn.

We thought of a trip afoot, but this mode of travel offered difficulties in the transport of luggage. A man is content with a change of shirt and underwear; but a woman needs a relay of fussy clothing and a hot-water bottle for a chilly night. Distances are long, moreover, in the west of England, and there was danger we would be caught by darkness on lonely roads. And again, the hills are too steep. For my instruction, when our trip was planned, I laid out a set of ordnance maps and checked the rise and fall of roads. Even in contemplation I grew short of breath as I considered the thousand-foot lift of the Porlock and the Countisbury hills.

"The sun shone, the bees swept past me singing; and I too sang, shouted, World, world, I am coming!" This is from Maurice Hewlett, but he was doubtless a youngster at the time of his excursion to the mountains.

So we agreed that we would settle on no one means of locomotion, and that we would travel each stage of our journey as its circumstance should dictate—afoot, by hired motor, by public bus or railway train, by whichever of these conveyances was most convenient. We would proceed to Dorchester by train, and make our start with a touch of Dorset before entering the western country.

At Southampton we had from our carriage window a view of broad water and a distant glimpse of ocean funnels. A far-off whistle in the mist was a liner starting for New York. The New Forest was smeared in downpour. At Bournemouth we threw off a few passengers and stuffed their luggage through the windows. On the station platform posters announced pathetically that here was a spot where Whitsun holidays might be spent in sunlight, but water was dripping from the sodden cardboard. Bournemouth was enormous— a sprawling district of hotels and obvious amusement, as if all of London fetched down its pail in August.

We crossed the edge of Hardy's Egdon Heath, which was appropriately clad in sullen weather out of compliment to the miseries of Tess who once had lived upon it; and presently our locomotive signaled to Dorchester that we had come.

And now the sun had another change of heart. As we climbed down from our railway carriage, it thrust out again its watery head and smiled a welcome. "I have no more than a half hour to spend on you," it seemed to say, "but if you two people will be good enough to step lively, I'll see you to your hotel before I turn on the cold tap again."

High West Street
Dorchester

III. WE STEP LIVELY

DORCHESTER appeared to possess only one motor-cab for station use, and by the time our luggage was hoisted through the window and piled around us, it had departed with brisker passengers.

"How far is the King's Arms?" I asked.

"No more'n a mile."

"And our bags?"

"Bill!"

A lanky boy, whose bolts needed tightening, pushed up a two-wheeled truck. On this he heaped our luggage. He then leaned heavily against it and we followed afoot.

My diary informs me that we passed a brewery from which issued a grateful odor of hops, and presently an avenue of trees that were a border of the denser town. It informs me that we entered a street of business and passed an ancient almshouse. Dorchester seemed to be a charming little city. But whether this impression arose entirely from the town's beauty in the fleeting sunlight, from the brisk traffic along its row of shops, or was the result of the high spirits that marked our travel's start, I must leave in question. On this Friday afternoon something of Saturday's holiday was already afloat. Housewives tried their thumbs on melons or pointed stubby umbrellas at upper shelves.

Dorchester's start was Roman, but it does not show its antiquity at first glance. What dowager today will dress in the flounces of her youth? And cities, also, change their house-fronts and are always new.

At the top of the street we came to a church and turned a corner to the King's Arms. It had a trim little entrance hall, with a glimpse of firelight in a lounge beyond.

"A double room," I said.

"Sorry," a girl at the wicket answered, "but every room is occupied."

"Is there another good hotel?" I asked.

The girl was not certain. It was evident she was not paid to advertise a rival inn. There was an Antelope Hotel up the street. We might try it.

We loaded the truck again. The lanky boy leaned his loose bolts against it as before. Up the hill he pushed it and around the corner. Here our luck was better. We were given an excellent room with windows on South Street.

Both of these hotels have a place in Hardy's novels. For Dorchester, as every reader knows, is Casterbridge—the novelist's home until his death and the center of his Wessex. No tourist enters Dorchester without a volume of Hardy in his pocket. The volume in mine was "The Mayor of Casterbridge." It was at the King's Arms, in an early chapter, that the banquet was given with Mayor Henchard in the chair at the peak of his prosperity. Time has swept away the Three Mariners across the street. The Antelope has a less important place in the story as the place at which Henchard appointed a meeting with Lucetta. But Mayor Henchard's great house must have been somewhere opposite our windows, and the sound of the feet on the busy thoroughfare, as we unpacked our bags, were old echoes from the days when his prosperity endured.

Below our window was the town pump—a tawdry pillar forced from business by the tavern. There is a legend that a passage once led under ground from this pump to the Maiden Castle several miles outside the city. Wherever one travels beyond the Atlantic he finds tunnels of this sort. Every stronghold in Europe has one, every English inn on the Channel once suspected of Popish plots. Legendary tunnels are as plentiful as Elizabeth's four-post beds. We have looked down a well at Rye for Jesuits. We have scrambled to the innermost recesses of Capri's Blue Grotto, seeking vainly the passage of the Pirate Barbarossa to his castle on the heights above. Now and then, just to whet discovery, one of these old tunnels proves to be real, like the one towards Cumae that Dante used in his Inferno. This one at Dorchester must have been the length of the Simplon, and is of course absurd.

And now the rain fell again. I ventured to complain of this to our landlady. "My barometer," I said, "still points to fair weather, even when I shake it."

The good woman sniffed. "I never knew one of those things that was worth its salt," she answered. "We used to have one in the hotel, and folks were always thumping it to make it work. You can tell better that rain's coming by the creaking of your joints."

"And what do the joints say now?" I asked.

My question was immodest, for no lady will discuss her legs with strangers.

"There is a saying in these parts," she replied evasively, "that a Friday's rain means wet weather through the week-end."

At dinner we noticed several young women together at a table, and, on inquiry, learned that they were a concert company that had come to town for a Saturday's performance. After the sweet, they went to the parlor of the inn where one of them played a waltz of Chopin. Whether the player's fingers were stiff with cold, or whether certain of the ivories were divorced from the strings, our diary does not say; but the slippery runs stumbled now and then. These concert companies are distinctive of England. This one at Dorchester was in the first flush of youth, but often they travel with a cough and limp.

In the inn's lounge there was the smallest of all possible fires in the smallest of all possible hobs, and against this we huddled close without warming our northern suburbs. The unnourished flame really needed no iron grill to hold it in. It sucked languidly at a single piece of coal, as if it knew the tiny morsel was its dinner and its breakfast. It made no more effort to escape than a tired horse would make to wriggle from its nose-bag.

And now, presently, there was no patter of rain on the pavement and we set out to see the town in the April twilight.

We were standing undecided at the curb when a man crossed the street and asked us if we had seen Dorchester's remnant of Roman wall. As we had not, he volunteered to guide us to it, as his own course lay in that direction. With shutters up, he was on his way to dinner.

We passed a half-timbered house where Judge Jeffreys had held his Bloody Assizes. No other person fills quite so black a page of English history; and his court, set to stamp out treason against James II, would fit the cruelest days of the Spanish Inquisition. We shall run against this rebellion of Monmouth's in several towns, for its consequence defiled all the west of England.

At the top of the street we came to the Roman wall. There is the merest fragment of it, and it is built into a modern wall that gives privacy to the city garden of a dentist. It was quite confusing—imperial Rome and present-day bicuspids. We were asked to think of the Latin centuries in the presence of prophylactic brushes. A buzz from a window was a molar being ground away. Time has strange companions in its wallet.

"Have you seen the Amphitheatre?" our guide now asked. "It's but a mile and is worth the walk."

Our acquaintance directed us, then wished us good night, as he lived near by. We followed what is called the West Walk, a pebble path under an arbor of fine trees that separates the town from the lawns and gardens of a public park. Here are a bowling green and paths rambling in a grove. The West Walk follows the course of the now demolished Roman wall.

The soft colors of the twilight had faded into dusk when we came to the Amphitheatre, just beyond the edge of town. As seen from the road, the great mound might have been the city's reservoir of water; but, when we had scrambled up its grassy embankment, we found a huge dry hollow at the center, cropped close by sheep. The pit was large enough to be a football field. The inner slope was marked in terraces where Rome's provincial populace had sat. There must once have been scooped-out caves for animals, but these were smoothed away.

In any light, even of noonday, the Amphitheatre must impress one by its size alone and by its lonely station; but the gathering dust offered also the shadows of the Roman centuries, and the night wind that played across the top was the murmur of the crowd's applause. Almost two thousand years unrolled themselves before us and caught our breath. The heart of Rome beside the Tiber is overlaid with the Renaissance and with trivial modern life; but here on the outskirts of its power, abandoned in the fields of England, one understands the might of Caesar.

In the parlor of the Antelope Hotel, on our return, Chopin was still in torture. We climbed the corkscrew staircase to our room. I turned to the pages of "The Mayor of Casterbridge."

"Listen to this," I said. "Here is Hardy's description of the Amphitheatre as he saw it when a child in the middle of the nineteenth century. It saves my diary trouble." And I read aloud:

" 'The Amphitheatre . . . was to Casterbridge what the ruined Coliseum is to modern Rome, and was nearly of the same magnitude.' " I mumbled down the page and started again. " 'Old people said that at certain moments in the summer time, in broad daylight, persons sitting with a book, or dozing in the arena, had, on lifting their eyes, beheld the slopes lined with a gazing legion of Hadrian's soldiery as if watching the gladiatorial combat; and had heard the roar of their excited voices; that the scene would remain but a moment, like a lightning flash, and then disappear.' "

"Mary, are you awake?" I asked.

There was a half-smothered answer.

"It says here," I persisted, "that a witch was once burned in the Amphitheatre, that it was used for prize fights, but wasn't much good for a cricket ground, as the pit seemed haunted by the witch. Stay awake for just a minute." And I read again:

" 'There still remained under the south entrance excavated cells for the reception of the wild animals and athletes who took part in the games. The arena was still smooth and circular, as if used for the original purpose not so very long ago. The sloping pathways by which spectators had ascended to their seats were pathways yet. But the whole was grown over with grass, which now, at the end of summer, was bearded with withered bents that formed waves under the brush of the wind. . . .' "

"Are you still awake?" I asked.

There was no answer.

Chopin, also, had succumbed to pure fatigue. I put out the light and stood at the open window. There were footsteps on the pavement of the street, a sound inseparable from English towns at night—footsteps that echoed back again the Roman legions in this island of the north.

I have long been meditating an essay on the night sounds of towns and cities. It will contain no more than a fretful paragraph on the American clang of wheels (the jarring advance of street cars and the honk of motors) and will concern itself chiefly with the sounds of Europe when the sun has set. In Catholic districts it will chronicle the bells of night—soft tones far off that assure one of safety in the darkness. It will tell what songs are heard on Italian streets, together with the strumming of romantic strings. In London there is a low moaning across the shadows, as if the city slept in uneasy dreams. And an English village is marked with footsteps—strange patterns that rise and blend and fade away to silence.

South Walk.
Dorchester.

IV. DORCHESTER

OUR DESCRIPTION of this charming county town declines to start. Our stagnation reminds us of a picture by
Doré, in which a cloud of insane fancies flies about Don
Quixote's head. We, too, are plagued by disordered memories which refuse to resolve themselves to sequence. And we
are at one with Cervantes, as we find. "Sitting once in a very
studious posture," he complained, with his paper before
him, his pen in his ear, his elbow on the table, and his cheek
in his hand—he could not make a start. Authors will recognize this position. It is the pest of writing—this start. In
what manner shall we deal with the incidents that lie upon
our path? " 'Pray, look better, sir,' quoth Sancho; 'those
things yonder are no giants, but windmills. . . .' 'It is a
sign,' cried Don Quixote, 'thou art but little acquainted
with adventures.' " This brave method does quite well for
Spain, but in England our feet must touch the ground. A
windmill is still a windmill there.

From the upper windows of Dorchester one can see the

rolling fields of Dorset, and the hills of Devon to the west. A ten-minute walk from the center of the town will convey one to open country. The compactness of this little city has been described by Thomas Hardy. "It is huddled all together," he wrote, "and it is shut in by a square wall of trees, like a plot of garden ground by a box-edging." Dorchester has no suburbs of sprawling houses. It is as compact, adds Hardy, "as a box of dominoes."

Nice people live in Dorchester and in the country roundabout, if one may judge by the wares in the merchants' windows, their wool fabrics and recent styles from Regent Street—if one may judge by the number of the bookshops, and by a general courtesy and the prosperous appearance of the house-fronts. Any comedy of English life could rightly spare an act from London and set it here in Dorchester. It would choose a drawing-room whose windows looked across a garden to the West Walk. It is that kind of town—a little city competent to furnish neighbors to Thomas Hardy.

To the casual eye, Dorchester is modern despite its heritage from Rome. But an almshouse is of Tudor stone and mullioned windows. There are several cottages whose foundations sprout from ancient cobbles. A graveyard, also, is close upon the shops; and its ghosts might employ the midnight by a perusal of boots and riding-breeches. On the line of the demolished Roman walls are long avenues of trees that provide a promenade almost around the town. There are old bridges, a market square and statues of William Barnes, the Dorset poet, and of Thomas Hardy. Except as a name, I am unacquainted with Barnes. Our guidebook, however, quotes him:

> Zoo now I hope his kindly feäce
> Is gone to vind a better pleäce

—whatever that may mean; and, for myself, I shall stick to Thomas Hardy.

There was gay sunlight across our customary kippers and frozen toast on the morning of Saturday, the twenty-fifth of April; but the sky was rimmed with clouds and we walked out quickly to see the town before the daily flood began. Had Noah's ark come to rest in England after its long excursion, the old admiral would have wisely kept its seams calked against a second inundation.

Mary had with her a pad and pencil and, although the brisk wind was chilly to her fingers, she soon halted in High West Street to sketch a picturesque cottage whose walls sprawled along the sidewalk. It was a house of cramped low ceiling, with bow-windows where aspidistras listened to the gossip of the cobbles. With later experience in such stoppages I would learn to read Hardy on the hoof; but, being still unpracticed, I walked on to see the town.

Traversing the streets of last night's exploration, I passed the Amphitheatre and headed into open country towards the Maiden Castle which the guidebook had recommended as a special relic of prehistoric and of Roman work. Maiden Castle is of ancient British origin in the days before Julius Caesar landed, and it occupies what was probably the first site of Dorchester before the town moved down from the hills to be beside the River Frome. For in England, as everywhere, primitive settlements chose the lofty ridges for their safety.

A signboard presently directed me to a lane through extensive meadows, beyond which at a distance of more than a mile there arose high land. I was far from shelter when it began to rain. Ahead of me, I could discern the position of the Maiden Castle on an upper level; but, as the storm was now slapping against my face, I turned about. There was not a tree or any house in sight. My blue nose was threatened with a long stalactite. Hardly was I once more inside the town when the sun came out again. It hinted that I turn once more to the distant hills, but I detected a dishonest purpose in its invitation.

I met Mary in a narrow street.

"How did the picture go?" I asked.

"My fingers are so cold," she answered, but she held up a sketch of the cottage. There were spots of rain on it. "Everytime my teeth chattered," she added, "my pencil got to chattering too."

In the kitchen courtyard of the Antelope Hotel we met our landlady.

"Have you seen Judge Jeffreys' garden?" she asked.

She opened a door from a disordered lumber-room at the rear of the inn. We could peer out upon a small grass plot, a tree and a pebble path that led to the back of the house whose half-timbered front we had seen on High West Street. It was a garden for a student or a poet, not for the cruel minion of a tyrant.

"It was in that house," our landlady volunteered, "that Jeffreys held his Bloody Assizes. But the room where he lodged is now a part of the Antelope. I'll take you to see it."

She gave her pantry keys to a servant. "Mind you use the joint that's cut," she said.

We followed her through a mesh of corridors, up steps and down. Two or more buildings had been laid together for hotel use without any nice adjustment of levels and they fitted badly, like strips of wall-paper whose pattern is askew.

"Watch your step," said our landlady, as we fumbled through the dark.

Quite at the rear of the hotel were two rooms, held by her for private use. In Jeffreys' time these two rooms were one apartment, before a flimsy partition had been thrown across it. At both ends of this now divided room were great fire-places of delicate carving. There was wide planking under foot, such as an honest tree puts down. Great windows looked out upon the kitchen yard. In its early state, before the par-

tition was up and our landlady's bed and dresser had soiled
its magnificence, it was a noble room.

"What a brute Jeffreys was," I said.

"That's what the books say," our landlady answered, but
she said it with a sigh.

For she seemed unwilling to add her condemnation to the
general low estimate of Judge Jeffreys. I fancy that, as his
former lodging was now her own, she had taken the habit
of regarding him somewhat in the light of a distant relative—
a black sheep, it is true, but of an ill fame so exalted as to
bring profit to her Antelope Hotel. He was good for a night's
bed, a dinner and a tip from unhurried tourists. Except for
him, no char-à-bancs would stop, nor would glasses clink in
her bar to help pay off the mortgage. And, as this world goes,
it is better to have an ancestor of widely acclaimed dirty
reputation—a very Judas on one's escutcheon—than to look
back on generations of quiet and decent living that are not
recorded in the books of history. Were all monuments and
oil portraits listed honestly in St. Peter's record, we would
find a good sprinkling of rascals among the saints of our
parks and galleries.

Dorchester, until Hardy's novels gave it a better fame, was
celebrated chiefly through Judge Jeffreys. All of its respectable citizens, from the rise of Rome to the present day, cannot fill so stout a chapter in local guidebooks as this one
miscreant who lodged here for several weeks of wholesale
murder. Nor is our present volume of better taste. As we look
through the rain-splashed windows of Jeffreys' room, we
shall review these events that are of common knowledge.

King Charles II of England entertained his exile at the
Hague in the summer of 1648 in a manner that is not entirely confined to Stuart monarchs; and in April, 1649, a certain Lucy Walters, "brown, beautiful, bold, but insipid,"
gave birth at Rotterdam to a son. The lady had been of such
easy hospitality to her several admirers that it was never en-

tirely proved that Charles was the father; but the English
king, to whom such episodes were not uncommon, chose to
acknowledge young James as his own child. For the lady in-
sisted; and when seed is so widely scattered, who shall deny
that a weed may spring up among the crop?

While James was still a child, the king summoned him
to London and lodged him fittingly with a subsequent mistress, to be reared as a little gentleman of the Stuart model.
Before the end of Charles's reign in 1685, young James had
so far won his father's affection that many titles and commands had been lavished on him, until, at last, as the Duke
of Monmouth, he was a favorite at the English court. During
certain lapses from his father's favor, Monmouth lived in
Holland, where he taught Dutch ladies the English country
dances. He skated with them on the frozen canals and be-
haved to them in private like any prince of the house of
Stuart.

Charles II, although more than suspected of Catholicism,
had been outwardly a friend to the protesting English
churches. His brother, however, James, the Duke of York
and successor to the throne, if Charles died without accepted
heir, was professedly of Roman dogma. In consequence of
this, a party of opinion saw safety to Protestant belief in the
succession of Monmouth, who boasted that he was opposed
to the Pope in birth and in his Dutch education. For had not
the sluices of those canals on which he had skated been
loosed once to stem Rome's invasion? Contrary to this opinion were the English Tories and those Whigs who feared a
disputed succession and the miseries of a civil war. It was
due to the rise and fall of these discordant parties that Monmouth was now petted with extra titles and commands, and
now sent to exile.

King Charles died in February, 1685, still asserting that
Monmouth was but a bastard and declining to disturb his
brother's title to the crown. Monmouth, at his father's death.

was living in Holland in company with a pretty lady and
many exiles and malcontents. It was at their joint persuasion
that he decided to claim the English throne. An attempt was
planned to raise Scotland and the friendly western counties
to his standard. While the northern conflict was still in
doubt, Monmouth sailed with three vessels, escaped the English fleet, and anchored at Lyme Regis on the coast of Dorset.
He was met by a popular enthusiasm which saw in him, not
a renegade of bad morals and less than mediocre ability, but
a Protestant hero who would save England from the Catholic
bigotry of King James and restore its liberty of thought and
worship.

At Lyme's market cross Monmouth raised his standard—
a green banner, marked "Fear Nothing but God." Gunpowder might have been more fittingly substituted, as events
proved.

A rustic army was now gathered around him and he moved
with much vacillation and divided counsel to Taunton,
where he was proclaimed king. And now further indecision
followed until, on July 6, 1685, an English army had been
encamped at Sedgemoor, near Bridgewater, where the pre-
tender's troops were quartered. Monmouth's untrained men
were outmatched, but the battle was still undecided when
Monmouth deserted his command and fled towards the
Hampshire coast, hoping to escape to the continent and the
pretty lady he had left behind. Near Ringwood, beside the
New Forest, he was discovered hiding in a field of grain.
He was taken to London, where he begged for his life by an
offer to turn Catholic, and a death sentence was executed
without delay.

King James determined to stamp out treason and he sent
Jeffreys to the west as the agent of his tyranny. He picked his
man with expert cunning. Jeffreys had risen to royal favor
by his insolent conduct of a criminal court and was already
Lord Chief Justice of the King's Bench and a member of the

peerage. He was of ungovernable ferocity and was an excellent tool for a cruel monarch in any work that promised preferment and dishonest profit.

The Bloody Assizes opened in Winchester, moved next to Dorchester, then to Exeter, to reap finally its greatest harvest in Somerset, where the rebellion had culminated at Sedgemoor. Eight hundred and forty-one persons were transported to Jamaica to be sold as slaves, and the profit arising from their sale was bestowed on those who were in the favor of Jeffreys and the King.

At the time when Monmouth had assumed the royal title at Taunton, a group of little girls had marched out of school to strew flowers upon his path. They had been mustered by a teacher and were as innocent of treason as if they had been released for a picnic in the woods. The Queen's maids of honor now asked permission to extort ransom from the parents of these children, many of whom were less than ten years of age. It was William Penn, the Quaker, who was the agent in this extortion. "He probably silenced the remonstrances of his conscience," writes Macaulay, "by repeating to himself that none of the money which he extorted would go into his own pocket; that if he refused to be the agent of the ladies they would find agents less humane; that by complying he should increase his influence at the court, and that his influence at the court had already enabled him, and might still enable him, to render greater service to his oppressed brethren. . . . If it be said," concludes Macaulay, "that it is incredible that so good a man would have been concerned in so bad an affair, I can only answer that this affair was very far indeed from being the worst in which he was concerned." We may judge from this that the brotherly love of Philadelphia had no progeny in England.

Three hundred and twenty persons were hanged—a greater number of traitors, Jeffreys boasted, than all the predecessors in his office had together hanged since the Norman Con-

quest. "At every spot where two roads met"—we are quoting
again from Macaulay—"on every market-place, on the green
of every large village which had furnished Monmouth with
soldiers, ironed corpses clattering in the wind, or heads and
quarters stuck on poles, poisoned the air, and made the
traveler sick with horror. In many parishes the peasantry
could not assemble in the house of God without seeing the
ghastly face of a neighbor grinning at them over the porch.
The Chief-justice was all himself. His spirits rose higher and
higher as the work went on. He laughed, shouted, joked and
swore in such a way that many thought him drunk from
morning to night."

It is a fashion nowadays to reëstimate historical opinion—
to overthrow a hero or excuse a rascal—and for this reason,
perhaps, Macaulay is accused of blackening a picture. Yet
the evidence against Jeffreys had been believed for two hundred years. If any rich man protested at this general sham-
bles, a corpse was suspended at his park gate for punishment.
Alice Lisle was burned alive for ignorantly sheltering a runaway from Sedgemoor. Little children, less than ten years of
age, died of fever and fright in crowded prisons. A fifth of
those who were shipped to Jamaica to be slaves died upon the
voyage and were thrown from their dungeons to the sharks.
It is perhaps no wonder that Jeffreys' name carries a fouler
connotation than any other name in English history.

But our landlady was still apologetic.

"I don't suppose he was as bad as he is painted," she said.
"You know what evil gossip does. When it's started—" She
lifted her hands in protest. "And, anyway," she continued,
"Judge Jeffreys may have hung his gorgeous robe of office
on that very hook."

"The whole room smells of him," I answered, and we
came away.

Jeffreys was rewarded by King James with the Great Seal

of England "for the many eminent and faithful services which he had rendered to the crown."

In the hallway of the Antelope Hotel there is a pleasanter souvenir than this of Jeffreys. It is a picture of Edmund Kean, with an inscription that he played in Dorchester in the year 1813. This was no humdrum appearance of a provincial tour, but an event of the greatest moment in his career.

As a child, Kean had been a tumbler at fairs and taverns; a little older, a vagabond with a vagabond mother who sold pomatums and perfumes across the country; a cabin-boy on the ocean; a theatrical drudge in small parts in London and through the provinces; then marriage and dismissal. He and his wife walked from Birmingham to Swansea to meet an engagement—two hundred miles, with a baby born on the road—"pale, hungry, and silent, twelve miles a day." In 1808, Kean was "a tolerable actor" on the Dublin stage. At Dumfries he played in a tavern for his shelter—"one auditor, and he paid sixpence." There was an engagement in London as a teacher of boxing, dancing and elocution—slim days with tightened belt—and then to the road again. At last Kean came to Dorchester in 1813, carrying to this city along the dusty roads his son upon his back.

It was this appearance that was to end his tedious years of misery and be the prologue to his tremendous fame as England's great tragedian.

It seems that for several years Drury Lane Theatre of London had been on the verge of failure and that its managers had been casting about for an actor to repair its fortune. In Dorchester, on the fourteenth of November, Mr. Arnold, stage-manager of Drury Lane, witnessed Kean's performance from a private box. The bill was a now-forgotten play called "The Mountaineers" and a pantomime written by Kean himself.

We have the story of the evening in Kean's own words.

"When the curtain drew up," he wrote, "I saw a wretched house: a few people in the pit and gallery, and three persons in the boxes, showed the quality of attraction we possessed. In the stage-box, however, there was a gentleman who appeared to understand acting—he was very attentive to the performance. Seeing this, I was determined to play my best. The strange man did not applaud, but his looks told me that he was pleased. After the play I went to my dressing-room under the stage, to change my dress for the savage, so that I could hear every word that was said overhead. I heard the gentleman of the stage-box ask Lee, who was the manager, the name of the performer who played Octavian. 'Oh,' answered Lee, 'his name is Kean—a wonderful clever fellow. . . .' 'Indeed!' said the gentleman, 'he is certainly very clever, but he is very small.' 'His mind is large; no matter for his height,' said Lee. By this time I was dressed for the savage, and I therefore mounted the stage. The gentleman bowed to me, and complimented me slightly upon my playing. . . . Said the gentleman, 'Will you breakfast with me tomorrow? I shall be glad to have some conversation with you. My name is Arnold; I am the manager of Drury-lane Theatre.' I staggered as if I had been shot. My acting the savage was done for. I, however, stumbled through the part. . . ."

It was on the night of January 26, 1814, that Kean appeared at Drury Lane as Shylock and "roused the audience to almost uncontrolled enthusiasm," assuring his own and the theatre's prosperity. We find a note of this first appearance of Kean as a lead in London in a notice written by William Hazlitt. "Mr. Kean," he wrote, " (of whom report had spoken highly) last night made his appearance at Drury-lane Theatre, in the character of Shylock. For voice, eye, action, and expression, no actor has come out for many years at all equal to him."

Kean, in his London dressing-room, with the applause

still sounding in his ears, what did he think of it? What can a man think when prosperous lightning burns away his rags?

"Where was the theatre in Dorchester where Kean played?" I asked our landlady.

"The building is a warehouse now," she answered. "It's just behind the hotel. But, if you don't mind my suggestion, there's a good cinema down the street where Ramon Novarro is playing."

Thomas Hardy's Birthplace

V. HARDY'S CASTERBRIDGE

THERE are villages of England that are held in almost feudal ownership by a single family. We shall later see Clovelly, whose buildings pay rent to a manor-house on the hill above the Channel. Dunster Castle is the general landlord of a town. But Dorchester is held in another kind of fee. It is the property of Thomas Hardy, as surely as Stratford-on-Avon belongs to Shakespeare.

Hardy's domain is Wessex, a misty kingdom extending from Oxford to Land's End, and Dorchester is its center. He was born near by in a farmhouse among a "few scattered dwellings called Upper Bockhampton . . . a lonely and silent spot between woodland and heathland." The easiest approach to the region of this slight hamlet, avoiding dust and mud, is along the pages of "The Return of the Native" and through the tragedy of Tess.

It was in Dorchester that Hardy attended school. This began in 1849, when he was nine years old. It was a long cross-country walk for a little lad. His memory has recorded men in the stocks, corn-law agitations, mail coaches and No-Popery riots. As a child he saw the Pope burned in effigy in the old Roman Amphitheatre.

Hardy returned to Dorchester in 1883, now a man of forty-three years of age, and built himself a house. In 1885 Max Gate, just outside the city, was completed, and there he lived until his death in the winter of 1928. The site of the house was at first undesirable on account of its newness; "but before the well-diggers had got deeper than three feet they came upon Romano-British urns and skeletons." Originally in a bare setting, the house is now buried in a grove of trees that Hardy planted. In the second story above the drawing-room he wrote "The Woodlanders." He moved his study to the back of the house for the composition of Tess. In a third room above the kitchen "The Dynasts" and all of his later poems were written.

At Hardy's arrival at Max Gate he was already famous as the author of "Far from the Madding Crowd," "The Return of the Native" and "Two on a Tower." "The Mayor of Casterbridge" was written but not yet published. The second Mrs. Hardy has described him as he appeared this year. "His smile was of exceptional sweetness," she writes, "and his eyes were a clear blue-grey. His whole aspect was almost childlike in its sincerity and simplicity, the features being strongly marked, and his nose, as he himself once described it, more Roman than aquiline. The nobility of his brow was striking. When young he had abundant hair of a deep chestnut colour, which later became a dark brown, almost black, until it turned grey. His hands were well shaped, with long deft fingers; his shoulders particularly neat, and his gait light and easy. He walked very rapidly. He was always a spare man, though not actually thin, and he never in his life allowed himself to be weighed, as he said he considered that to be unlucky."

During these forty-five years of residence Hardy was Dorchester's great citizen—a man of simple habits, shunning formal society and publicity, absorbed in his work, but seen frequently on the streets and in the shops and private dwellings—a friendly man, we think, of wide and chance acquaintance, but of a lonely mind and of a melancholy face that was engraved with the hundred tragic plots of his uncompromising pen.

We think he must have been a man of homely ways of thought and action, of little harmless eccentricities that endeared him to his friends; for, when his monument was dedicated in the summer of 1931, Sir James Barrie came down from London to remark as he stood beside the unveiled statue of his old acquaintance, "I hope it has grown so true of him that I shall even know what is in his pocket—probably a piece of string and an old knife." We like to think of this—of Comedy standing beside Tragedy as a life-long friend, and offering in admiration its loving jest.

Hardy's first publication after his return to Dorchester was "The Mayor of Casterbridge," and as we might expect, he sets its plot in the setting he remembered when, as a child, he walked to school across the country—Dorchester, as it appeared just before the middle of the nineteenth century and the repeal of the corn laws. This novel has set Dorchester forever on the map of letters.

Time's industrious fingers have been at work for more
than eighty years since then, but the town's essence must be
the same. We can read its inventory of life and occupation.
"Scythes," he writes, "reap-hooks, sheep-shears, bill-hooks,
spades, mattocks, and hoes at the ironmonger's; beehives,
butter-firkins, churns, milking stools and pails, hay-rakes,
field-flagons, and seed-lips at the cooper's; cart-ropes and
plough-harness at the saddler's; carts, wheel-barrows, and
mill-gear at the wheelwright's and machinist's; horse-embro-
cations at the chemist's. . . ." For today we might add loud-
speakers and motor tires.

In "Hardy's Wessex" by Hermann Lea there is a chapter
on Dorchester—a study of the streets and squares that have a
place in the novels. But a tourist, with his nose in such a
book, will miss the living city and will probably be run
down by a Baby Austin. Joined to the building that was
used by Jeffreys for his Bloody Assizes is the house, "over the
china shop," where Henchard told Susan to take lodging.
Farfrae's fête was held in the West Walk. The two bridges
of Hardy's city may be found, to recall the unhappy men and
women who had leaned against their shabby parapets, to spit
upon the stream and curse their luck. In these bankrupts,
planning death, we find the cause of those melancholy eyes
of Hardy's that saw life at so dark an angle. A tourist can
discover the Ten Hatches Hole where Henchard, in his evil
days, saw his effigy floating in the pool. But change has fallen
on the Corn Market and on the disreputable district of
Mixen Lane where the Furmity Woman and Mother Cux-
som planned the skimmity-ride that killed Lucetta. It is
strange that a little city that lies so bright and happy in
the intermittent sunlight should arouse such tragic fancies—
that these persons who now barter on the streets and go
about with smiling faces should be the legatees of those
former persons who had nought but evil to leave behind.

Hardy pursues so pitilessly the logic of character and circumstance. He sets down the qualities of his people, and by these he dooms them. Even if they seem to escape for some brief interval, fate drives them back to tragedy. In this there is the quality of Greek drama. Jude the child is already Jude the failure. The curse of an evil temper, dispelled by prosperity, returns to Trenchard to drag him in the mud. The d'Urbervilles are in Tess's blood. Elfride Swancourt's ruin is predestined in the soft fiber of her character. In Hardy, life is logical. It is water that seeks its level—a ball that rolls where it finds a slope.

I was recently discussing Hardy with a man whose judgment I respect. "The tragic endings," he said, "as logic goes, are necessary. But life is not as cruel as Hardy paints it. Tragedy is not predetermined by character, for life is not logical. Or, if it be really so, it depends on too many circumstances for us to foretell the end—a tenth unsuspected fact may outweigh the other nine. In every one of us there are dark spots—black streaks enough for disaster—but it is this tenth factor that sometimes saves us. And life, so often, is merciful. We are seldom crushed as Tess and Jude were crushed. The very weakness of our natures saves us from the realization of our defeat. Have you never wept," he asked, "at the calamities of a play or novel, to discover, to your amazement, you yourself have had similar unhappiness and that it has not crushed you? Your life has jogged on and you have had your share of laughter despite the fact that Hardy or Ibsen would have done you in. No," he added, "life is rather hit and miss, illogical, and when we ought to sit and cry, we think of something comical."

Things do seem to be blacker in novels and on the stage than they are in life. A real Becky Sharp would have been quite contented in her final lodgings—would probably have hooked another old gentleman for a happy ending. Lear would have comforted himself at Cordelia's hearth. Not half of Ibsen's ladies would have used poison or the knife.

The realists who write these painful scenes have had many years of practice in composing tragic phrases, in gathering circumstance together to make an audience weep. They are clever showmen, or they would not be successful writers, and they employ every trick of their profession. They know the very moment at which to drop their black curtain when misery has reached its height, choosing to omit an aftermath of forgetfulness and laughter. The fact is that few of us have the ability to think with sustained intensity—to be the heroes of realism's stark and gloomy drama. A jest keeps breaking through our troubles, like this English sun that pops out now and then its head. For most of us, a decent funeral will close a life that, on the whole, has contained more comedy than suffering. After all, it is better to weep with fictitious Tess and Jude, and to laugh with our actual neighbors across the fence. And if we must think of those brooding eyes of Hardy's, let us punctuate our thought with Barrie and his speech that chronicled a jack-knife and a piece of string.

- Corfe Castle -

VI. TO CORFE CASTLE

TOWARDS noon the sky still threatened. It had been our plan, when we sat at home with maps, to hire bicycles at Dorchester for a circular trip to Corfe Castle and return. Roundabout, the distance is rather more than forty miles, mostly on the level, and we thought this could be managed in two days. But our plan, which was so easy in slippers on an ordnance survey, took no account of rain. Time was when maps showed what weather might be expected—Cupid's heads that spat out tempests on the monsters of the deep— but the British survey confines itself to contour lines.

Under a gray sky we bargained for a motor. It was a tour-ing car, converted to the uses of bad weather by sliding windows. These were so small and low that my head soared above them into the motor's dim vault. Only by cramping my breakfast kippers could I get a view.

"Chauffeur," I said, "we are strangers in these parts. Name us the famous sights as we go along. And speak loudly so that you will wake me."

It was just outside of Dorchester that our driver announced Max Gate, the home of Thomas Hardy until his death. I crooked my spine in time to see a wall and, in the briefest of glances, a house set among trees.

"Shall I stop?" our driver asked.

"By no means," I answered. "We can consider it checked off."

Later I bought a colored postcard to supplement the impressions of my cramp—a house of moderate size that offered several bow-windows as possible outlooks for the novelist's desk.

It was in June, 1885, that the Hardys moved in, and almost the first visitor was Robert Louis Stevenson. "I could have got an introduction," he wrote, "but my acquaintance with your mind is already of old date. . . . If you should be busy or unwilling, the irregularity of my approach leaves you the safer retreat." It was the Stevenson of the Bournemouth period. "Treasure Island" had been published as a volume less than two years before. "A Child's Garden of Verses" was just out, and "Dr. Jekyll and Mr. Hyde" was already in contemplation. We wonder what these widely different men talked about. Neither of them, as far as we know, wrote the record of the evening. Stevenson was an invalid, soon to undergo a serious illness, an exile seeking sunlight, high-strung, his eyes looking past the facts of life to far-off Pacific islands, the poet of childhood.

> In winter I get up at night
> And dress by yellow candle-light.

In summer, quite the other way,
I have to go to bed by day.

He was a strange visitor to the author of Wessex tragedy.
"The world is so full of a number of things," Stevenson perhaps remarked. "Yes," was Hardy's answer, "but I wonder if
kings are ever really happy."

I have read "Cakes and Ale" by Somerset Maugham. The
Edward Driffield of this satiric novel is obviously Thomas
Hardy, for he is described as "one of the greatest novelists of
our day." He was the last of the Victorians, "an enormous
figure. His novels have as good a chance of surviving as any
that have been written in the last hundred years." No one
but Hardy quite fits this description. Driffield, moreover,
when the story starts, has just died in circumstance that
accords with Hardy's—a home in a country town that has
been the scene of his youth, a second wife much younger
than himself, England's adulation to its dean of authors,
longevity, novels that concern the district at his door, a
diffidence toward formal society. Even the bow-windows of
Ferne Court where Driffield wrote are matched by the windows of Max Gate.

But at this point Maugham's plot runs into whole-cloth
fiction, and deals with the wish of the second Mrs. Driffield
that certain early passages of her husband's life be suppressed
by his biographer—chiefly his early marriage and the un-
savory character of his first wife. It is she who is the skele-
ton of Maugham's sub-title—the secret that the second Mrs.
Driffield tries to hide in a closet. For the first Mrs. Driffield
had been a barmaid and a woman of such easy immorality
that she had given herself to all of her husband's friends.

This is entirely fiction. The first Mrs. Hardy was the
daughter of a prosperous solicitor of Plymouth and was well
educated in a private school. At her sister's marriage with a
clergyman of Cornwall, she went to live with them to help

in the parish duties, and it was in her new home at St. Juliot, near Boscastle, that Hardy met her when, as a young architect, he was sent by his employer to inspect the church and to draw plans for its repair. She was a young woman of excellent character and taste, resembling somewhat in circumstance, but in circumstance only, the Elfride Swancourt of his "Pair of Blue Eyes." In the early chapters of this novel we find many incidents that are suggested by his visit here at St. Juliot; for these are confirmed by her diary—"music in the evening," excursions to the cliffs of Boscastle. Hardy's poem, "When I Set Out for Lyonnesse," is a further record of this week.

That this young woman of St. Juliot aided Hardy towards his ambition in the field of letters we have excellent proof; for later we find him sending her the broken and disordered sheets of "Desperate Remedies" for her to iron out and smooth for publication. They were married in 1874 and lived together until her death in 1912, when Hardy was about seventy-two years of age—thirty-eight years of married life. These facts are enough, we think, to prove Maugham's tantalizing novel fictitious.

Another character of the story hints at Hugh Walpole, and this doubtless is another stuffed figure quite untrue. Maugham has a habit of using living men for his plots or of digging into recent graves. There was Gauguin of his "Moon and Sixpence." And the murderous lady of "The Letter" is said to be recognized at Singapore. Maugham, challenged for these resemblances, rushed to print not long ago. "We authors of course try to be gentlemen," he wrote, "but we often fail and we must console ourselves by reflecting that few writers of any consequence have been devoid of a certain streak of vulgarity."

We find "Cakes and Ale" contemptible; inasmuch as any reader who will not put himself to the trouble of learning the truth about the first Mrs. Hardy, will be influenced to

think that the facts of her life have been suppressed, even as
the first Mrs. Driffield's life was suppressed. The springs of
his faith will be poisoned by this baffling blend of fact and
fiction, for dirty gossip will always find its audience. He will
conclude that inasmuch as the second Mrs. Driffield was able
to obliterate a barmaid, so perhaps the second Mrs. Hardy
was equally successful as regards her predecessor.

There is a chapter in "Cakes and Ale" that seems to describe Max Gate shortly after Hardy's death—a chapter in
which Driffield's widow displays her husband's desk, his
books and manuscripts, in which she purrs her recollections,
basks in his fame and turns it to her advantage. And in all
this an actual Hardy blends so cunningly with a fictitious
Driffield that we seem to stand inside a cyclorama where
certain figures are partly real but are joined to the painted
creatures of a canvas wall. It is a brilliant but contemptible
book. One wonders if it was read at Max Gate—whether
Hardy's friends all around the world protested at its shoddy
attempt to get a profit out of untrue scandal. We are informed that a parody was written called "Gin and Bitters,"
and that its author removed her gloves to give Maugham the
spanking he deserved. "Life is vulgar," said Maugham. We
would like to have been present in the woodshed.

We were again on our way towards Corfe Castle when a
tall policeman stepped out from a crossroad with lifted hand.
It seems, however, we were not arrested for speeding, and
that he was merely asking for a ride. When we were crossing
the old bridge in the village of Wool, the officer directed our
cramp to a farmhouse.

"Tess lived there," he said, "just after her marriage."

I kinked my kippers and looked through the motor window. It was rather a pretentious dwelling. Hardy refrains
from exact description and contents himself with saying
that the building was once a "portion of a fine manorial

residence, and the property and seat of a d'Urberville, but since its partial demolition a farm-house."

Readers of Tess will remember it was here that she and Angel Clare came directly from their wedding. They will remember the old portraits inside the house that "haunt the beholder afterwards in his dreams." They will recall the necklace that came as a wedding gift and how the man put it around her throat, tucking back her bodice to simulate evening-wear. They will recall how tragedy lurked behind this man and woman all that evening, to break at last upon them when Tess followed his confession with her own.

It was long after noon when we entered the town of Wareham. We ordered food and then sought to warm our chilly fingers at the hearth of the Black Bull Inn. It was a sickly fire and there were, moreover, two English persons squeezed against the grate. They sat whispering together in a refined undertone that disregarded our frozen condition at the back of the rug.

It was at Wareham, probably, that the first Hardys landed from the Isle of Jersey in the fifteenth century.

Wareham was once a seaport on Poole Harbor, but was later silted from salt water, like so many other of the Channel ports. It would scem as if nature, having speculated in real-estate at Southampton and Liverpool, had been in a long trade conspiracy with the ocean to wreck the general Channel's prosperity in favor of those ports where its particular profit lay—dumping sand at Rye, drowning Winchelsea by a tidal wave and otherwise stifling competition. Certainly, during the hour we were at Wareham, we did not suspect that the ocean was so near at hand, gloating at its destruction.

"It is probable that Wareham was originally a riverside stronghold built by the Bronze Age Celts." In the first century of our era the Romans reënforced its walls. During the northern invasions its history is a chronicle of disaster. Sometimes the Danes held it, and sometimes the Saxons, until at last Canute reduced the town to a heap of ruins. King Stephen burned it. It suffered in the civil wars. A Jeremiah would be needed, says our guidebook, to tell of all its lamentations. On this day of April, however, it seemed a pretty little town that had chosen to forget its ancient tragedy.

After lunch we motored to Corfe Castle. It is a remnant of a Norman fortress that was built on the Saxon footings of a hunting lodge. It stands at the top of a steep hill that commands a valley to the sea, and must have been in the later years of the Conquest an important stronghold. Our guidebook informs us that in those days it was "well-nigh impregnable," then goes off on such a rambling history of its adventures from Saxon days to its destruction in the civil wars of parliament and king that, in mercy to a sleepy reader, I skip the digest of its mournful life. It is enough to say that Corfe Castle has been the residence of kings, a prison for kings less fortunate who had lost their crowns, the scene of siege and torture, of murder and destruction.

Today the castle is an interesting old wreck—"no noise, but silence and eternal sleep"—towers without roofs or floors, battlements without a staircase—a few steps that start to climb—casements void of glass, foundations here and there that give no hint as to the sort of buildings that they held. A gatehouse is tumbling down a hill, shattered by the guns of time. Walls have been carted off as from a quarry. There are grasses growing on the dungeon tower; and the meadows, storming up the hillside, are today its last assault. William's impregnable stronghold has been captured by daisies and the blue and yellow blossoms of the spring.

And now, after much scrambling to the hill-top, we braced ourselves against a brisk wind for an extensive view of other hills that rose above us, of a narrow valley to the sea, of cluttered roofs below the castle gate. The village of Corfe,

says our guidebook, lies "at the foot of its Castle like a
faithful hound." Corfe's only life are the sea-birds that
wheel about its barren towers and find their nests in the ivy
of its walls. The few people that wandered up and down the
sloping meadow were obviously looking only for a spot for
a picnic tea. Mary sketched the great tower and dotted the
sea-birds against the sky, while I sat in a corner of a wall
where I was intermittently guarded from the fitful wind. In
picturesque setting and in its suggestion of battles far away,
Corfe is one of the wholly satisfactory English ruins.

- Lulworth Cove -

VII. LULWORTH COVE

OUR RETURN to Dorchester lay not through Wareham,
but by a narrow winding road close upon the sea and under
the ridge of the Purbeck Hills. The quarries of this tumbled
country furnished marble to the English cathedrals. Wherever the core of a column is encircled with engaged shafts

of grayish green, these shafts are likely to be of Purbeck marble. When first cut, the stone takes a high polish; but it flakes off and grows rusty until, at last, it resembles a downspout of unpainted metal. A waggish friend of ours, standing in Salisbury's hard cold light from its unstained windows, once remarked that plumbers had been too careful to drain the roof.

Our driver now wished to give us the view from the ridge of the Purbeck Hills and he took us up a narrow lane on a steep detour. On all sides lay bleak and empty country, and it was surprising that such unfrequented spaces could be contained in such a little island. To the north stretched heath and woodland, all contained in the district that Hardy calls Egdon Heath. We saw this under gray clouds and in a gale of wind, and these fitted the spirit of the novels. The scene needed but the fall of night and the rising of shadows to fill these hollows with Hardy's tragic gloom. One recalls here the first chapter of "The Return of the Native." "The face of the heath," it is written, "by its mere complexion added half an hour to evening; it could in like manner retard the dawn, sadden noon, anticipate the frowning of storms scarcely generated, and intensify the opacity of a moonless midnight to a cause of shaking and dread."

The dyer's hand "is subdued to what it works in," and Hardy's plots are always stained by the dark shadows of this bare country at his door. It is the black spirit of the heathland that is his constant hero; and if puny men and women attempt to guide their lives, they are lost in these overpowering spaces and swept from their paths by storm. Companion to King Lear is the tempest where he lost his wits; and Hardy's people are maddened also by these bleak hills of Dorset. This must be true of many writers. One can name them in any random cast. One realizes the long Norwegian nights in Ibsen, in Dickens the mysterious filth of London.

Wordsworth explores the new continent of nature just discovered, and his verses are reflected from the still waters of
a northern lake.

And now, after our descent from the ridge of the Purbeck
Hills and when sleepiness was already settling down on me,
we passed Lulworth Castle. It is a "solid square building of
much solemnity" and still possesses a roof and a family as
its tenant.

It was hereabouts that we were lost. The road had dwindled to a mere lane across rolling meadows, with now and
then a cattle-gate to open. In my drowsy state I was dimly
conscious that our driver was inquiring his way to Lulworth Cove from any stranger that we met. Then presently
we came to West Lulworth, a half mile distant from the sea.

This village must formerly have been of great beauty, but
it is now spoiled by new villas and the general appearance
of offering tea to excursionists from Bournemouth. However, on this April day of doubtful weather, the pavilion of
refreshment was not yet opened for the season and the village
was pleasantly deserted. We had tea at a small inn in front
of a small fire that begged for another lump of coal.

Lulworth Cove explains the chars-à-bancs from Bournemouth. It is a sheltered pool of sea water that rests in a
round hollow under Bindon Hill, whose sharp cliffs rise to a
height of four hundred feet. The narrow entrance of the
cove admits no more than a ripple from a storm. No wind
can swoop so low as to ruffle the clouds that lie reflected in
the water. It is said that a child once fell from the cliff and
by a miracle of fortune escaped without permanent injury,
although her clothing was torn to strings upon the jagged
rocks. Lulworth Cove must be of a soft beauty under the
warm skies of summer when its surface is blue and the cliffs
are of a dazzling white, nor could April's intermittent rain
entirely spoil it.

A legend of Lulworth Cove contains the genesis of one of

the greatest poems of the English language. In August, 1820, John Keats was condemned by his physician to a winter in Italy on the chance that it might save him from advanced tuberculosis. "This journey . . . haunts me horribly," he wrote. "I shall endeavour to go, though it will be with the sensation of marching against a battery." He sailed from London in a merchant brigantine with his friend, Severn, as his companion. No sooner was the cramped little vessel in the Channel than it met dangerous storms and put into Dungeness for safety. In the calm that followed it anchored at Portsmouth and again at Lulworth Cove. There is a record by Severn of the hours spent here upon the cliffs as the vessel waited for the rising of the wind. It was at night, when the vessel had sailed and he had seen forever the last of the English coast, that Keats, writes Sidney Colvin, "borrowed the copy of Shakespeare's Poems which he had given Severn a few days before and wrote out fair and neatly for him, on the blank page opposite the heading *A Lover's Complaint,* the beautiful sonnet which every lover of English knows so well."

Bright star, would I were stedfast as thou art,
   Not in lone splendour hung aloft the night
And watching, with eternal lids apart,
   Like nature's patient, sleepless Eremite,
The moving waters at their priestlike task
   Of pure ablution round earth's human shores,
Or gazing on the new soft-fallen mask
   Of snow upon the mountains and the moors—
No—yet still stedfast, still unchangeable,
   Pillow'd upon my fair love's ripening breast,
To feel forever its soft fall and swell,
   Awake forever in a sweet unrest,
Still, still to hear her tender-taken breath,
   And so live ever—or else swoon to death.

For this last view of England, Lulworth Cove is hallowed. Its little roar of August's chars-à-bancs must fade forever from an ear that is tuned to these old melodies of our greatest lyric poet. On any summer night, from Bindon Hill, there must be lights sailing in the mist towards exile.

Hardy knew this cove and Keats's tragic story; for one hundred years later, in 1920, he composed a poem. "Had I but lived a hundred years ago," he wrote:

Had I but lived a hundred years ago
I might have gone, as I have gone this year,
By Warmwell Cross on to a Cove I know,
And Time have placed his finger on me there:

"You see that man?"—I might have looked, and said,
"O yes: I see him. One that boat has brought
Which dropped down Channel round Saint Alban's Head.
So commonplace a youth calls not my thought."

"You see that man?"—"Why, yes; I told you; yes:
Of an idling town-sort; thin; hair brown in hue;
And as the evening lights scants less and less
He looks up at a star, as many do."

"You see that man?"—"Nay, leave me!" then I plead,
"I have fifteen miles to vamp across the lea,
And it grows dark, and I am weary-kneed:
I have said the third time; yes, that man I see!"

"Good. That man goes to Rome—to death, despair;
And no one notes him now but you and I:
A hundred years, and the world will follow him there,
And bend with reverence where his ashes lie."

Hardy's genius falls upon its knees in worship of other genius. Shelley and Keats are buried in Rome near the pyramid of Cestius.

Cestius in life, maybe,
Slew, breathed out threatening;
I know not. This I know: In death all silently
He does a finer thing,

In beckoning pilgrim feet
With marble finger high
To where, by shadowy wall and history-haunted street,
Those matchless singers lie. . . .

- White Horse -

VIII. A VISIT TO A PAIR OF NOVELISTS

ANY READER of current books will know Llewelyn Powys, the author of "Black Laughter," and it is almost as likely that he will know, also, his wife, Alyse Gregory and her several novels. Mary had been a friend of Miss Gregory in her old home in Norwalk, Connecticut, and I had met her once or twice in Greenwich Village. I recall a dinner at a foreign restaurant on a narrow street at which our host was

Tinckom-Fernandez, then a writer on the old *Nation*. Each winter it was his habit to gather together a strange company picked from here and there among the writing slaveys of the city, and to set them down to dinner at a charge of eighty-five cents a plate, including tip. The restaurant for this particular dinner had descended from the Orient, for I remember that the bread was unleavened and was baked in flat discs like chair pads. I have no doubt but that the bad wine was scooped up from the sacred Ganges.

I had not seen Miss Gregory since that night of the Pentateuch, and now it seemed that she and her husband, Llewelyn Powys, were living on the Dorset coast just to the west of Lulworth Cove. It was Mary's suggestion that we pay them a visit on our way back to Dorchester.

"They live at White Nose," she said to the driver. "Can you find it?"

The driver scratched his head until an idea sprouted in the furrow. "It's rather a wiggly way," he said.

We left the highroad at Watercombe and turned south on a lane that presently dwindled to little more than a path across the meadows, with here and there a gate to be opened and signboards informing us that we were trespassing. And now, after several miles, we came to high land that bordered the cliffs where there were meadows without a tree. To the south was the waste of the Channel, flecked with white and swept by changing patterns. There was a moment when it seemed likely that our motor might be bogged in the soft grass; and then ahead of us there stood a lonely house in bare outline like a man's finger held up to judge the wind.

It proved to be a series of attached houses for several families—almost a city dwelling—with a broad front facing the ocean. Our driver informed us that it had once been the station of the coast-guard. As this service is now performed largely by the use of telephones, the several apartments of the house are let to summer residents. There were no doors in front as I recall but a general path led along the back of the building and offered entrance to the kitchens. Little plots of grass here were sheltered from the wind.

The Powys family popped in sight.

"Do you recall sitting on a loaf of—" I started.

"Well, of all the people," Miss Gregory cried, "if it isn't Mary!"

We were at once in Norwalk and Sheridan Square. Miss Gregory was kind enough to recall the chair-pads at Tinck's dinner.

Llewelyn and Alyse Gregory had just returned from a long tramp across the cliffs. He was dressed in corduroy and flannel and was a man of handsome and intelligent face. Wind-blown, he seemed a creature of the rain and storm. There was also something of Pan in his composition, as if on search I might have found a reed in the pocket of his coat. She wore tweeds and heavy boots.

Powys is a native of Dorset. This surprised me, for his name suggests Wales and a more fanciful and Celtic tradition than we attribute to this south of England. He was born in Dorchester, and he told me that since boyhood he had been familiar with White Nose and all of this coast. He and his wife live part of the year in America, but his health is delicate and he finds improvement on these wind-swept cliffs. The bedlam of New York has left no mark on him. He seemed like a man who would look beyond tall buildings to the stars.

The four of us walked out of the cottage for the view— white headlands to Portland Bill, the smoke of distant steamers, the ocean ribbed by April breeze and covered with a broken roof of running clouds. For twenty miles, east and west, there was no tree—only green meadows, the cliffs and a floor of water that was streaked with sunlight.

Llewelyn and Alyse Powys had spent the winter here at White Nose, and their house had been the target of gales that had rattled their windows and eddied beneath their doors. One might think that storms would be content upon these windy cliffs of Dorset, yet all through the blustering months they had come tapping on the casements, moaning dismally for shelter. As a studio for writing the Powyses use the old coast-guard's lookout at the edge of the cliffs. It seems that in some previous storm the roof of this building had been blown away and that the damage had been repaired by laying a smuggler's boat upside down across the top and anchoring it so securely to the walls that the tiny structure was tight against the rain.

Alyse Gregory had just published a novel and Llewelyn Powys was at the time editing selections from Anthony à Wood. I fumbled in my memory to find this man, made a guess and was wrong. It seems that he was a seventeenth-century antiquary of Oxford. Mr. Powys now asked me if I had ever seen samphire growing. Here I was better, for I quoted Lear:

Hangs one that gathers samphire, dreadful trade!

Mr. Powys leaned forward and plucked a tiny plant that grew on the facing of the cliff just underneath its dizzy edge. The ocean was five hundred feet below; yet I had no fear for him. It seemed impossible that Pan could fall from rocks that were his home.

. . . the murmuring surge,
That on the unnumber'd idle pebbles chafes,
Cannot be heard so high.

I have looked up samphire since to learn why men gather it in such danger. "The young leaves," I find, "are highly esteemed for making pickles." It seems a bit of a let-down. Having now seen it growing on the Dorset cliffs, I shall in future confine myself to Heinz and watermelon rind.

We went indoors and sat in a pleasant confusion of books

and papers. Miss Gregory and Mary went back to Norwalk; while Mr. Powys and I discussed publishers and royalty, the poor taste of a public that neglects us for the *movie* and the wireless. I had always thought of him as of an author of prodigious sales. He informed me, however, that as his thoughts grew more serious with the advancing years and turned from the writing of lighter fiction, in that degree his sales were falling off.

"In the communistic state that is surely coming," he said, "I wonder if there will be a place for books and writers."

"And is the soviet sure to come?" I asked.

He paused.

"I have heard in gossip," he replied, "that the director of the Bank of England said lately that the country would look back upon this bad year as a prosperous one."

Mr. Powys' face suggests poetry—not any raw product that is turned outward with a crank to please the masses—but the face of one who should have lived in some first dawning of an era, of one who should have known Keats or have talked with Shakespeare—a face of rare beauty, with eyes that are gentle and invite confession and the truth.

I reminded Mr. Powys that he had once reviewed a book of mine, and that he had scored me for neglecting a just description of Westmoreland. This he had forgotten. He had allotted me a half page in the New York *Times*. For all practical purposes of sale, a half page of somewhat unfavorable notice is better than a paragraph of unstinted praise, so doubtless I am in his debt. For the public judges us by the bulk of our advertisement, the inches of space we fill, and the size of the type. A friendly little light under a bushel sells fewer books than a destructive conflagration that is sprawled across a page.

"How about this book of Maugham's," I asked, " 'Cakes and Ale'? How much of it is truth? And how about the barmaid?"

"I knew the first Mrs. Hardy," Mr. Powys answered. "She was of excellent western family, a woman of good education, a woman in no wise like the person of the novel. All that part is fiction. Nor is the second Mrs. Hardy at all the kind of woman that Maugham describes in the person of the second Mrs. Driffield. She is a direct unaffected person who would never dream of distorting the truth of her husband's life. We know her very well. We were in America when 'Cakes and Ale' was published; but Maugham, as I recall, issued a statement that its characters were fictitious."

"A statement very few would see," I answered.

"Of course," he replied. "The book must have done a bit of mischief."

The sun was now almost level over Portland Bill, so we took our leave. Few tourists can have the privilege of seeing White Nose, for it is far from the highroad and guarded by many gates and signboards not to trespass.

We dozed to Dorchester and spent the evening by the hearth. Chopin, who had been last night in torture, had packed his bag and gone. The old piano rested from its classic effort; and, as if to show that it was not snootily hospitable to nocturnes only, a broken sheet from London's music halls now rested on its rack. "It's you, my dear, that I'm a-dreamin' of." The inn's small fire still had its nose in its iron feed-bag. There was a brush of wind against the windows, and the faces of the night and storm looked in upon our comfort.

Maiden Castle

IX. TOWARDS DEVON

ON SUNDAY morning we repacked. We had four bags and as our travels required but two, we now found it possible to leave the others in the linen room of the Antelope Hotel, to be sent forward when needed. To such assistance the English inns are accustomed, and I have never found them careless to instructions.

A slim housemaid tried, until I prevented her, to stagger down the corridor with these two monstrous bags. These little slaveys of country hotels move at a trot all day and no work is too heavy for them. They rise with the summer sun and they are busy every minute. Our own stout Sadie at home must have her afternoon nap and she gets the chauffeur in to lift a rug. And yet an excellent servant, as I am told, can be employed in London for a pound a week, which is less than the amount we Americans pay for an extra waitress at dinner—a young lady who will sit in the kitchen afterwards and load herself with duck and apple sauce at our expense.

There was another flash of ironic sunlight across our morning kippers, but the sky was still rimmed with threatening clouds.

And now we hired yesterday's motor to convey us to Bridport on the way to Devon, with a detour to the Maiden Castle, which is not far distant from Dorchester across those fields where I had been caught by rain.

A superlative burst of ink would be needed to describe adequately Maiden Castle—Mai-dun, in Celtic, meaning hill of strength. Its origin is obscure, but it is supposed to have been already a fortified British town when the first Romans landed; and certainly of all the Celtic remains of the British Isles, it is the largest and most imposing. It consists of huge concentric circles of earthwork that gird a flat, high table-land above a treeless plain. Inside the inner ramparts, this flat top is of forty-five acres, and the whole compass of the earthworks covers more than twice that area. The ramparts rise to a height of sixty feet and are still sharply pitched.

"This gigantic structure," writes Sir Frederick Treves, "was made by men who worked with horn picks and with hatchets of stone or bronze. When the inhabitants left the camp centuries ago they left it forever. It remained as desolate as a haunted glen. It became a solitude; no man meddled with its walls, so that its great valla became merely shelters for sheep. Thus it is that Maiden Castle survives in perfect preservation. . . .

"Maiden Castle, to the mind of the Celt," he continues, "lacked nothing in perfection as a site for a founding of a town. It realized to the fullest his ideals of a home. Here is a hill on an open down, a height so commanding that none can approach it unseen, a place ready to defend, with all around it grazing land for sheep and no patch of cover for wild beasts or the creeping foe. At its foot are the lowlands of the Frome, where could be grown such crops as the man had knowledge of, and where he could find fish for his eating and the wherewithal to build his mud and wattle huts. In primitive grandeur—in the grandeur of the sheer cliff and the Titanic rock—there is nothing in Dorset to surpass this hill-town, this city of refuge, with its grass-covered ramparts rising, tier above tier, against the skyline."

"This grandeur of Titanic rock" is a bit strong, we think. Englishmen have a habit of looking at the British landscape through an enlarging glass; and if any tourist think to discover in Maiden Castle a Sicilian hill-town such as Mola he will be disappointed. I once traveled in Wales, reading George Borrow, and found no mountains as high as his description. It was Sam Johnson who made little fishes talk like whales. I have a grudge against certain English castles because I saw them first through the gloriously false imagination of Turner's paintings.

We stood for a half hour on the heights of Maiden Castle. Far across the meadows to the east we could see the line of the Roman road that had once clattered with Caesar's legions on their journeys from the coast to Dorchester when first its walls were new. This was a part of a famous road that led northeast from Portland Bill upon the Channel to Silchester and to London, that branched at Dorchester, once Durnovaria, to bind Exeter to Roman rule. And in still more ancient days there was a trackway here to connect with the great track along the ridges of southern England whose use and traffic must forever remain in the field of doubt.

Dorchester's higher towers peeped at us on tiptoe. To the west were the hills of the Devon border. The whole country was deserted, save for a farmhouse here and there and grazing sheep. Our own motor at the foot of the rampart was the only discordant note in this solitude around us.

Maiden Castle lacks the shrill advertisement of Stonehenge, which in contrast is but a trifle; and, of a consequence, chars-à-bancs go snorting across Salisbury Plain to lay out their pennies for colored postcards. Stonehenge on bank holidays is a noisy picnic ground. Maiden Castle, except for the brisk whistling of the wind, rests in silence. Of the Celtic remains of England that I have seen, it is the most tremendous. It is a ray of light across the dark centuries from the age of bronze—a stroke, as of lightning, that reveals movement and color in the blackness of the night. Its vast construction must be older than the Coliseum by a thousand years, and its earth ramparts are more durable than the crumbling stones of Rome that became a quarry. It is of equal age, no doubt, with the forgotten Etruscan foundations beneath the Palatine, as old as the swamp that once rankled in the Forum. And all of this stands intact and deserted in the wide plains just beyond the modern streets of Dorchester.

England's open fields are its best museum. For towns, in their prosperity and growth, destroy all vestiges of their forgotten youth. A wall is overthrown by disaster and becomes a quarry for new buildings. An ancient pavement is broken up to be a modern surface. The wattles of a prehistoric house become the fuel for the hearth of a dwelling made of stone. And Time is a careless housewife and it allows dust to seep in upon its treasures. But where these vestiges are in cheaper meadowland they remain unregarded and unchanged through countless ages. So here in Dorset, the Romans chose the site of Dorchester for their camp and stronghold as more convenient to running water; and their road from Weymouth had no commerce with the Celtic town upon the hill.

The ordnance map of all this district is dotted with British memorials—barrows, tumuli, camps and footings whose use may only be guessed. And it is fitting that our approach to the west of England should be across fields that tempt one with their antiquity. For Devon and Cornwall are still Celtic —the home of legends whose origin can never be discovered, of superstition and of magic twilight. The map of eastern England is marked with Saxon and with Danish conquest. Except in the west one can trace everywhere the Roman roads. But now, as we journey towards Land's End, we shall come to districts where the southern legions never marched, where the hill-tops and the narrow winding valleys were mostwise a guard against invasion. Here every moor and upland meadow will be dotted with Celtic names, and Rome will be forever but a rumor across the hills.

It was towards noon when we came to the town of Bridport and stopped at the door of the Greyhound Hotel.

"A double room with a coal fire," I demanded.

"And lunch?"

"And lunch," I added, "with a plate of strawberry jam and clotted cream."

For we were now near Devon's border where every cow is on its toes to serve the tourist.

Our bags were lifted from the motor. They were hoisted by the porter up a broad stairway lined with engravings and colored prints. The landlord walked in front and threw open the door of his best room. A damp wind floated out.

"May we have a fire?" I asked.

"Yes, sir. Very well, sir. It's a shilling, sir."

"It's cheaper than a headstone," I replied.

- West Bay -

X. BRIDPORT

WE HAVE vainly searched our diary for any commendation of Bridport. Sir Frederick Treves, in his afore-mentioned book on Dorset, calls it "a wholesome, homely, county town, with an air about it of substantial simplicity. It has no more pretense or assurance than has an honest yeoman's wife in homespun. . . . It boasts of no antiquities and of no particular past." But Treves is the same man who swelled up the Maiden Castle. He is a native hereabouts and a local historian, and he should not, therefore, be entirely trusted in his praise; for it is his business to sell the locality to tourists from overseas. One reads his pages agreeably, but his argument must be attended with some of that incredulity that is bestowed on those who deal in real-estate.

On this Sunday afternoon when all of its shops were closed we found Bridport dull. The shutters of the High Street and the deserted pavements seemed to proclaim a Presbyterian moratorium. From our window we saw a sign on a house-front announcing that in the year 1651, when the building had been an inn, Charles II had there spent a night; but King Charles's sleeping quarters grow monotonous in the south of England. One wonders if he ever stayed awake; or whether, like Queen Elizabeth, he went forever about the country trying new beds. Another signboard proclaimed that a certain Doctor Roberts was the maker of an ointment called "The Poor Man's Friend." It must have failed sometimes of a cure, for another placard near by on the wall informed grieving survivors that funerals were furnished from the premises inside.

Bridport, although never on the sea, was once on a river navigable for shallow bottoms.

But if we slight Bridport, we offer as a substitute a particular description of our bedroom at the Greyhound Hotel. It was a large slice cut off from the end of the coffee room by a thin wood partition, whose great double doors squeaked in any draught. Here was assembled a discord of old furniture. In front of an ornate marble mantel, in which was squeezed a fire of one dimension, there stood a square table of a size for a family dinner when all the cousins have arrived. On top of this arose an aspidistra under dust. The room was lighted by gas in asbestos filament that only wavered with the spark and seemed designed to display no more than the general gloom. One vast bed would have fitted the splendor of a palace and the other possessed a thin and sagging mattress. A clothes-press was large enough to hold a dozen family skeletons. On the walls were crayon portraits in tarnished frames of white-bearded ancestors in black cloth and Sunday collars—men who would have detested the frivolity of a game of checkers. And there were mice in the partitions that nibbled all the night.

Having eaten England's standard lunch of a cold joint and loaf cabbage, we walked out to find the ocean which lies about a mile and a half from Bridport. For it had happened that an enthusiast whom we had met at a dinner in London, had recommended to us the village of West Bay on the Channel. We should have questioned his taste, for he had called Bridport "the gem of the west." It may have been some excellent Scotch that had whetted his enthusiasm. The road followed a sluggish river that had once been deep enough to carry Bridport's ships. It wiggles now without a job at the bottom of a sightly valley that is spoiled by the straggling suburbs of the town. We passed a hoarding with an advertisement in great letters: "Oh, Yes, Baby, It's Quite True that Exeter's Cup Team Will Play. And After the Match a Non-Stop Dance Will Rage from 9 to 1 A.M. at the Church House." We were still, it seems, in Merry England.

We were at quite a distance from West Bay when we heard the roaring of the sea. This noise was loudest from far off, for the narrow valley between headlands acted as a channel of the sound.

In another mile, quite on tiptoe with expectation, we came to West Bay. But we were disappointed. It was a bare place and it offered only a beach of smooth stones, two piers that served as exit to the river and a high meadow to the east where men were playing golf. This high land was cut sharp to the ocean, exposing a white chalk cliff—in itself majestic, but unsupported by any beauty of the town. The largest structure offered summer lodging to a hundred families and was hideous. Against the stony beach, however, there was a pretty inn, and to the west a pavement for pedestrians stretched for some distance beneath the cliffs. A few decayed vessels lay in a shallow basin. West Bay had once ambition to be a port of commerce, and of this there was evidence in the mighty rings and bollards around the basin where its ships had been tied. A line of warehouses, rusty with disuse, still remains. On such a stormy day as the one of our visit, no ship larger than a rowboat could have squeezed between the piers without being mauled and scraped.

We walked by the ocean until our shoes were full of stones. A notice, "Don't Cart Away the Beach Without Permission," seemed to refer to us. We watched the waves pounding at the pier-heads. We gazed at the sea. Then, when rain splashed in our faces, we went inside the inn and ordered tea. Two Englishmen had surrounded the hearth, and the fire's comfort could not get through. This inn boasts, also, of Charles II and tells of his escape from parliament's policemen.

In an interval of better weather we walked back to Bridport. Behind a Tudor front on South Street a Conservative Club was once lodged and still had its sign on the door. We peeked on tiptoe through the window, but saw only a litter of papers and disorder. Perhaps every one in England is turning pink.

My diary records a Methodist church at the foot of a nest of narrow lanes in which King Charles might have hidden once. It is emphatic that a most unusual number of black cats walk in Bridport's streets. It says that on our return we stirred the fire in our room and thawed our icy fingers under the shadow of the aspidistra.

All night, as often as I awakened, there were strange squeakings in our partitions—mice in the walls, perhaps, hiding from Bridport's black cats. In a nightmare (for there was strange infection in the chilly room) I seemed myself to be a larger mouse. And when I waved a frightened tail at the cats' assault, all the bedclothes tumbled to the floor.

*The Parade,
Lyme Regis*

XI. LYME REGIS

THE FOLLOWING morning we advanced to Lyme Regis on a road that was a foretaste of Devon. At Chideock we were at stream level, at Hardown perched aloft with the ocean far below. In the mist the water was indistinguishable, and the declining slope ended in an eternity of sky that had fallen from above. Into the valleys the highway descended recklessly, found a sheltered village in a hollow, then climbed a farther height above the level of a church spire. It was Devon, except for the fantastic outcropping of stone that marks the moors. Once we stopped to see a fragment of a British temple at the roadside. It was a circle of upright stones, and cattle nibbled in the grass roundabout unsuspecting its antiquity.

In our descent to Lyme Regis we saw evidence of the danger of this road that we had traveled. A motor lorry coming into town had failed to make a turn and had crashed headlong into a building at the curb, carrying away the wall so that the roof had fallen in. This accident was in its newest excitement and a crowd was still chattering beside the ruin. The driver of the lorry had not been hurt, but his motor and cargo were demolished. A smell of hops betrayed the nature of the lorry's load. Our own American purveyors are forced to drive with better care. In the window of the building there still hung out a sign that teas were furnished, but the tables were under a weight of plaster and splinters from the roof.

And now, having dipped to the level of the ocean, we climbed again to the western edge of the town and to the entrance of the Alexandra. This excellent hotel sits in a garden and looks upon the Channel. There would come a day before we left Lyme Regis when warm sunlight would flood this stretch of lawn, but as yet the sky was cold and gray.

We were given a room with a bow-window towards the garden and the sea, and with a fire that warmed us. The English landlord always places a dresser to block a view, setting it squarely against a window. This custom will perplex one until he realizes that this red-cheeked nation is never content to look on nature darkly through a glass, but calls for its boots if it wishes to see the world. We hoisted the dresser to one side. I wish to mention also that always on our travels, just when our room was growing warm with an open fire, a maidservant who had been watching her chance through the keyhole, would suddenly pop in and lift the windows in order that the rain might refresh the moss on the carpet.

There was once a man who lived in the swamps above Toledo, Ohio, before this district had been drained and when ague was still about. When asked how he escaped the shivers, he had his answer. "Well, neighbor," he said, "when

I wake up in the morning I look out of the window; and if it is foggy, I take a little bitters and go back to bed. And then in an hour I look again. If it is still thick, I take another little bitters and go back to bed again. Sometimes I have to tåke a dozen little bitters"—he paused—"but that is when the morning is demnition thick." But England's curse is rheumatism. If you will look through the pages of *Punch,* you will find that most of its old men and women limp. The lion rampant of Britain's royal arms is waving aloft an inflammatory paw. That flicking tail of his, that angry jaw, are protesting against the dampness of his English cage.

Lyme Regis is of considerable interest to a sentimental traveler. The stone cobb that outlines its artificial harbor has for its grandsire a breakwater erected by Edward I. The cobb now existing was built in 1825, when its shallow water was deep enough for the period's small vessels. From the cobb and from the hills behind the town, the folk of Lyme Regis watched the passing of the Spanish Armada with Drake snapping at its heels. The town successfully endured a siege by Prince Maurice in the civil wars. On June 11, 1685, the Duke of Monmouth landed here to claim foolishly the English throne. It was on the beach below our window that he offered a prayer for his success; and in the marketplace he enrolled the first country-folk for the army that was to be scattered at Sedgemoor and hanged by Jeffreys.

From Lyme Regis came a certain Arthur Gregory with an "admirable talent of forcing the seal of a letter in such a way that it appeared untouched." Walsingham used Gregory for ferreting out the treason of Mary Queen of Scots. Tennyson came to visit Francis Palgrave here at Lyme. Palgrave, famous for his anthology of poetry, was a Jew and his name was Cohen. Mary Mitford stayed a bit upon this coast. Whistler came here to paint.

But Lyme's great person is Jane Austen. She spent only a

month of holidays, and yet she bulks larger in the annals of the town than either the Armada or Monmouth. Lyme Regis points out a small house of tipsy walls as hers. It prints in its guidebook the paragraphs of her descriptions. It shows a flight of steps on the cobb called "Granny's Teeth," and says it was down these steps that Louisa Musgrove fell in the novel, "Persuasion." As this accident is almost the only exciting event in any of her stories, it is a shame to throw discredit on the steps that are offered to tourists. But besides the fact that her description does not fit them, there is an added objection that "Persuasion" was finished several years before the present cobb was built. Guides suppress this disconcerting fact and whenever chars-à-bancs arrive, sentimental ladies peep down the dangerous stairs and drop a tear.

Jane Austen, as a set of leather backs on a library shelf, stirs me with pleasant thought. Here is a range of books, I say, that some day I shall read complete. When I am an old man with teeth fit for soft food only, perhaps then I shall read them roundabout in endless circles as so many excellent critics have done even before their teeth gave way.

But now, today, like certain other authors of high repute, Jane Austen disappoints me. Her young ladies are so prudish and they talk of grandpapa and our dear mamma in such stilted phrases. They are too perfect in their respect for age, too careful to keep behind a chaperon, too unsuspicious of all folly. Blushes, emotions packed in ice, little feet peeping in and out like mice! We feel like crying out with Sir Andrew Aguecheek, "Legs and thighs. Let me see thee caper." We have no praise for loose manners; yet fashion runs to extremes, and if these women of Jane Austen had only forgotten their primness now and then, perhaps our own age would have been more moderate in its discard of petticoats and underwear.

One of these young ladies elopes, it is true—I forget which

one—and to her I feel gratitude that she alone could break convention. One wonders how Jane Austen ever heard of an elopement. She must have been reading a naughty book. As for Miss Louisa Musgrove, who fell down the steps at Lyme, I can only wish she broke her neck. She was being "jumped down" the stairs by the handsome Captain Wentworth. And being "jumped down" once, she wanted to be "jumped down" again. "In all their walks he had had to jump her from the stiles; the sensation was delightful to her." And, of course, she jumped too soon, before the Captain was ready to catch her. I think that the book was written with its author's hand cramped in a kid glove. Yet I have known persons of unimpeachable taste who run through the novels once a year, who keep them on a table by their beds, who find in each rereading a greater depth of reality. At Lyme Regis and at Bath one should, if anywhere, be able to find truth and beauty in "Emma" and "Persuasion," and at both of these towns I tried these novels with poor success.

Lyme Regis is described in "Persuasion." A great carriage-load of Jane Austen's people cross the hills on a certain November day for a brief visit here. It is written "that they were come too late in the year for any amusement or variety which Lyme, as a public place, might offer. The rooms were shut up, the lodgers almost all gone, scarcely any family but of the residents left; and, as there is nothing to admire in the buildings themselves, the remarkable situation of the town, the principal street almost hurrying into the water, the walk to the Cobb, skirting round the pleasant little bay, which, in the season, is animated with bathing machines and company; the Cobb itself, its old wonders and new improvements, with the very beautiful line of cliffs stretching out to the east of the town, are what the stranger's eye will seek."

Lyme Regis lies in the channel of a narrow valley to the sea; and its streets and lanes, nowhere upon the level, run here and there as they find safe footing. The valley's stream, as the old traveler, Leland, puts it, "cometh fleeting on great stones" to fall beneath a stone bridge that over-arches it near the sea. Decayed buildings lean forward on this brawling runnel or they offer it their gardens at the rear. Lanes, in indecision, wander hereabouts, crossing the streamlet on a stone span above a momentary pool, threading their devious ways up hill and down, quite lost, but always with water splashing at their feet.

The houses of Lyme are placed on whim, without order or design. It is said that, like the Gadarene swine, they "appear to be running down a steep place into the sea." There is a High Street that wiggles on a winding hill between rows of shops, gets no more than a brief view of the ocean, then climbs on a hard journey to the west. At one point a house divides this street, with the roadway on one side and a footpath on the other. Bicycles need no pedals in Lyme; for one is forced by the stiff gradient to push them up afoot, and each incline downwards is an easy coast. Small boys are so reckless that one shivers at the thought of broken brakes. At any hour of a summer morning, there are chars-à-bancs wheezing on the slope. Old ladies in funny hats and feather boas inch along, and rheumatism limps upwards on its cane.

There is a hotel that boasts of entertaining Tennyson, who once thought of settling here, a building that lodged Lord Chatham and the younger Pitt. There is a mill whose great wheel rests forever, a museum of native fossils. Near the mouth of the stream is the Town Hall—such an ornate structure "as would be found in a German toy box of building bricks for boys." Or, if a tourist is restless among these little sights, he may climb from Lyme to Golden Cap, six hundred feet above the ocean, or by easier journey up through meadowland to see the colored roofs of Lyme nestling below him on the coast. Every guidebook is full of hints

Broad Street
— Lyme Regis —

of these excursions roundabout; but our own hint to one who sets out afoot is for heavy boots and an umbrella.

But Lyme's chief attraction is the ocean and the cobb, the long parade beside the water, with its tea signs and placards announcing that rooms are to be let with "hot and cold laid on." On this broad walk, as once in August when I strolled there, little concert companies, rather worse than that of "The Good Companions," pitch their one-night tents, while their hawkers announce in rasping voices that their galaxies of stars have sung at the king's command, although they leave it in doubt whether it be the British monarch or some crown of make-believe. In France there would be a jolly Punch-and-Judy show with a noisy rough-and-tumble; but England delights itself sadly in a melancholy performance in which each tenor has a cough.

The cobb is a stone crescent, with a further point of masonry as an extra protection in a storm. On the cobb is a decayed customs house and a still more battered placard of tariffs, now so rubbed by time and exposure that one is certain that nothing now larger than a fishing vessel ever finds its way to shelter to be taxed. At low tide these boats lie on their sides in the anchorage behind the cobb and seem to snore; then they slowly right themselves as the first trickle of the rising water marks its ripples on the sand.

After the exploration of the back lanes that lose themselves behind the High Street towards the mill, after peeping through doorways into hidden gardens and thumbing the shelves of the bookshops ("Persuasion" in all of its editions) —after all this, then one wanders to the ocean and thinks of Monmouth and Jane Austen, of the many years of commerce that have now sunk to stranded fishing boats. He sits in a shielded cranny of the cobb with his collar up and reads about Louisa Musgrove until the wind echoes back the plot. He strolls on the parade and counts the women's funny hats

that seem to date from the coronation of Queen Victoria and
have had no fresh ribbon since. Certain other modish little
numbers—we have Mary's word for this—were in their bloom
of youth and hardly more than four years old. Dogs go
sniffing at the iron benches. A wheel-chair carries an invalid
out for air. Children are digging wells in the sand.

Roofs · Lyme Regis

The waves sweep in without a break and leave a careless
rim of lather, yet there is shingle at the edge. With eyes
closed, one can know the composition of a beach—the smooth
sucking of sandy atoms that run through the fingers of the
tide, and here at Lyme the rattle of little pebbles, as if the
ocean were shaking dice.

We remained at Lyme Regis for five days. On our first
morning I cashed a traveler's check at the bank and I asked

the teller to direct me to the steps down which Louisa Musgrove fell.

"It's on the cobb," he answered.

"And I suppose that any one thereabouts can tell me where," I persisted.

The teller shook his head. "It's not likely," he said at length, "but all natives can tell you where all of our taverns are."

We inquired in which house Jane Austen had stayed. Two dwellings dispute this honor, so we chose the one that was the most picturesque—a tipsy building that stood above the beach and was crooked at every angle. We knocked at the door. It was probably our American accent that gained us admittance, for the English woman who now rents the house has a cousin living in Chicago by the name of Smith "and did we know her by any chance?" Never was another house so crooked. No floor was at the right relation to the walls, no window that did not sag from its original design. The tenant, it seems, had grown so used to these defects that it was only in one furious winter storm, when the ocean's spray was dashing against her windows, that she had doubts of her safety. I was looking sentimentally from the windows, thinking I was in the room where "Persuasion" was written, when she informed me that the novel was begun many years after Jane Austen's brief sojourn here.

Lyme once owned an ichthyosaurus. This old creature had been dead for a few hundred thousand years when a little girl of ten discovered him. The meeting, says our guidebook, was another strange encounter of "Beauty and the Beast." Both made the other famous, but a stained-glass window in Lyme church commemorates the little girl.

From the parade and from our garden we watched the varying colors of the ocean—the dull gray of a sunless morning that changed to a pink twilight spreading its pigments on the cliffs and sky and waves. We watched the procession of the clouds—a mirror, as it seemed, of our changing world under Time's upheaval. In a theatre's cunning motion pictures we have seen a plant grow before our eyes. Here at Lyme we saw a continent in swift transition—its harbors and rocky shores that nature in its slower tempo would carve through a thousand years—evolution at a gallop.

With our afternoon tea each day we ate Devon's clotted cream on toasted scones and laid a fat coating of raspberries across the top. Later on our travels, when my belt was slipping to its last hole, I would deny myself my lunch to have a good conscience for this feast; but as yet I was unafraid.

And while Mary sketched, I read "Persuasion" in contented boredom.

All of this was our entertainment during these five days at Lyme Regis, but I may not omit the severe cold I caught and several doses of aspirin. Mary always carries a few of these pellets in her handbag and they are always dusty.

We end the chapter in slippers by the fire, while rain sweeps its fingers across the vibrant strings of right.

In such snug circumstance one thinks of all the heroes of British fiction and their entertainment in small hotels— of Tom Jones and Smollett's rascals, of Mr. Pickwick and his companions. In a bookcase of the Alexandra I found a volume of Hazlitt, himself a mighty traveler among English inns, and I read his yellow pages until the fire was white with ash.

Ottery St. Mary Church -

XII. OTTERY ST. MARY

THERE was a public bus billed to Exeter, but I struck a bargain for a private motor that would give us on the way an hour at Ottery St. Mary, where Samuel Taylor Coleridge was born. Nobody leaves Stratford out of his travels, and few of them omit Ambleside or Stoke Poges. Now and then a curious tourist finds himself at Winterslow on account of Hazlitt. But we have never heard of any traveler, except Elihu Burritt, an American blacksmith of seventy years ago, who ever took the pains to read the signboards and turn aside to Ottery. If one is not a student of sorts he has never heard of this small town; and, with better information, he will know that Ottery is to Coleridge no more than the faint horizon of his youth and the mere cradle of his undeveloped fancy.

Coleridge was born at the vicarage of Ottery St. Mary in the year 1772 and remained there until the end of his ninth year when, by the charity of a family friend, he was sent to the Charterhouse School in London for his education. Only a few anecdotes of his childhood are preserved in his writings. He was a devourer of fairy stories of the bloodier sort and, when their plots were hot within him, he walked about the graveyard near his father's house striking at nettles with a stick pretending that they were giants. He never joined in games, but always sat reading or in thought. He must have been a little old man even when in dresses; and later, at his school in London, when he was still of an age for jam and crumbs, he was already reading the Greek philosophers. His precocity matched that of Macaulay and Hazlitt, of John Stuart Mill, who had read Herodotus in the original before he was eight. Not even the humor of his Charterhouse play-fellow, Charles Lamb, could make Coleridge entirely human.

An occasional letter or poem of his mature years recalls his childhood in his father's vicarage—a plank that was a tiny bridge above a stream where willows bent across the margin, a release from study to launch in the pool a paper navy against the scarlet armada of October's drifting leaves, an old church tower whose bells were a poor man's only music.

But these visions, recalled from childhood, are seldom concerned with happiness or the playthings of a normal youth. Specters haunt the graveyard and rub their gaunt noses on his window as he tries to sleep. There are nights of fever with "armies of ugly things" bursting in upon him. There is a flight from punishment when he lies all night in the wet grass beside the River Otter. And darkness always waits breathless for the comfort of the dawn. Perhaps the lives of all great poets have begun in nightmare—in wild imaginings that have outstripped in growth their frail bodies, to be the ugly trumpeters of beauty's long procession that shall later pass before their eyes.

If Coleridge had possessed the ability to depict childhood as his friend, Charles Lamb, possessed it, Ottery would be a place of pilgrimage. For who is there who does not know

the pattern of each room at pleasant Blakesmoor and wish
that this village could be found upon the map? We have
ourselves in vain scanned Hampshire. "Every plank and
pannel of that house," Lamb wrote, "for me had magic in
it . . . the cheerful store-room, in whose hot window-seat
I used to sit and read Cowley, with the grass-plat before, and
the hum and flappings of that one solitary wasp that ever
haunted it about me—it is in mine ears now, as oft as summer returns. . . ."

Coleridge's lonely hours of youth had fed themselves on
sickly meditation. How different is Lamb's boyhood! "The
solitude of childhood," he wrote, "is not so much the mother
of thought, as it is the feeder of love, and silence, and admiration." But Coleridge, casting back upon his early days,
wrote frigidly of Pierian springs, of zephyr-haunted brinks,
of elfin tribes and of Solitude, the wood-nymph; and Ottery,
in consequence of these chilly phrases, is a deserted shrine.
Lamb carried forward his childhood with him into the reality of the nineteenth century, while Coleridge left his behind to keep stilted company with the ghosts that the French
Revolution had killed forever.

When Coleridge left Ottery at the age of nine, he left it
for life. At most he returned for one or two brief holidays,
but they lent no magic to his pen. Later on our travels we
shall pass through Nether Stowey and see the house of his
mature years; and there we shall find Coleridge and reality,
his pen dipped in no artificial Pierian spring.

We crossed the breezy hills from Lyme Regis, entered
Ottery and halted at a book-shop.

"Perhaps," I said, "you will be good enough to direct us
to the house of Coleridge."

"Which Coleridge?" was the answer.

This was disconcerting, for I had forgotten there was more
than one Coleridge whose birthplace was worthy of a visit.

"The poet, of course," I replied. "Who else is there?"

"Lord Coleridge lives at the top of the street," the book-man answered. "The vicarage where the poet lived has been pulled down these many years."

I looked around the book-shop. I saw no edition of the poet's verse or any volume of his prose—nothing, not even a biography or any colored postcard of his face. There was a riffraff of cheap novels of crime and excitement, a whole shelf of Oppenheim, of Fletcher and of Edgar Wallace, a display of monogram notepaper, boxes of bouncing balls, children's dolls and folderol, London's evening journals and little plaster casts of Charlie Chaplin and his flat feet, priced at six-pence. It was evident that we were in the prophet's country.

"If we inquired at the church," I asked, "could any one tell us where the old vicarage once stood?"

"That's as it might be," the bookman answered. "But the sexton would be sure to know."

A little girl had entered the shop and the merchant turned away to help her choose a rubber ball.

At the top of the town we came to St. Mary's Church. It sets in an ample graveyard on the slope of a hill above the level of the near-by buildings in the High Street. Later in our travels farther west, we shall discover hill-tops whose lonely church towers are solitary fingers pointing to the sky; but here, on this tamer edge of Devon, the hills are of easier slope and of a less extensive outlook. At Ottery St. Mary's, as is proper in a parish churchyard, the view included only the houses of the town and their homely chimney-pots and windows. The evening bell blends with the sound of traffic on the cobbled streets.

I have remarked in another book how intimately an Eng-lish village surrounds its graveyard and how children swing upon the sagging gate or pick daisies among the tombs. To any grandsire whose day has come, the transit is so short from his aspidistra in his window on the green to his lilac

just beyond the graveyard wall. Death is so slight a change
of lodging that he will still hear the children at their games.
Something of this intimacy with the life hereafter is true of
Ottery; but on a second view we saw near by the great house
of the present Lord Coleridge and in such a presence no
child surely would swing unembarrassed on the graveyard
gate.

The name of Coleridge is on many headstones and but
seldom without a title. Poorer stones of less important families across the path bend forward in obsequious gesture. Inasmuch as the poet's father was the half-paid vicar of the
parish and the mere master of an undistinguished grammar
school, with too little wealth to educate all of his sons except with outside help—inasmuch, moreover, as the poet
died without wealth or title, I was confused by this grandeur
of the Coleridge family. It seems, however, that a nephew
of the poet married money and that the nephew's son
achieved distinction in the law, to be made in time the Lord
Chief Justice of England. Ottery St. Mary, therefore, in its
present magnificence of wealth and social station, acknowl-
edges Samuel Taylor Coleridge as merely collateral and a
poor relation.

St. Mary's is a lovely building of irregular and mixed types
of architecture. Inside there is an amazing seventeenth-century clock which, although it seems to work on the theory
that the world is flat with the obedient sun and stars revolving around it, does nevertheless contrive with tolerable accuracy to tell the hour of the day and the position of the
moon. In the churchyard old stocks are set up for curious
display. Adjoining the graveyard, in a plot of ground now
covered with newer headstones, is the spot where the vicarage stood in which Coleridge was born. I could find no
memorial of him in St. Mary's. He died July 25, 1834, and
was buried in Highgate Churchyard of London. The trees,

however, of the parish of his youth, were reciting his verses
on this windy day of April of our present visit.

All seasons shall be sweet to thee,
Whether the summer clothe the general earth
With greenness, or the redbreast sit and sing
Betwixt the tufts of snow on the bare branch
Of mossy apple-tree, while the nigh thatch
Smokes in the sun-thaw; whether the eave-drops fall
Heard only in the trances of the blast,
Or if the secret ministry of frost
Shall hang them up in silent icicles,
Quietly shining to the quiet moon.

Our Pickwickian industry finds another celebrity in Ottery—Joanna Southcott, once famous throughout England
and now forgotten. This old fraud in petticoats was born
near by in the year 1750, and has had her life recorded by
Baring-Gould. She was a domestic servant at Exeter until
her head was turned by the shrieks of a crazy preacher in a
Methodist revival; whereupon she set herself up to be a
prophet and a seer. In 1791 she was already "beginning to
see visions." Later, being now famous and the leader of a
sect of her own contrivance, she earned her living by the
sale of "passports into heaven"—six or seven thousand of
them, mostly at a guinea each. Such a scheme was not entirely new, being somewhat a cousin to Roman indulgences,
but she bettered the old dogma by taking all the profits for
herself. St. Peter had distributed them more generously inside the Vatican and out and had even built a mighty church
with them.

In 1801 Joanna Southcott began to publish books of
prophecy—partly in rhyme, which she asserted to her followers was the direct word of God to his inspired amanu-
ensis. "Once she declared," writes Baring-Gould, "that she
had scratched the devil's face with her nails, and had even

bitten off one of his fingers, and that his blood tasted sweet."

Presently she announced that she was pregnant, by no one in particular it seems, and that her unborn son would be Shiloh, another savior of the race. Gifts from the faithful came pouring in. "One wealthy proselyte sent a cradle . . . another sent a pap-spoon . . . and that nothing might be lacking at this accouchement, laced caps, infant's napkins, bibs, mantles, some of white satin, pap-boats, caudle-cups arrived." While Joanna was in this delicate state, certain physicians said "a baby," while others called her figure dropsy. And it was in the midst of this uncertainty and excitement that the lady died.

But this was not the end. Joanna, it seems, had foretold her death to the friends who were gathered at her bedside and had assured them that she would be dead four days, at which time she would revive and be delivered of her son. It was but decency, therefore, that she was wrapped in warm blankets and that a hot-water bottle was placed against her chilly feet. The fourth day passed with unavailing watch, and then poor Joanna was laid away. This was in January, 1815.

Nor was this the end. The sect lived on, attending to all rumors that there was any disturbance of the graveyard sod; for her resurrection, although delayed, was still expected. In January, 1817, probably on or about the second anniversary of Joanna's death, a conclave of her church at Leeds inhibited those of the faith from going to their shops or business in order that they might be at hand and in a proper religious mood for the lady's somewhat dusty reappearance. In London her disciples assembled and made their way in a procession down the Strand, past Temple Bar, and to St. Paul's Churchyard. They were decorated with white cockades and carried a huge trumpet that was larger than Gabriel's, although the purpose of both horns was quite the same. And here a leader arose and shouted out to the throng

that Shiloh had come again. The brazen trumpet sounded.
The crowd shouted its welcome. But it was not Shiloh but
a company of London bobbies that appeared. There is no
law of England against new prophets, but it is a serious mis-
demeanor to obstruct traffic in the Strand.

Baring-Gould informs us that Joanna's sect lingered on
for many years, still hoping for Joanna's resurrection and
Shiloh's birth, but that gradually it fell from faith until at
last only a few of her disciples were left.

We can ourselves add a postscript to his narrative.

In the winter of 1928, one hundred and thirteen years
after Joanna's death, I passed a day at San Diego in Southern California, and went for lunch to the vast hotel that
stands on Coronado Beach. As I crossed the paved circle
where motors are left standing, I observed that one of these
motors was wrapped about in a printed canvas, as if it advertised a circus or a patent medicine. I stopped to read
what the canvas offered, wondering if it would tell me of
bareback riders or of a cure for Bright's disease. It was a
notice that Joanna Southcott was still expected to return to
the glimpses of the moon, and that in the meantime a wicked
world would do well to heed her warnings of the hell to
come.

I walked all around the motor, read each sentence and
then stopped.

"What is the price today," I asked, "of a passport into
heaven?"

There was no response from inside the canvas, for the
driver and his saintly crew had gone to lunch.

I pulled off a handbill from a package that was tied to
the extra tire. It was a demand that the prophetic writings
of this lady of Ottery St. Mary, now deceased and waiting
for her special trumpet, must be read by every one who
wished to curry favor with St. Peter—that, at last, there were
portentous stirrings in an English graveyard.

California is the home of ecstasy and strange religions, of new churches that are built on novel heresies and those reborn on old. It was fitting, therefore, that Joanna Southcott should have lugged her poor old bones there for resurrection.

And now, having seen the best of Ottery St. Mary, we climbed into our motor, where I fell asleep. Across my dreams there was a low whir and murmur, until I awoke at the door of the Royal Clarence Hotel in Exeter.

I stood shivering on the curb while our bags were pulled out.

"A double room with an open fire," I demanded from a young woman at the office wicket.

Exeter Cathedral—

XIII. THE ROYAL CLARENCE

THE ROYAL CLARENCE is of respectable antiquity and fame. It stands inside the cathedral close with a near view of the great building's embroidered front, its towers and crumbled walls, its stretch of cloistered lawn. From the hotel's windows, on any rainy day, one can see a dean or bishop stepping across the puddles, or a family hand in hand. It is a museum, and its corridors and parlors are crowded with curious pictures and mementos that impede one's progress into dinner. For who would hurry down to beef and cabbage when a pair of King Charles's boots sits in a glass case for his inspection? I am not precise about these boots, for in so great a clutter of precious souvenirs one's memory fails.

The food and beds of the Royal Clarence are excellent. There was, it is true, no key to our room. I complained of this, and an aged porter came up to look. At first he attempted to put me off by telling me that no person of Devon would ever think of stealing, and that hardened thieves turned honest when they came across the border. He had served the inn, boy and man, for fifty years, and in all that time no one had ever demanded a key. Then he went off to see what could be done about it.

The key that he produced proved to be competent in securing the door; but had not the faintest notion of how to unlock it. It was, so to speak, a one-way key. What a key has joined together, let no man put asunder. It was only after much fumbling and squinting through the hole, by rattling the door and pounding a knee against it, that we could get out at all. As this seemed dangerous in case of fire, we tossed away the key and piled up the table and the chairs.

We had asked for a room with an open hearth, and we obtained our wish. It seems, however, that where there is a fireplace there is no central heat in the Royal Clarence. However, by feeding the flame, as one might coax a puppy, we finally lifted the damp chill to moderate comfort.

And now, while we are in a picksome mood, we would mention the electric lights of provincial England. It is an American prejudice that an incandescent globe should be really incandescent and that it should serve for dispensing light. A British landlord's theory is different. A light is enough if it makes darkness visible and keeps a traveler from knocking his shins against a table. A tiny globe hangs from a cord in the center of the room, like a murderer with a noose about his neck, and the spark of life that wiggles at the core suggests that the strangling is about accomplished. Now and then an inn will put a table beside one's bed, but there is never a light on it. Years ago, when inns had candles, it was possible to cut one of them into four pieces and have a cheerful celebration, but progress has put its dead hand on this.

We are in a bad mood and can't be stopped.

All American travelers speak of the English bathtub, and we must add our bit. The British regard it as something to be hid under a bushel—to be put, at least, at the far end of a chilly corridor where only patience will find it. And if an inn is so fortunate as to possess several levels to a single floor and little flights of steps that are hiding in the dark, it is down these treacherous steps that one must tumble to his bath. If any one will listen in the twilight of the dawn, he will hear tourists slapping along the corridors in their slippers, and then a little squeal of anguish as a toe is knocked away. Some inns also possess low doorways to their bathrooms in order that a traveler's head may be cracked as he descends.

In the provinces one never asks for a private bath, for such exclusiveness does not exist. It would be like asking for cream in coffee, for relief from loaf cabbage, for a baked potato. As for ourselves, after two months of communistic tubs, when at last in a larger city we had the opportunity of getting a bathtub that was all our own, we did not want it. It seemed wasteful to have a great hulk of painted iron standing idle all the day. And the tub seemed immodest, as being a shameful thing that should really be hidden in a far-off closet at the end of a murky hallway.

There is a printed menu at the Royal Clarence, a wine

list that hints a spacious cellar, food that surpasses the English standard. There are parlors with open fires, and from
most of the windows a view of the cathedral.

- English Hedges -

XIV. EXETER

EXETER is the chief city of southwestern England. Men of
Cornwall, as well as of Devon, regard it as their special own.
It has been the west's voice in the plans of Britain—sometimes of loyal utterance and again discordant. Exeter has
been the home of lost causes and on such occasions it has
been a sore thumb in England's fist. Usually, however, this
western thumb was folded with the other fingers to a common cause, as when Perkin Warbeck, plotting against Henry
VII, petitioned Exeter's help in vain—as when William
landed on the Devon coast from a journey out of Holland
and was proclaimed king at Exeter, to live happy forever

afterwards in London. And in England's greatest cause of all, the contest against Philip II, Exeter was of sturdy help to Queen Elizabeth; for its merchant adventurers boarded ship at Plymouth to help in the sinking of the Great Armada.

Exeter's obscure source is British. It was rebuilt to be a Roman city, and a farthest stronghold toward the untamed moors. It was Saxon for a season, and its castle still shows a remnant of those hard years. Even when England bowed to Woden it kept its Christian faith unstained. Exeter played its part in the Norman Conquest; and the Saxon castle, greatly altered and improved, was named Rougemont to fit the tongue of the invaders. Most of the marks of Exeter's early history are swept away, but we know the sites of its Roman walls and gates. There is Rougemont still standing to be examined, and the Norman towers of the cathedral are a commonplace to every tourist. Elizabethan England is preserved in a number of half-timbered houses in the High Street and in a nest of narrow lanes whose old structures lean forward from the curb. "There be divers fair streets in Exeter," wrote Leland towards the middle of the sixteenth century, "but the High Street that goeth from the west to the east gate is the fairest." Progress, however, has spoiled much of this former beauty.

Churches preserve our best contact with the past. Now and then in England we find an ancient inn that has endured—an inn of heavy walls and deep-splayed windows, of hospitality's blackened beams and tipsy hallways. Or we may discover an almshouse or a guildhall whose origin is lost. But a church is time's best sanctuary. Here alone, safe from innovation, antiquity reposes—old beliefs that would be jostled in the street, a handicraft neglected beyond its protecting walls, a faith that grows lukewarm in the traffic of swift motors. Churches, like the forgotten meadows and their Celtic stones, are the best museums of the past.

So if one walks on the High Street of Exeter or among its lanes and thinks to see a city that is marked thickly with antiquity, he will be disappointed. There is a guildhall arcaded above the sidewalk, a cathedral close of picturesque and ruined house-fronts, an almshouse and several churches that took their start in Saxon days and are of subsequent restoration—but these alone are left. Exeter's High Street is lined with prosperous shops, with London's fashion in the windows and a crowd of strictly contemporary noses against the glass. An electric tramcar runs on a modern trolley. There is a *movie* theatre, with a porter in uniform and brass buttons, tea-rooms and book-shops, public bars, millinery, gowns and boots, riding-breeches of recent cut, shooting-sticks and farm utensils. It must be that Exeter is unconcerned with the Roman soldiers who once walked here and with the Saxon monks who trotted in their sandals outside their convent walls.

Exeter has been too prosperous to be content with the relics of the past. Nor almost until our present days—until Sir Walter Scott roused England to the beauty of its ruined walls—has there been anywhere an interest in antiquity. One needs but to glance at old prints—at these Exeter plates of Dugdale, for example—to see what havoc has been made even in recent times. The old street corners of their yellowing pages are now swept away. The small leading of house-fronts are become great sheets of machine-made glass. Tumbled romantic brick is replaced by iron, and surveyors are employed to give a smooth direction to a wall of buildings.

In the High Street of Exeter there is a tavern of half-timbering; and an anecdote of this building will serve to show under what destructive pressure these ancient structures still exist. It seems that but yesterday a mighty corporation that operates a chain of stores—perhaps Woolworth itself—coveted the site of the old tavern for its own tall emporium of steel and glass. It offered a price that must have tempted the owners, who were subsisting on such a rental as arises from the small sale of beer and cheese. But at this point the city fathers interposed to save a cherished relic of Tudor days. The business corporation, to move the council in its favor, offered as a bait a guaranteed employment of thirty girls to serve its counters, and it was hinted that the great structure of the project would bring a boom to town. Times were bad, thousands were without a job, the offer was a tempting one. It was, however, finally rejected. Beer and Cheddar cheese were saved. We are reminded by this of the circus that had Canterbury on its summer route and found in advance that the elephants were too tall to get in through the historic gate—of the proposal that the gate be taken down in order that an English Jumbo might collect his shillings.

I was told this tavern anecdote in Rougemont Castle by a man in a shabby coat and with the listless bearing that goes with want of work. Plainly he was disgusted with Exeter's lack of progress. He had once been in New York City. He was afire with enthusiasm for tall buildings, and already in his fancy he saw Exeter's sky-line pierced by lofty towers of commerce.

There are a few cities of England where, if one is careful to restrict his gaze narrowly between blinders, he will see no modern structures. In a measure, except for suburbs, Chester is such a city with its arcaded shops. There are certain angles of Canterbury that are wholly old. Bath, at its center, is consistent with its circuses and crescents, its pump-house and parades. And almost anywhere in Chipping Camden the eye will be affronted by nothing newer than the seventeenth century. But in Exeter, mostwise, it is the eye of fancy that reconstructs what time has demolished. Such an eye will change a pavement into mud. It will clear the street of tourists and bring back the wool-laden donkeys of the past when Exeter was a buying market for English and

Flemish looms. In that old tavern we have mentioned it will
place a row of pig-tailed sailors at the bar. And if that eye
possess an equally gifted ear, it will listen to these seamen
as they boast of Virginia and the Northwest Passage.

Exeter was once a famous market for wool—Devon fleeces
spun by cottage labor "in lonely farms and homesteads upon
the moor" and fetched here to be sold. In a single week, it is
recorded, as many as fifty-six pack-horses arrived, and there
were buyers from every part of England.

In Exeter we saw a beadle. I had always thought of beadles
as creatures that perished with antiquity, or at most lingered
on in the pages of "Oliver Twist." And remembering
Oliver's experience with abuse and starvation, I had pic-
tured them as vicious dirty persons, particularly opposed to
second helpings. But our beadle of Exeter was entirely different—a pleasant fellow with a smile and jest. We met him in
Tuckers' Hall—now a museum, but once the seat of the guild
of tuckers, weavers and shearmen. On our first meeting him
he was just a tall old man who took our shillings at the door.
He showed us an oak-paneled banquet room where the tuckers met, a ballot-box with three keys to prevent a dishonest
counting of votes—a tricky little box with two small openings under cover in order that no one might observe into
which compartment the wooden ballot fell. He showed us a
great pair of shears inside whose mighty handles the shear-
man stood, and dried thistles that were used for combing
broadcloth. It was at our request and at an extra shilling
that he took out of a three-cornered box his three-cornered
hat, put on his long official coat, took up his staff and became
instantly a beadle. His face was gentle and refined, but his
voice was of the droning sort that opens meetings pursuant
to adjournment.

We inspected several ancient churches and guessed which
parts were Norman and which of modern restoration. We
visited the sites of the town gates and explored the line of

the demolished wall. We visited Bampfylde House, now the office of the English-speaking Union. It is a fine old building that is advertised to be "the most perfect specimen of Tudor architecture remaining in Exeter."

We gossiped with the keeper of the guildhall. A meeting of farmers was about to start for a discussion of market prices; and but for lack of time we would have sat among them. Except for modern phrasing about futures and hogs strong in closing, we wonder if their conference would differ much from those of long ago. Such talk seems strange in a room that was built to be a chapel.

We walked on Southernhay, a quiet street that marks the line of Roman wall on the southeast edge of town; and here, if anywhere in Exeter, I would choose to live, despite the fact that it seemed a bit snuffy with doctors' offices and old houses let to boarders. Another little backwater of life—a mere court that led to nothing—suggested the setting of the play, "Pomander Walk," except that it had no stream across the foot and there were no comic people sitting at the windows.

Exeter, except for Plymouth, is the chief city of the west of England. One must not from this assume immensity. It is of slight dimensions and from the hill of Rougemont Castle one can see the entire circle of meadowlands and of the hills beyond. Nor has Exeter such suburbs as most cities have. It ends abruptly at open country without that ragged edge of houses that are the work neither of God nor man. Far off to the east was a touch of moorland and just outside the city the bare outlines of a prison. A shabby fellow lifted an instructive finger to point out the death chamber. There was sunlight on the hills and the trees were stirring in a wind with happy tunes that fitted badly to those gloomy windows.

The hill of Rougemont Castle is a public park, with broad lawns and woodland across its moat. Few city parks have so unique a beauty or are so pleasantly sheltered behind Norman walls.

We sat in Exeter Cathedral, whose interior Mary thought of sketching. This is so usual a request that it seems to be a nuisance. The bishop and dean, therefore, in full conclave, have decided the privilege is worth two shillings. Exeter Cathedral is lovely to the eye with its shadowy vaults and spaces, but there is something about it that leaves me cold. Frankly, I am prejudiced. I have been in Exeter several times and on each occasion I have been bullied by some one who looks like a petty sexton. Once it was at the hour of service. I knew that. Not for the world would I have walked about and disturbed the congregation. But I was met at the door by a hard face that seemed to ask me if I had come to pray. In my momentary hesitation he condemned me. I watched Exeter's gentry pass in Sunday black and heard the organ from the chilly vestibule. On another occasion I got inside, but was warned of a dead-line I might not pass. The Catholics handle these matters better, and even heretics are made to feel at home. And now this same old sexton asked me for two shillings, if Mary wished to sketch the transept. There was a time once when money-changers were ejected from a temple, but probably there was no gold standard in Jerusalem.

We did our bit in the knickknack shops that line the cathedral close. Every tourist to Exeter buys a brass hook or a door-knocker. Our hook holds a Celtic pixie and it holds also my pajamas in the bathroom. In this shop we met a teacher from Vassar College who was buying brass hooks with a reckless gesture for all of her students. We were obliged to buy ours or seem to affront her taste. The good lady was on the Grand Tour from Rome to Dublin, but she had fallen ill at the Royal Clarence and was now at last sufficiently convalescent to get about. We left her flirting with a dozen pixies all of brass.

With our tea we had our first clotted cream in Devon. From now on it will be a habit.

In the evening we went to a *talkie* from Hollywood. It was with this taste that we entered the Royal Clarence, passed the glass case of King Charles's old boots, and entered our room, where a fire still smoldered. When our lights were out, we looked across the shadows of the close and saw the moon above the cathedral's towers. Gone were my complaining thoughts of the sexton and his two shillings. Hollywood was lost among these ancient walls and in the silver moonlight of the grass. Here was sanctuary for travelers.

We piled four chairs against our unlocked door and slept in moonlight and the flickering glances of the hearth.

Devon Houses

XV. DOWN THE DEVON COAST

ON SATURDAY, May the second, we left Exeter by public bus. It had been our first plan to hire bicycles for our trip into Devon. The road through Dawlish to Torquay, except for one or two steep pitches, is quite level; and it had seemed possible to harden ourselves here for the rougher country beyond. Our change of plan was fortunate; for our bus rattled at a furious speed around narrow turns, grazing walls and hedges, and on bicycles we must have been in continual alarm. The intermittent rain, moreover, would have drenched us.

Exeter's small suburbs are mostly to the south, like water draining to the sea, and we had gone several miles before we were in open country. The road to Dawlish follows at first the valley of the Exe. Presently we saw across the meadows to the east the town of Topsham. This town is now a decayed port at the top of the river's shallow navigation, but was once of importance in the chronic wars with France and in trade with Newfoundland and Virginia. Below Topsham, the River Exe at high tide is a broad sheet that fills the valley; but when the tide runs out, there is left only an idle ribbon of water winding in the sands. The ocean cleans its cities like a Dutch housewife, and except for its scrubbing brush the docks of commerce would be always dirty. The moon is the general laundress of our coasts—filling its tubs each day and draining them of soapy water.

In the years of Elizabethan prowess, when all of Devonshire was the snug harbor of deep-sea sailors, Topsham's taverns must have been crowded with salty pig-tails ridding themselves of Spanish gold and an ocean thirst. Of days later than these, its fairest chronicles are of contests with French privateers. One of these fights has found its way into an old pamphlet whose title at least is worth quoting. We copy it down from the pages of Baring-Gould. "A True and Exact Account of the Retaking a ship, called the *Friend's Adventure* of Topsham, from the French; after She had been taken six days, and they were upon the Coasts of France with it four days. When one Englishman and a Boy set upon seven Frenchmen, killed two of them, took the other Five prisoners, and brought the said Ship and them safe to England. . . . Performed and written by Robery Lyde, Mate of the same ship. London, 1693."

With such an ample title one need not peruse the entire details of the exploit. It is a tale such as Falstaff told at the Boar's Head. One man of Devon and a boy against seven Frenchmen! Two *mounseers* killed and five made prisoners! A sword hacked like a hand-saw! A plague of all cowards, I say. It was boasts like this that filled Topsham's taverns when grog was flowing.

Below Topsham our bus rattled past Powderham Castle, the home of the Courtenays. It will suffice that French

Courtenays before the Conquest founded a Cistercian Abbey
in the eleventh century, that they went on crusades to the
Holy Land, that one of them was an emperor at Constantinople, that English Courtenays have been conspicuous in
public affairs since the days of Henry II. A Courtenay fought
at Crécy and was a founder of the Order of the Garter.
Another was at Agincourt on that famous day of Crispin
when a French army was demolished. There was a Courtenay at Bosworth Field. It was a Courtenay who defended
Exeter against Perkin Warbeck, and another of them rode
with Henry VIII at the pageants of the Cloth of Gold. They
were prelates of the church and chancellors of Oxford. They
were the companions of kings and in less flattering days
their titles lapsed by attainder and they were beheaded on
Tower Hill.

And now we have come to Dawlish on the English Channel. This town's chief business is the entertainment of summer visitors. There are several hotels and a clutter of smaller
houses whose signboards offer rooms and board. A river
wanders across the town and stops to read these placards as if
it needed but slight persuasion to unpack its bag. There are
trinket shops and a beach, a bandstand for Sunday concerts
in the crowded season. It is the kind of town that offers
weekly rates with meals included and balconies for drying
bathing suits. Here come widows, and wives whose husbands count pennies in Lombard Street. It has a movie
theatre, paths for strolling up the stream, and as much sunlight as the English know how to relish.

This is the district that is sometimes called the English
Riviera. The south coast of Devon and of Cornwall boasts
of so mild a winter that oranges and palms do not entirely
sicken in a frost. The performance, however, of these semi-
tropic trees is really not satisfactory, and one thinks of Dr.
Johnson's comment on dogs that go walking on their hind

legs. "It is not done well," he once remarked, "but you are amazed to find it done at all."

The palm in both Europe and America is chiefly a landlord's bait. He exports them at great expense and sets them out in little tubs beside his door so that every tourist will be sure to see them. They are a seeming proof of warm and sunny days. "Spend the winter here," they say. "Ours is a little pocket that is shielded from the wind and safe from frost." But the palm and orange are no more evidence of this than does the presence of an Abyssinian monkey in a northern circus prove the equator to be near. All three of them are strictly boarders, and they look homesick for their native jungle. We shall see palms in many of the resorts of southern Devon and Cornwall, and they do not deceive us. We know them to be endurance tests against fog and rain— a false assertion that one can go about in winter in summer flannel. For it is now the second of May and I am wearing wool fuzzies and a raincoat, and the sun is of a watery chill.

I protest, also, against the custom of likening these Devon contours to the Bay of Naples; for there is no Vesuvius burning in the night or any dim Capri rising from the sea. The coast of Devon is beautiful, perhaps quite as lovely as the southern shores of France and Italy, but so different that all terms of comparison are futile. The south paints its pictures of ocean and of mountains in definite unmelting lines that are like those of a hard engraving, whereas the north draws a thumb across its softer colors and smudges all the hills in mist.

I am informed that certain modern artists are not satisfied with nature's softly blurred lines such as one sees in evening fog. Moved by that subjectivity which is now the rage, they hold their watercolors below the bathroom's dripping tap; and they have discovered that this extra smear of their burning souls gets them a place in exhibitions which would have been denied to saner and older-fashioned methods. Or, perhaps, in the case of sketches that are of England (no bath-tub' being handy) they merely kept on working out of doors in a downpour that puddled by sheer accident their canvas into genius. Some of Mary's pictures in this book would have been ultra-modern, if she had owned a tighter raincoat and had sat out longer in a drizzle.

But I digress. In Italy there is no apparent atmosphere, and a lovely coast is as clear of outline as a picture postcard. In the south there may be clouds, but they are mere flakes on the background of the sky. In the north, on the contrary, gray clouds are the background; and they are, at best, patched here and there with blue.

There is a homelike aspect also beside these northern waters—cottages from whose chimneys smoke is curling forth. In Italy and France we look on dizzier and homeless mountains, where abandoned Saracen towns are clinging at the top.

Nor is the difference wholly of scenery and dwellings. The resorts of eastern Devon have none of that gay spirit that animates Cannes and Monte Carlo. There is no roulette in a gilded palace. There are no doubtful duchesses ogling rich Americans and casting their chips at fortune. The east coast is not smart. It has no sunny restaurants out of doors with caviar and champagne in buckets. No soft music floats upon the night. Its casinos are bare of that pleasant riot that marks the south. They are, rather, bleak halls where one's footsteps only raise an echo. The benches on Cannes's Croisette are filled with people who seem to boast that they have leisure. Here in Devon in a summer season is a crowd of persons who are ashamed of the time they waste. They sit empty-eyed upon the beaches in any rift of sunlight and wish they were at their London counters measuring ribbons. England's smarter folk go to the continent for their holidays; and their own resorts are filled with last year's hats. Devon is a Riviera of respectable but unexciting boarding-houses for England's turbans of ancient date.

At Cannes, as we are told, ladies follow at a wink. In Devon there is a stiffening of the nose. In such decent Methodism, the legs of the French Riviera and the one-piece bathing-suits of the Venetian Lido would seem unfitting on the beach. Unfitting! We chose the very word. On English beaches, by some mysterious maladjustment, fat folk are always too tightly clad, whereas thin shanks go about in bags and wrinkles. It has been remarked that the British take their pleasures sadly, and this is attested by the crowds who merely sit and stare.

We have only to add that these Devon beaches on this chilly May morning as we motored by, were quite empty, and that the number of window placards showed that the summer crowds had not arrived.

Near Dawlish are two rocks in the ocean that are called the Parson and his Clerk. It seems that a worldly preacher, guided by his clerk, once traveled by night along this coast and they lost their way. In anger the parson cried out, "I would rather have the devil for a guide than you." The outcry brought help. A countryman appeared who offered to lead them into town. But we are in Devon, which is the land of witches, and the countryman was the devil in disguise, as you have probably guessed. To make a long story short, he presently hurled the parson and his clerk from a tall cliff. Two rocks sprouted up that night from the water, to bear forever afterwards their holy titles.

At Teignmouth, to avoid sharp hills, our bus circled up the valley of the River Teign to Newton Abbot, then rattled on to Torquay, which is the center of all this district of mild amusement.

Torquay

XVI. TORQUAY

TORQUAY occupies a rocky headland whose northern side looks towards the coast of Dorset, while its southern slope faces Torbay with the old town of Brixham at a distance across the water. Torbay is of yawning mouth and it is only when winds are blowing from the west that it offers protection to shipping. Except for Brixham, therefore, which sits in a safe inlet, it has no ancient city. For Devon and Cornwall lived aforetime in fear of the French and Spanish, and of any alien merchantman who might hoist suddenly a black flag and come ashore for plunder. No harbor was judged safe unless its headlands were so narrowly spaced as to be connected by a chain.

Such reasoning was not confined to southwestern England. One has only to study the map of Europe to realize the prevalence of pirates in ancient days and the consequent danger of building cities on unguarded coasts. A usual site for a city that wished the benefit of water communications was at the top of a river's navigation. London, Paris and Rome! Bristol was built on the Avon quite distant from the Channel. Rotterdam and Antwerp, Hamburg and Bremen are all inland, but connected with the sea. Of such cities as existed at the fall of Rome, only those were safe which had

no direct exposure to Viking raids; and in the later days of
wide-flung commerce when England, France and Spain were
engaged in their long conflicts, this policy of protection was
kept alive by continuing necessity. It is not wholly for commercial harborage that the cities of America are on guarded
bays and inlets—that New York stands on Manhattan and
not on Staten Island. The instructions for the settlement of
Jamestown provided precisely for a site that would be beyond the attack of Spanish pirates. Wherever we find an old
city on a seacoast, as in the case of Naples, we may be sure
that it led a stormy life and was frequently burned and
pillaged. Naples was assaulted so often that even today its
population is a blend of Saracen and Greek, Norman and
Bourbon. From such a seething pot it is no wonder that
strange smells arise.

And so here in southwestern England we find that Dartmouth and Fowey were protected by chains across their headlands. Looe was built on a river, Topsham at the head of
navigation, Plymouth inside a sound with a narrow mouth
and with a secondary defense at Cattewater. Torquay, therefore, on an open bay is not an ancient city.

It is a new town and a general terminus for summer tourists. It is to this district of eastern Devon what Ilfracombe is
to the north coast—the end of the railway and the major bus-
routes—a town that supports itself on the profits of a hundred hotels that are filled in August with trippers on holiday
from London. Torquay is a seine. Some few thousand travelers filter through a net that is set by greedy landlords, but
no other resort along the coast lands so many cockney fish.

There is a tiny stone-locked basin in which coastwise vessels and pleasure craft are moored, warehouses of none too
prosperous appearance that sleep as they wait for better
times. Whole streets cater to visitors. There is an excellent
book-shop with several rooms of dusty titles. There are
hotels at every turn. An amusement pier holds a casino

where one may drop a sixpence in a slot and pull out his picture or gamble on tin horses that run inside a glass case. It was here we had lunch—a rather dingy dish of what the cook was pleased to call a Welsh rabbit. At the end of the room was a loud-speaker dispensing jazz from London.

We saw merely the town's south slope and the harbor front; but I am told that a pretentious hotel in a northern suburb above Anstey's Cove gives housing to the city's smarter clientele. We hesitated at the foot of a street that extended in its direction, but the pavement climbed a hill and its length discouraged us. I had once spent a night at Torquay, and we saw on the south headland my hotel. A warship had been anchored in Torbay, and all of the streets had been filled with blue-jackets and the butts of cigarettes. This hotel was pointed out to us as the present lodging of the mother of the recent queen of Spain. This lady is English and the governor of the Isle of Wight, with a residence at Carisbrooke Castle. On this very day her banished son-in-law visited her at Torquay.

If the town had tempted us, we would have laid over at Torquay. But there were too many bare hotels from which to choose. It seemed too obviously waiting for trippers—a theatre whose doors had just been opened and whose aisles and seats were still empty.

Torbay's broad crescent has had several chapters that are parts of history. It was always a lurking place for suspicious French vessels that would presently assail ships from Dartmouth and Fowey. A whole French fleet in one of the wars of the seventeenth century had once anchored in Torbay, to sail north and sack the fishing port of Teignmouth. English smugglers used Torbay for landing rum without the payment of the excise tax.

Torbay's greatest event, however, happened on November 5, 1688, when William of Orange landed, to be proclaimed in Exeter the king of England. His first footprint

on Brixham quay is commemorated by the impression of a
Dutch boot. This wasn't really made by William, of course;
and it has not, therefore, the interest that attaches to an actual hoof-mark of Mary Pickford that shows in the pavement
of the Chinese Theatre, Hollywood. Were the great William
to come now in our more progressive days, a fresh bed of
concrete would be laid at the end of his gangplank.

For the narrative of William's coming, we quote from the
diary of a certain Mr. Whittle, who was a chaplain of the
fleet. "The sun," he wrote, "recovering strength, soon dis-
sipated the fog, insomuch that it proved a very pleasant day.
Now every vessel set out its colours, which made a very
pleasant show. By this time the people of Devonshire there-
about had discovered the fleet; the one telling the other
thereof, they came flocking in droves to the side or brow of
the hills to view us; but the standard of the Prince, the
motto of which was 'For the Protestant Religion and Liberty,' soon undeceived them. . . . The major part of the
fleet being come into the bay, boats were ordered to carry
the Prince on shore with his guards; and passing towards the
land with sundry lords, the Admiral of Rotterdam gave
divers guns at his landing. . . . The people came running
out at the doors to see the happy sight. So the Prince, with
Mareschal Schomberg and divers lords, knights and gentlemen, marched up the hill, which all the fleet could see over
the houses, the colours flying and flourishing before his
Highness, the trumpets sounding, the hoit-boys played, the
drums beat, and the lords, gentlemen and guards shouted,
and sundry huzzas did now echo in the fleet from off the
hill, so that our very hearts below in the water were even
ravished for joy thereof."

"Twenty-six regiments," continues Arthur Norway, "had
been landed at Brixham before night fell, and the news was
spreading far and wide. It is curious to see how little fear
was inspired by the landing of fifteen thousand foreign sol-

diers. People actually walked over from Totnes after morning service the next day to see the army, in absolute confidence that no violence would be offered them; while as for
the peasants, they did their utmost to bring in supplies for
so great a number of men, and coming to the top of the
hills set apples rolling down into the town, where the soldiers scrambled for them. Surely never in all history was the
work of the invader so fully done from the moment of his
landing. The country was won. The county magnates were
already meeting in secret to decide their attitude; and those
who were for supporting King James were few. A few days
of hesitation and anxiety ended in the accession of Sir Edward Seymour of Berry Pomeroy, and thenceforth the game
was won."

The Duke of Ormond, attempting unsuccessfully to land
here when Queen Anne had died, has no interest. The Duke
thought it was his turn to wear the English crown. He anchored in the roadstead and fired three guns "as a signal for
the gentry to rise to his assistance." No one rose, however,
but customs officers who asked, probably, if he had any silk,
tobacco or perfumery to declare. And as no one can be a
hero while his bags are rummaged, presently the Duke sailed
off and was drowned in getting back to France.

After two hours on Torquay's harbor-front, we hoisted
our Welsh rabbits up the steps of a public bus and went
bouncing across the hills to Totnes.

The River Dart flows past the footings of this town; and
at a bridge, with a garden on the stream, stands the Seymour
Hotel. It shows a pleasant invitation to the road, so down we
lumbered with our bags. We stayed for a week, with much
tea and clotted cream beside the river's moving tides.

The Bridge at Totnes.

XVII. TOTNES

TRAVEL'S greatest pleasure, as we are told, is to be at home again—to sit at our familiar window, unfretted by railway schedules, and to review our recollections in slippers. Beyond the poplar of our garden we may watch Italian sunsets change to the softer colors of the British Isles, the Coliseum tumble to the outline of a Devon cottage. The very snow upon our lawn by some strange reckoning becomes the slope of Etna, and trees that are tipped with snow hold the almond blossoms of the south. But travelers are a pest when they start to talk, for no one wishes to listen. We have ourselves sat through a horrid evening pinioned under the meticulous narrative of an excursion around the world.

Nor would we be justified in letting our memory throw an Italian glamor over England. English canvases are the subdued work of such a one as Constable as against a Veronese. They are not done in paint, but are, rather, quiet etchings—a village whose smoking chimneys hint of supper, a lake sleeping in the hills, a stream too small to turn the wheels of commerce. But in the room of our memory where these slight etchings hang, on some choice wall we shall suspend the memory of our week beside the Dart.

Totnes lies on the motor road from London to Plymouth; yet most travelers allow themselves only an hour for a cup of tea at the Seymour Hotel. They may, perhaps, look across the lawn and see the river drifting in or out upon the tide; then remarking that it is a charming spot, they rise and dust themselves of crumbs, call loudly for their reckoning and hurry to their motors. Before they have crossed the first hilltop to the west, their chins are already inside their collars.

These tourists are too hurried to waste a day in Totnes. They are ignorant that at the very center of the town there is a castle that commands a wide outlook up and down the valley, that narrow lanes behind the High Street are worthy of a visit. They have no guess for the beauty of the Dart, its hundred curves among the hills, its towns and villages, until the river passes between headlands to the sea. There is a delightful walk through meadows by this stream; but it is not the possession of any swift motorist bound to Plymouth.

One out of every dozen of them may see Berry Pomeroy Castle, three miles out of Totnes; yet even these fortunate tourists have not climbed down a pathway through the heavy woods to see the ruin from the streamlet far below. At most they have craned their stiff necks to look upon a tower and pronounce it Norman, have stood before crumbling walls and called them Tudor. But never have they had time to climb the tower and lie on the soft grasses at the top, high above the tallest trees, to watch from this outlook springtime's cloudy pageant in the sky. The church bells of Berry are of softest tunes on Sunday mornings and there are lilacs and laburnums in the graveyard—but these are unremarked in a tourist's diary.

We stayed at Totnes for a week, and our memory holds title to all this beauty roundabout.

It was early in the afternoon when we arrived at the Seymour Hotel. Our bedroom windows looked pleasantly on the River Dart, with a sidelong glance at the bridge and its occasional motor. Beyond was Totnes rising on a hill with a church tower at the top above the roofs. We had asked for a room with an open fire, but could get nothing better than a hearth with a flicker of blue gas that crept up an asbestos sheet.

We went out at once to explore the riverside. In the hotel's garden little tables were already set for tea; but we passed them by and issued to a lane that ran downstream at the back of a row of decayed one-storied warehouses on the water front. Although Totnes is almost two hours from the ocean by a chugging steamer, the town once had considerable commerce with the coast and with river ports whose sailing vessels landed produce here. Totnes is at the top of the tide, with muddy shallows just above, and it is only when the moon permits that any boat larger than one with oars can make now the journey from the sea. The warehouses, in consequence of this, are empty. And this is just as well, for their romantic desolation suggests spicy bales from across a southern ocean. Below the warehouses there is a landing stage for the river's two passenger steamers; and here, as often as they sail, arises the town's prime excitement. This happens once or twice a day, depending on the hours of flood. It is quite the proper thing to stand around then with your hands in your pockets and to call the skipper Harry.

Totnes is said to have been founded by Brutus—not Shakespeare's *Et tu, Brute,* but a gentleman descended from that Aeneas who had sailed from the fall of Troy and has been plaguing schoolboys ever since. English towns, wherever possible, claim descent from the Trojans; with now and then a variant like Colchester, which boasts of Old King Cole—or like Bath, which looks back to an eleventh generation of Venus as its progenetrix. But Troy, like the *Mayflower,* indicates the bluest of blue blood.

After wandering about among the islands of the sea, Brutus came at last up the River Dart and announced his satisfaction with the valley in a poem of modern English and bad rhyme.

> Here I am, and here I rest,
> And this town shall be called Totnes.

If one is inclined to doubt the truth of this legend, he needs only read the history of Geoffrey of Monmouth to find his landing recorded. England was inhabited at that time, it seems, by a race of giants. "Wherefore," says our historian, "after exploring certain districts of the land, they drove the giants they found to take refuge in the caverns of the mountains, and divided the country among them by lot according as the Duke made grant thereof." Among others of these giants there "was a certain hateful one by name Goemagot, twelve cubits in height, who was of such lustihood that when he had once uprooted it, he would wield an oak tree as lightly as it were a wand of hazel." In a wrestling match between this giant and a member of Brutus's crew, the Trojan hero "gathered up all his strength, heaved him up on his shoulders and ran with his burden as fast as he could for the weight to the seashore nighest at hand. Mounting up to the top of a high cliff, and disengaging himself, he hurled the deadly monster he had carried on his shoulder into the sea, where, falling on the sharp rocks, he was mangled all to pieces and dyed the waves with blood." If one distrusts this history of Monmouth, he can see the stone on which Brutus sat while he composed his poem. It lies in the pavement at No. 51 Fore Street, and this should be proof enough.

Arthur Norway, who is our informant in these and other matters, is disposed to put his tongue in his cheek at this legend, but he does not dismiss lightly, however, its implication. "Even sceptics will admit," he writes, "that the Brutus story is probably an indication of some very early invasion and conquest of the aboriginal tribes; and it must be borne in mind throughout Devon and Cornwall that their situation, facing directly to the west and south, exposed them to the first impacts of those successive waves of commerce and of civilization which radiated from the Mediterranean in ages far beyond the range of history. Very scant and few are the records of early voyages among these northern seas; but those writers are rash who disregard them, or who pretend to set limits to the enterprise of sailors of whom all we know is that they were bold and daring, and had no difficulties between them and Britain save such as they were well able to overcome."

We are inclined, therefore, to let Brutus sit forever on his Totnes stone and compose bad rhymes in English. Our only regret is that blind Homer did not take this same journey for an epic; for he would have stuck to his native Greek and served up something pretty about this River Dart. "All day long," he had written once, "the sail of the running ship was stretched. Then the sun sank, and all the ways grew dark. And now the ship reached earth's limits, the deep stream of the Ocean, where the Cimmerian people's land and city lie, wrapt in a fog and cloud. Never on them does the shining sun look down." Who of us knows the truth. This fog would seem to indicate that Odysseus also reached the British Isles.

Totnes has an ancient castle on a hill-top, and its keep is of Norman origin. For a shilling one may obtain a key from an old lady who sells small wares in a shop outside the gate, and he may climb by a wooded path to a ragged crenelation for an extensive view across the valley. He will see the high line of Dartmoor in the north and east, its tors like answering castles. He will see the narrow valley through which the River Dart issues to the ocean, the cluttered disorder of the Totnes roofs that confess no streets among them. He will hear the song of birds and the leaves that whisper to the wind. Then leaving the castle's keep, he may climb up and down a wooded hillside, looking curiously at the dry marking of an ancient moat, or over fences into a pleasant nest of back-yards that are living wholly in the present and are concerned only with a Monday's wash that stretches through the week.

In this early season of the year, before the hum of motors is on the road from Plymouth, a tourist may possess this hilltop's solitude for the payment of a shilling. Nor would the castle's enclosure be crowded in August; for Totnes, we repeat, is a town that motorists hurry through. Their diaries confess at most to a blurred succession of house-fronts, to a sharp turn upon a hill, to a long stretch downward on which their motor races.

On the crenelations of the keep I met an English couple who were searching the horizon for a glimpse of Hay Tor. And when I laid my map and compass on the wall and found it for them, we were friends at once. They had just spent two weeks of idleness at Salcombe on Devon's southern shore. As this vacation town lies outside our travels, I may be permitted to give their opinion that it is worth a fortnight of holidays, that its situation is beautiful and that its hotels are excellent and of moderate price. This last qualification will keep most Americans from it. An English friend asked on our return if we had been to Salcombe. "It has a jolly beach," he said, "and a great cliff above the sea."

My Totnes acquaintances lived eight and a half miles from Hyde Park Corner near Slough, where they had an acre of ground with pear trees and new potatoes. The man had lived for eighteen years in India before his marriage, and he was a bit discontented with a single acre. He preferred a certain cottage at Salcombe with a view of ships. London, moreover, so he said, had a habit of extracting guineas where a half-crown was quite enough. His wife, however, had put her foot down in favor of Slough and her new potatoes, and it was evident that the cottage would not be purchased.

"James," she said, "wants nothing but an old harbor to poke about in and a fisherman to talk to."

The three of us came out of Totnes Castle together, and each of us rattled the gate to be sure that it was locked. It seemed only decent to be quite sure, when the Normans had been at such pains to build a dungeon tower strong enough for siege. There was a display of German cannons at the entrance, taken in the recent war. The woman disapproved of this as she had lost a brother in the trenches.

"Have you seen the guildhall?" she asked presently.

I had not, so they walked around the square to save me a search, and they left me at the door.

"You should go down to Salcombe," said the man, "and see my cottage."

"Slough," was his wife's reply.

They turned the corner and were lost forever.

I was met on the guildhall's doorsill by a young woman with a mop.

"You mustn't come in," she said. "We've been scrubbing the floor and you would track mud on it."

It was a tone such as cooks use at a kitchen door when there are children in the house.

"Please," I answered, and I rattled a shilling.

She relented and stretched out her palm. " 'Cue," she answered.

I entered.

"Just keep off the part that's wet," she added, "and you might scrape your boots."

On the wall inside was a painting of the poet Ossian reading aloud his verses to an audience of the third century. The picture was made in a year that still believed in the reality of Ossian's poems, before they were shown to be fraudulent and the composition, wholly or in part, of Macpherson in the eighteenth century—like the verses of that Priest Rowley who was conceived entire by Thomas Chatterton. In the guildhall also was a prison cell with its grill for bread and water—a prison now unused. There were village stocks and other souvenirs. But now the mop was in fierce assault against the stone floor, and the dirty island on which I stood was dwindling into nothing, so I came away.

Totnes has a parish church with a Norman charter, walls that are mostly of the fourteenth century, and a furious peal of bells that are frightfully alive. The town has two ancient gates, a remnant of original ramparts, a book-shop, and a *movie* theatre. It has a picturesque steep-pitched High Street.

But our best memory concerns the garden of our hotel, where we could watch the rise and falling of the tide and mark it on a flight of wooden steps. It concerns tea and clotted cream, the steamer-landing and the long walk along the meadows. Totnes is best in memory when, with the day's labor of sights behind us, we leaned against the stone railing of the bridge and watched the leaves floating in the twilight towards the sea.

— the River Dart at Totnes —

XVIII. THE MEADOWS OF THE RIVER DART

MARY'S pencil was busy with the roofs of Totnes. My book was of Thomas Hardy. Cattle were grazing in the soft grass. Far off rose a church tower. Out of silence came a steamer and left silence in its wake.

England's coal mines cannot compete. Her looms lack buyers. Her cities are crowded with men who live upon the dole. In every port vessels lie rusty in the mud. A hundred years of wealth are followed by collapse. Yet of all this there is no echo across these meadows of the Dart.

France grumbles on her pile of gold. New forts along her eastern front are thick with guns. Her air fleet could be a plague of locusts on the lands beyond the Rhine. She is thinking again of Napoleon and of conquest. Mussolini wears Caesar's imperial toga. Germany totters, with empty hand outstretched for help. Spain is in a first raw experiment. There is bankruptcy in South America and war in China. Russia is a workshop of forced labor that underbids democracy. But the Dart's vista is of a golden age.

Our chart is license. We have scrapped our morality, to start again from nothing towards Utopia. Tradition is a chain, and we have cut it from our ankle. Art is a cracked mirror for the diseased image of our thought. Letters follow a nasty lead. Music is the clamor of ungreased gears. But there are birds in the meadows of the Dart, and they sing the songs of David.

I was roused by the crack of a rifle. A man was climbing across the wall.

"What is that?" I asked.

"It comes from a practice range," he answered. "There is a target down the river."

"Does the world need practice in destruction?" was my reply.

Nor is Totnes entirely peaceful, even with the exception of its rifle range. For presently, while we sat at tea, the bells of its parish church suddenly went mad and performed a terrible racket for a full half hour. One would have thought they had taken a hint from my discordant meditation and were clanking up a Russian revolution.

- Berry Pomeroy Castle -

XIX. BERRY POMEROY

TOTNES is a convenient center for tours. Our first of these was to Berry Pomeroy to see the village and the castle. These two are a mile apart and both of them hide in the foldings of the hills. Berry Pomeroy has been for several hundred years the home in absence of the Seymour family— its actual home until the castle was shattered and unroofed. These Seymours have held since Tudor days the title of the Somersets. You will find them everywhere in English history. Jane Seymour was number three in Henry VIII's matrimonial waiting list—his only wife who died naturally and undivorced within his lifetime—an accomplishment for which we must give her credit. The Lord Protector of England during the youth of Edward VI was another Seymour. There were Seymours in the wars with Cromwell. They were bishops and soldiers, men of ability, of virtue spotted now

and then with vice, but they were always in the public eye.
And their title still persists to be, except for Norfolk, as I am
told, the premier dukedom of England.

Our trip to Berry Pomeroy was sentimental, urged by
neighbors who are Seymours. I once looked up in England
the sister of a gardener of a friend, and she gave me tea in
her cottage. Our present errand, however, although it moves
among coronets and plush, offers no tea to strangers.

It seems that a certain Richard Seymour—a younger son
of the duke, no doubt, sailed for America about the year
1642. He carried with him a patent from the king for a
frontage on Long Island Sound and as great a depth of lot
as could be traversed in a day. For so the legend states. He
landed on the shore of Connecticut and struck inland to
claim his royal gift. It was bad going, we may be sure,
through the unbroken forests of an undiscovered country.
But spurred by greed and the terms of his patent, he succeeded in encompassing the site of the present Norwalk,
where we leave his offspring for nearly three hundred years.
This original Richard Seymour is said to have been buried
in a certain graveyard that still exists in Norwalk beside the
river, although no stone marks his grave to save the site from
speculation. All this is probable enough, but it is unsupported by documents and lives in legend only. And of a consequence, it has become the habit of American Seymours to
visit Berry Pomeroy and to consult the vicar of the parish
church for any proof that may exist in his records. And
scriveners in London at the Herald's College have also
wrinkled their foreheads and raked up documents for a
usual fee.

One of our Seymours at home is a neighbor just down
the street. And if the question is put point-blank to him for
proof of his family's claim, he answers that in Berry Pomeroy's parish church there is an angel carved of stone, reputed to be a likeness of the original Richard, and that it

has a strong resemblance to his Cousin X—, a certain confidence of posture that proves them close of kin. This evidence would not move the decision of a court of law, but it weighs heavy on our street. In Cousin X—'s veins flows, unquestionably, the blood of the Somersets. Let us confess the truth. Mary is herself one of these Seymours that look back upon a Devon home. Our visit, we repeat, was sentimental.

It was on a Sunday morning that we set out afoot for Berry Pomeroy. We climbed a hill from Totnes on a road that was being widened from a pretty lane to a broad highway of concrete for motors. Far to the north stretched a green valley, with woods on a farther range that hid the castle.

It was at the hour of service when we entered the churchyard of Berry. Already the bell was ringing and village folk, heavy with psalters and hymn-books, were coming up the path. Was it better to attend service and then accost the vicar? Or would it be more profitable to postpone our questions until we had paid our visit to the castle in order that the leisure of a Sunday afternoon might give us ample time? Vicars, perhaps, are more talkative after they have dispensed their sermons and have had their naps. The latter method seemed the better, so we turned away at the last echo of the bell and trudged uphill along a country road.

It was such a morning as only Devon offers in the springtime—green meadows rolling to the hills and the trees waking into blossom.

Presently, in a mile or so, a signboard informed us that the castle was near and that its key was kept at the porter's lodge. We found the lodge. We knocked at the door. A shrewish face was thrust out from a narrow crack that was just wide enough to repulse a beggar.

"Please," I said, "we want the key of the castle."

"You can't have it. The castle's closed until two o'clock on Sundays."

"But the porter of our hotel said the gate was open at ten."

"Which ain't nothing to me," the wrinkled woman answered.

"You don't understand," I persisted. "We are distant cousins from America. Perhaps you have heard of Richard Seymour who died in Norwalk in the seventeenth century. We are his grandchildren—both of us—and we are asking only for a key and not a fatted calf. We would be grateful for tea and slap-cake, but we don't insist."

"The fire's out," she answered.

"But surely the good duke—"

"The duke ain't here. And orders is orders."

The door was slammed. It was an ungracious greeting for prodigals returned from the land of wooden nutmegs. If some poor relative of the Great William had arrived from Normandy, he would have been admitted and bedded in the straw. It is evident that the feudal system is dying out.

I looked at my watch. It was barely noon. Across these hills as far as the eye could see, there was no restaurant. And it was evident that Cousin Ed, the Duke of Somerset, was not expecting us.

We went around the lodge to the rear. An old man was squatting in a shed sorting potatoes. Obviously he was not his excellency. I rattled a shilling, for he seemed the kind of man who would heed that kind of tinkle.

"What would happen," I asked, "if we climbed the fence and went to the castle without the key? Are there any bobbies in the woods?"

"You couldn't get inside the castle," he replied, " 'cause it's locked."

"And I suppose there's no pantry window left unbolted." He sniffed.

"But we could sit under the trees."

"We've nothing against that."

"And at two o'clock, perhaps you would be good enough to bring us the key."

He looked up, like one who plans to spend his Sunday afternoons in a hammock and doesn't wish an interruption. I held out two shillings.

"Well, perhaps I could," he answered.

We left him pawing his potatoes and climbed the fence.

We were on a road that descended a valley of shadowed beauty, and at the bottom of the slope we stood before Berry Pomeroy's Norman towers. Beyond these the land drops sharply to a river far below.

I have no doubt but that this stronghold in its pristine state could have successfully endured assault; but our own attack was thwarted, not by its weight of ordnance, but rather by a mesh of barbed wire—by this and a line of broken bottles on the top of a half-fallen wall. By great effort, I got my chin above the dangerous glass, but could not hoist myself across it. I scratched my front buttons and was snagged by wire, but Berry Pomeroy did not surrender. England's mightiest castles are no longer secured by boiling oil poured through their crenelations, yet a tourist must always wait, nevertheless, until an old woman tosses out a rusty key.

We walked around as much of Berry Pomeroy as the sharp pitch of the hill permitted and, finding no cranny for our entrance, we decided on a siege until two o'clock. There was a convenient bench for this, and here we sat while Mary sketched the Norman towers.

Presently an Englishman and his wife came down the road with an air of persons who were out on holiday. They took but a moderate interest in the castle, but were eager to find a wishing-tree that was mentioned in their guidebook. I helped them find it. Consulting their book again, they discovered that the tree gave out its magic only to those who succeeded in walking backward three times around it. As the tree rose from a sharp decline and a tangle of exposed roots, the task was harder than it sounds. However, the three of us got down on all-fours and by much scrambling somehow got around it. My own wish concerned Old Potatoes, with a hope that he would not fail to fetch his key at two o'clock. I now offered to these English tourists a general lecture on Berry Pomeroy, its architecture and its antiquities; but they yawned and moved off among the trees.

The Castle from the Valley —

Presently a larger group arrived—at first a frisking of youngsters, to be followed by older folk who came puffing up the hill from the river dropping sweat. They laid down a cloth and emptied a basket. There was a genial pop of corks and a clank of knives. Had they thrown a chicken bone my way, I would have seized it like a hungry dog, for I was hungry. And now they also had departed, without a remaining crumb.

As Mary's sketch was now done, we set out to explore the woods. At the stream-side there are footings of an abandoned mill and a view of the castle far above. There were primroses and other wild flowers in the woods—paths that show the park to be a common picnic ground, but quite unspoiled by refuse.

Old Potatoes arrived promptly at two o'clock. We applied his mighty key to a barnlike door beneath the Norman towers and went inside.

The manor of Berry Pomeroy, as it first appears in the paragraphs of history, was of Saxon ownership. In Isaac Taylor's "Words and Places"—a meaty book that is perhaps not to be wholly trusted—the manor is spelled Bury-Pommeroye, and it is asserted that the syllable *bury* conveys in Saxon "the notion of inclosure or protection." It comes from Germanic origin and is cousin to *borough, burgh, brough* and *barrow.* Like the Celtic *dun,* it means a hill-fortress. These German syllables, he adds, sometimes "denote the funeral mound which gave shelter to the remains of the dead, but more frequently they mean the walled inclosure which afforded refuge to the living." Of Saxon days we can discover only that Berry Pomeroy during the reign of Edward the Confessor belonged to a certain Alricus.

We have spent a zealous morning in an attempt to dig out the history of a certain Ralph de Pomeroy, with whose arrival in England the castle's connected narrative begins. The Conqueror gave him fifty-eight lordships in Devon from which to choose a site for a castle against the Saxons. But Thierry's Norman Conquest omits him from its index. The Britannica, among its million names, does not include his. The author of "England Under the Normans and Angevins" tosses not a sentence in his direction. It is the plague of authorship that one cannot find what one is looking for. Our local guidebook, however, states that the "records of the castle . . . having been lent by the eleventh Duke of Somerset to a friend" were not returned. Perhaps this is an answer to the Britannica's silence, and the pride of the Pomeroys is saved.

Be this as it may, Ralph de Pomeroy selected Berry from

among his scattered lordships and built a strong castle on
this wooded crest of hill. A Pomeroy married an illegitimate
daughter of Henry I, and from that event to the reign of
Henry III they were admitted to the House of Lords. They
then lost the benefit of peerage, although still retaining a
somewhat empty title. And so for nearly five hundred years
they had their seat at Berry, until in the reign of Edward VI
a certain Thomas Pomeroy in one of many legends forfeited
it by treason. This is but one legend, for another states he
sold his castle and made good money at the price.

And now the Seymours enter the plot at Berry—a family
originally from St. Maur in Normandy where, if an old story
be believed, a certain parent of the family was a monk who
forgot his vows. But Jane Seymour married Henry VIII, and
her younger brother became a member of a council that
was to govern England after Henry's death during the mi-
nority of Edward VI. That Jane's brother was made the
Duke of Somerset and the Lord Protector of the Realm, that
he built Somerset House in the suburbs of London on the
Strand, that he was for a term England's most powerful poli-
tician and was embroiled in intrigue to hold his place, are
matters of general history. He fell at last and was condemned
to death on Tower Hill.

One account says that the Lord Protector purchased Berry.
The other affirms that at the treason of the Pomeroys, it was
given to him by the king. In this second legend, the Pomeroys returned a saucy answer to the royal command that all
the castles of England be dismantled. A siege of Berry Pomeroy followed. When at last the walls were forced, the Pomeroys, declining to surrender, blindfolded their horses and
spurred themselves to destruction from the hill-top.

The Seymours, now in the reign of Edward VI possessing
Berry Pomeroy, were not content with its Norman towers.
For thick walls and crenelations were gone from fashion and
were mere relics of fiercer days when a Saxon countryside

must be kept at heel. The Reformation had checked the building of churches (heresy had space enough without new walls) and architectural genius had turned to the erection of country houses—buildings that borrowed something of what is called English perpendicular, but dwarfed to fit a drawing-room. What we call Tudor is dotted all through England, and in its political suggestion it indicates a countryside safe at last, lending its luxuries to the rich.

Berry Pomeroy, as we see it today, is of two distinct types of construction. If one wishes evidence of the iron hand of William the First, he need only stand before the Norman towers. Inside the enclosure, in front of the airy range of buildings that the Seymours put up, he will see how elegance followed security.

The roofs and floors are gone, the windows are unglazed like martyrs that have lost their eyes in torture. There is scarcely a staircase left, and their broken stumps climb to sills that open merely into space—staircases like that which David Balfour climbed blindly in the night when a villain wished to kill him. Great fireplaces remain, one above another, and they are still marked with Elizabethan hospitality. Grass grows within the shadowed spacing of the walls and is a sunny fringe along their tops. Nor can I leave these waving grasses of Berry without a recollection of an essay by Alice Meynell in which she comments on a similar runaway growth of summer. "It breaks all bounds," she writes, "flies to the summits, lodges in the sun, swings in the wind, takes wing to find the remotest ledges, and blooms aloft. It makes light of the sixteenth century, of the seventeenth, and of the eighteenth. As the historic ages grow cold it banters them alike. The fragrant flourishing statue, the haughty façade, the interrupted pediment . . . are the opportunities of this vagrant garden in the air." Miss Meynell is writing of Rome, but her description fits a Devon ruin.

While Mary sketched these Tudor buildings of her far-

off and controversial great-great-grandsires, I climbed one of
the Pomeroy's Norman towers. And there I found a padding
of soft grass where I watched the clouds until I slept.

Berry Pomeroy Church

XX. A VISIT TO THE WARDEN

IT WAS now the middle of the afternoon. It was, therefore,
likely that the Vicar of Berry Pomeroy, having completed his
heavy dinner and his siesta, might be in a mood to tell what
he knew of the Richard Seymour who had journeyed to
Connecticut.

We halted at the castle lodge.

"You don't suppose," I said, "that they have postcards for
sale. It would be nice to send one to Cousin X— and tell
him that his roof needs mending."

I had once mailed a card of a particularly ruinous castle to a friend and had marked a battered tower as being my room. But my friend missed the jest and thought it was really a picture of my hotel and that I was lodged in the attic.

Downhill we went to the village of Berry. We inquired for the vicar's house, but a gardener informed us that he was absent on a holiday.

We stated our errand.

The gardener scratched his chin.

"You might enquire of the warden," he replied. "I'll show you where he lives."

We crossed the churchyard and knocked at a door. We gave our errand and waited in a stiff parlor where a large square table suggested that the room was dining-room as well. It was the kind of room where a marble statue of Florence Nightingale, an aspidistra and a pot of tea could feel equally at home.

And now there were clumping footsteps on wooden stairs outside. A woman's voice cried out from a kitchen beyond, "Mind the mud on your boots." There was a sound of obedient scraping, and then a tall man of more than middle age entered. I had expected a Trollope's warden, a bent and scholarly figure in Sunday black. But the warden of Berry Pomeroy was dressed in corduroy riding-breeches, although his upper half was compromised by a Sabbath tie and collar. He was neat and clean, but he looked as if he had entered from the stable—as if, indeed, he was accustomed to regard the parlor as a room wholly for evening use and as rather a womanish place when the sun was up. He was the kind of man who would scratch a pig's back with a walking stick and enter a stall to slap a favorite horse. Trollope's warden, if I remember rightly, composed a history of hymns.

The Warden of Berry Pomeroy halted at the door with almost a suspicious surprise. We might have been a demand on the mortgage. Then a friendly wink twinkled in his eye.

"What can I do for ye?" he asked.

We restated our errand.

"Have ye heard the bad news?" he interrupted. "The duke died this very morning. We have just had word."

We were silent, not knowing what remark might be expected. The warden shut one eye and seemed to think. "I have served under six dukes," he said, "and now there will be a seventh." A wink ended his serious meditation. "Perhaps ye have come," he added, "to claim the title."

This, possibly, was not wholly jest; for the duke whose death had just occurred had been of collateral line rather than of direct descent from his predecessor. It was only after a long examination by the House of Lords into the legality of certain marriages that the title had been at last conferred on him.

The warden knew nothing of our Connecticut Richard Seymour, except what we already knew ourselves—that a certain angel inside the church was said by legend to be a likeness of a man who had that name.

"I can show you him," he said, "a jolly little fellow singing hymns with all his might."

"Perhaps there are parish records," Mary suggested. "The gardener said you had the keys."

"Perhaps there are and perhaps there ain't," he answered. "But you will have to consult the vicar when he gets back. Sorry," he added, "if it was pigs or horses, I could help you."

We took down the vicar's name and left. We saw the angel. Our errand, although unsuccessful, had at least gained us entrance to an English cottage.

We walked to the Seymour Hotel and as we had missed our lunch by several hours, we did unusual justice to cakes and clotted cream. The tide was running down the Dart, and leaves and twigs were drifting out to sea.

Dartmouth Harbor.

XXI. DOWN THE DART

OUR NEXT trip from Totnes was down the River Dart. It was a sunny but uncertain morning with more than enough blue than was needed to patch a sailor's breeches. But if any reader thinks that blue patches are an indication of continuing sunlight in England, we hope that he also leaves his umbrella at home and is drenched.

There is a general belief that of all the rivers of southwestern England the Tamar between Devon and Cornwall is the most beautiful—that it offers a variety of scenery unparalleled elsewhere on this lovely coast, and that the Dart is merely second in its attractions to the tourist. I have never had the good fortune to travel up the Tamar; for at Plymouth, a week hence, the boats to the top of its navigation were not yet running on their summer schedule. At this present writing I can only affirm that the Dart is as beautiful a river as I ever followed to its mouth. The steamer trip of less than two hours from Totnes to Dartmouth is through a range of hills, whether one considers the shallow river at the top or the deeper channel near the sea.

The steamer's schedule is altered each day to fit the changing of the tide. Nor is the inconstant moon entirely faithful in its promise of sufficient water; for on rare occasions, through some lunacy above, the boat is stranded and must wait until the Queen of Night comes back upon her job.

The Dart that seems so safe and peaceful, has rather a bad reputation for calamity, and this is attested in a country rhyme.

> River of Dart! O River of Dart,
> Every year thou claimest a heart.

But on a May morning under summer clouds, it is hard to believe these tales of shipwreck.

We boarded a small vessel of large overhanging decks, above which a canvas is stretched in rain—tardily, of course, after every one is wet and really doesn't care. It was the kind of ship that has a skipper who himself tosses off the mooring line and clambers across the rail just when you think he has been left behind—a skipper whose name is Harry to any deckhand and whose only badge of office is a blue cap.

But Harry was a friendly fellow and presently in a gust of rain, he invited Mary to stand beside him under cover at the steering wheel as he guided his craft around the river's tricky curves. Later, in wider waters, he gave the wheel to his mate and became a salesman along the deck to dispose of his stock of colored postcards and a descriptive map and circular of the Dart. He called out his wares with that galvanized enthusiasm that comes from years of repetition. "Here ye are, ladies and gents! Here ye are! It's yours fer a sixpence! Everything ye need to know. Confirmed Hinglish 'istory! Only a sixpence while they last! And ye ain't seen the river proper unless ye know what it's all about!"

The ship's fireman, meantime, having loaded his furnace

with coal, sat on the steps of his dirty pit and smoked an evil pipe that seemed to be doing its bit to keep the vessel's steam up. Occasionally he spat into the blackness at his feet.

In a stuffy cabin halfway below the water sandwiches of uncertain date were offered, and tea at its proper hour.

We bought a guidebook for future use in order that we might plague a reader with its dullness. Here and there on our travels we bought dozens of pamphlets of this sort, together with any books that celebrated a town or village. And when the burden of these had so swelled our luggage as to leave no place for underwear, we tied them in a bundle and mailed them to America. On my desk at home on my return I would find forty-seven of these packages.

The channel of the Dart shifts at every turn to escape a sand-spit and find deep water. It offers beauty unparalleled. Our enthusiasm declines restraint. Were we Baedeker we would set a double star upon it. It is of continually fresh surprise, offering in succession villages and great estates, unbroken woods and headlands, an unrolling panorama that is the very heart of friendly Devon.

There is always suggestiveness in the place-names of an English countryside, and here along the Dart we find Windwhistle Cottage, Sharpham, Greenway Farm, Dittisham Ferry, Killgate, Bosomzeal Cross, Fleet Mill, Cuckold's Head, Stoke Gabriel, Tuckenhay, Sandridge and World's End. That so many of these names are Saxon in this Celtic land reminds us of Germanic invasions up the Dart. Bosomzeal Cross hints of later days and suggests that this village was named by seventeenth-century pietists who had fought alongside Cromwell and now affirmed their zeal in the solemn business of a Presbyterian God. Cuckold's Head indicates domestic complications of Elizabethan days. World's End may record the ambition of a deep-sea sailor dreaming of the Northwest Passage. Windwhistle Cottage is an honest

confession of winter storms, and therefore it belies the
oranges and palms in the tubs of Devon landlords.

Sandridge was the birthplace of John Davis, who gave his
name to a strait towards America's Arctic Ocean, and Froude
has written of Greenway Farm in an essay entitled "England's Forgotten Worthies." "Some two miles above the port

Dartmouth Castle

of Dartmouth," he writes, "once among the most important
harbours in England, on a projecting angle of land which
runs out into the river at the head of one of its most beautiful reaches, there has stood for some centuries the Manor
House of Greenaway. The water runs deep all the way to it
from the sea, and the largest vessels may ride with safety
within a stone's throw of the windows. In the latter half of
the sixteenth century," he continues, "there must have met,
in the hall of this mansion, a party as remarkable as could
have been found anywhere in England. Humfrey and Adrian

Gilbert, with their half-brother, Walter Raleigh, here, when little boys, played at sailors in the reaches of Long Stream; in the summer evenings doubtless rowing down with the tide to the port, and wondering at the quaint figure-heads and carved prows of the ships which thronged it; or climbing on board, and listening, with hearts beating, to the mariners' tales of the new earth beyond the sunset. And here in later life, matured men, whose boyish dreams had become heroic action, they used again to meet in the intervals of quiet, and the rock is shown underneath the house where Raleigh smoked the first tobacco."

Here along the Dart we are in the land of heroes—of sailors who guided their cockle-shells in the storms of the seven oceans, who planted colonies and mastered native tribes, who sowed the seed of England's empire. Froude quotes a letter of Humphrey Gilbert to Queen Elizabeth on the eve of a voyage of discovery. "Give me leave, therefore," he concludes, "without offense, always to live and die in this mind: that he is not worthy to live at all that, for fear or danger of death, shunneth his country's service and his own honour, seeing that death is inevitable and the fame of virtue immortal." It is a sailor's phrase and worthy of bronze.

And now during gusts of rain Mary stood protected in the wheelhouse with the merry skipper, who pointed out the sights. The room was too small for a person of really honest girth, so I went below to the stuffy cabin, where I saw the shore darkly through the bull's-eyes that were like dirty little moons. And my nose was offered a stale odor that once was cheese.

We passed several pretty villages and the Royal Naval College. Here, said our skipper, Spain's recent king has enrolled his son for education. And then as the river broadened towards Dartmouth, we encountered a long line of steamers anchored in the stream. A few of these were large passenger steamers taken off their Atlantic routes during the present depression of trade. But most of them were carriers of freight—England's oak walls, now of steel, that lacked a job. All of these ships were deserted, except that here and there a line of drying underwear of both sexes suggested a watchman and his wife. The ships' sides were stained with rust, and there were twenty of them, bow to stern, floating in shallow water, out of use during the calamity of unemployment. In every tidal waterway of southwest England we shall discover such ships that are out of service.

Dartmouth is ahead, and Kingswear to the left across the river.

And now we have come to the heart of Elizabethan adventure, for Dartmouth was the rival of Fowey, Falmouth and Plymouth. It is proper in this port that we pay obeisance to these sailors and to their great historian, Richard Hakluyt. Tired readers may sit in a beer-shop near the dock, and we shall be back in just a few minutes.

If Dartmouth had been in Hakluyt's index, we would have compiled a pretentious list of famous seamen who had used this port. But Hakluyt is neglectful of English harbors in his zeal to chronicle journeys over seas and strange adventures on foreign shores. The ports of Devon and Cornwall, together with those of the Thames, the Avon and the narrow channel, are seldom mentioned except in general gesture. We know, for instance, that Richard Coeur de Lion sailed from Dartmouth on the third crusade, yet Hakluyt, skipping all the needless pageant of the start, embarks him at Marseilles. Sir Humphrey Gilbert despatched his vessels from the River Dart to seek a northwest passage to the Pacific Ocean, but he is chronicled by Hakluyt only when he has cleared the headlands and is proceeding west from Plymouth. Hakluyt, like so many of us who sail for Europe, seemed to wish no one on the pier to say good-by. Our reading, therefore, is not local to Dartmouth; and it is only by inference that we can re-create the glamor of this sheltered harbor, the smell of tar and bilge, the weighed anchors, the last excitement of the taverns, the housewives on the cliffs above the ocean waving a farewell to husbands who may not return.

It was Hakluyt's mighty task to gather through all his lifetime the narratives of English exploration. These he copied from the logs of sailing vessels that had returned from the ends of the ocean—logs that dealt in commonplace with the ports of Russia, America and China, logs that narrated a journey around the Horn or through the Northwest Passage, that sailed from Good Hope to chart the seas towards India. There are logs of inland excursions down the Volga, across the Persian mountains, into worlds that had not been guessed.

In Hakluyt one may read the articles of instruction for trading stations, rules for laying down a colony and its governance against sedition and starvation, charters of merchants into Muscovy and wherever there were goods to buy, letters written by Queen Elizabeth craving for her agents decent treatment among the monarchs of the east and south. Monsoons and lonely islands, catalogues of fighting ships and their equipment, soundings in unknown straits, foreign manners as they affected commerce, triumph and defeat—all these things season these endless pages.

Readers of Hakluyt will learn on the authority of Tacitus that London was a famous market in the reign of Nero. They will discover how King Canute bargained with the Pope for the comfort of English merchants in order that they might go to Rome in peace and return in safety. William Malmesbury, as they will find, describes Bristol as a safe receptacle of ships bound towards Ireland, Norway and "other outlandish and foreign countries." There is the text of a treaty between England and the Emperor Barbarossa for the governance of trading back and forth. Edward the First, doubtless with an eye to reciprocity, grants permission to the merchants of the continent that their ships shall not pay wharfage at any English port.

There are descriptions of Russia—its northern ice and danger, its southern spice, musk, ambergris and rhubarb that fetched a profit. Here is a narrative of exploration by Sir Hugh Willoughby, who died in Lapland, together with the names of his mariners down to the very swabbers of his vessels' decks. Corpus Christi Bay, the River Volga, Cape Race, Moscow and the Caspian Sea, Tartary horses, journeys by sleds, the rites of marriage and of hospitality, burial customs, the drinks and foods of Russia—all of these are a part of Hakluyt's wide-flung plot.

There are letters to the sophy of Persia, commissions for discovery southeast by sea, voyages to Constantinople, to the ports of the Holy Land, to Egypt and Algiers, to all such harbors of the Mediterranean as offered profitable exchange of commodities. We find letters of protest on behalf of merchants who have been cheated, complaints of ships that have been fired upon against a treaty with threats of war hanging on the issue, wrangles over customs duties and false imprisonment.

India is in Hakluyt's pages, with speculation as to the nearest and safest route. We may read of the River Ganges, of Babylon's hanging gardens, of Siam and the coral islands, of Ormus and Cathay, and can know each town through all the Orient where ginger, aloes, pepper and fine silk are bought for London's use. There is a warning against tempest-spitting devils in all these oceans of the south.

Or perhaps we are more eager to learn of western discovery towards America. Here is John Hawkins, sailing to the West Indies in the good ship *Jesus* of seven hundred tons in the year 1564. Sir Walter Raleigh sailed two pinnaces out of Plymouth to the Azores. There are letters patent of the year 1497 to John Cabot and his son, together with their journey out of Bristol in an English fleet to the Island of

St. John and down the coast to Florida. The ship's log of John Davis is set down day by day, with his discovery and description of the Davis Strait. Martin Frobisher searches for the Northwest Passage. Humphrey Gilbert sets out for Newfoundland. There are letters patent to Sir Walter Raleigh for the founding of a colony on the River James which in later days will be called Virginia. We can read how Sir Francis Drake captured the town of St. Augustine in Florida, how he sailed through Magellan and up the coast of California, how at last he charted a course around the world. When his *Golden Hind* anchored at last at Deptford, we can imagine the excitement among the wherries of the Thames.

This task of Hakluyt involved him in dangerous travel and heavy labor. He transcribed old records and spent years in the searching of libraries and the ledgers of merchant companies. He entered on a vast correspondence, talked with sailing masters and with common seamen, with capitalists who had ventured their purses, and with roustabouts lifting cargo in the dock. It was his life's great work, and the result was an English epic whose excitement depends neither on rhyme nor measure.

As a preface to all this business and adventure, there is Hakluyt's own dedication to Walsingham, the Queen's great secretary at Hampton Court.

This dedication is written with a mastery of English whose phrases echo Shakespeare. One must always be impressed by the beauty of Elizabethan prose. Even if its document deals in the mere stuff of the counting-house and street, there is yet a flow of words that carries poetry along its stream. We have read enactments of a Tudor parliament—bills concerning this or that huddled together for decision—and they are always set to a kind of music. Even today, when times are fallen into plainer prose, there lingers still in the circum-ambulating phrases of the law some last remnant of stately

English. *Know all men by these presents* might come from the King James version of the psalms of David. Perhaps the general excellence of Elizabethan prose explains the mystery of Shakespeare. If wisdom cried out in the streets, as he has told us, we may be sure that its words were not discordant. Shakespeare is the most considerable peak in all the range of letters because he rises from a lofty tableland. If we in this less gracious day of ours think to pile our sentences to a lofty hill, it is to our disadvantage that our basic rock starts from a valley of sloven speech.

From the dedication by Hakluyt we gain an inkling of himself and of the circumstances in which he took up the study of English navigation. For our ease we shall change these paragraphs to modern spelling and punctuation. Tired readers may order a second round of beer. When we end our quotation we shall take them for a walk around Dartmouth.

"I do remember that being a youth," Hakluyt starts, "and one of her Majesty's scholars at Westminster that fruitful nursery, it was my hap to visit the chamber of Mr. Richard Hakluyt, my cousin, a gentleman of the Middle Temple, well known to you, at a time when I found lying open upon his board certain books of cosmography, with an universal map. He, seeing me somewhat curious in the view thereof, began to instruct my ignorance, by showing me the division of the earth into three parts after the old account, and then according to the latter and better distribution, into more. He pointed with his wand to all the known seas, gulfs, bays, straits, capes, rivers, empires, kingdoms, dukedoms, and territories of each part, with declaration also of their special commodities and particular wants, which by the benefit of traffic and intercourse of merchants are plentifully supplied. From the map he brought me to the Bible, and turning to the one hundred and seventh psalm, directed me to the twenty-third and twenty-fourth verses, where I read that they which go down to the sea in ships and occupy by the great waters, they see the works of the Lord and his wonders in the deep. Which words of the prophet, together with my cousin's discourse (things of high and rare delight to my young nature) took in me so deep an impression, that I constantly resolved, if ever I were preferred to the university, where better time and more convenient place might be ministered for these studies, I would by God's assistance prosecute that knowledge and kind of literature, the doors whereof (after a sort) were so happily opened before me.

"According to which my resolution, when, not long after, I was removed to Christ-church in Oxford, my exercises of duty first performed, I fell to my intended course, and by degrees read over whatsoever printed or written discoveries and voyages I found extant either in the Greek, Latin, Italian, Spanish, Portuguese, French or English languages. . . . In continuance of time, and by reason principally of my insight in this study, I grew familiarly acquainted with the chiefest captains at sea, the greatest merchants, and the best mariners of our nation . . . men full of activity, stirrers abroad, and searchers of the remote parts of the world. . . .

"Which of the kings of this land before her Majesty," he continues, "had their banners ever seen in the Caspian Sea? Which of them hath ever dealt with the Emperor of Persia, as her Majesty hath done, and obtained for her merchants large and loving privileges? Who ever saw before this regiment an English ligier in the stately porch of the Grand Signior at Constantinople? Who ever found English consuls and agents at Tripolis in Syria, at Aleppo, at Babylon, at Balsara, and which is more, who ever heard of Englishmen at Goa before now? What English ships did heretofore ever anchor in the mighty river of Plate, pass and repass the unpassable (in former opinion) Strait of Magellan, range along the coast of Chili, Peru and all the backside of Nova Hispania further than any Christian ever passed, traverse the mighty breadth of the South Sea, land upon the Luzones in despite

of the enemy, enter into alliance, amity and traffic with the
princes of the Moluccaes and the Isle of Java, double the famous Cape of Bona Speranza, arrive at the Isle of Santa
Helena, and last of all return home most richly laden with
the commodities of China, as the subjects of this now flourishing monarchy have done?"

Another half pint, good man. One more paragraph and
we are done.

"Having," Hakluyt reminds us, "for the benefit and honour of my country zealously bestowed so many years, so much
travail and cost, to bring antiquities smothered and buried
in dark silence, to light, and to preserve certain memorable
exploits of late years by our English nation achieved, from
the greedy and devouring jaws of oblivion . . . what restless nights, what painful days, what heat, what cold I have
endured; how many long and chargeable journeys I have
traveled; how many famous libraries I have searched into;
what variety of ancient and modern writers I have perused;
what a number of old records, patents, privileges and letters
I have redeemed from obscurity and perishing; into how
manifold acquaintance I have entered; what expense I have
not spared; and yet what fair opportunities of private gain,
preferment and ease I have neglected. . . . This being the
sum of those things which I thought good to admonish thee
of (good reader) it remaineth that thou take the profit and
pleasure of the work: which I wish to be as great to thee, as
my pains and labour have been in bringing these raw fruits
unto this ripeness, and in reducing these loose papers into
this order."

The Butterwalk,
Dartmouth.

XXII. DARTMOUTH

DARTMOUTH'S first history, except for legend, begins at
the fall of Rome when England was invaded by the long
boats of the north. Such assaults will account for those villages of Saxon names that we have found beside the River
Dart—Germanic place-names interspersed with Celtic, as if
perhaps, here on this remote southwestern coast, annihila-
tion was not so complete and savage as it was in those districts of the narrow channel which bore the heavier brunt
of conquest. In Kent we find few Celtic names surviving,
scarcely any Saxon names in Cornwall—facts of importance
in the placing of those old invasions and determining their
ferocity. Perhaps the southwest offered less attractive loot.

After America had been discovered, Dartmouth prospered in the fish of Newfoundland. It was a port of Mediterranean commerce that dealt in wine, oil and salt. In the continual wars with France, it was a nest of loyal pirates that sailed against vessels that issued from the harbors of Brittany. It hoisted its flag against Spanish galleons.

> Four-and-twenty Spaniards,
>   Mighty men of rank,
> With their Signoras,
>   Had to walk the plank.

These were rough days, but they trained sailors for Francis Drake against the Great Armada.

The town has been several times invaded by the French. Dartmouth's Castle was built by Henry VII—"a strong and mighty tower and bulwark, with lime and stone, and . . . a chain in length and strength sufficient." In the civil wars, Dartmouth, garrisoned by the king, was stormed by Fairfax of the parliament army.

Arthur Norway describes Dartmouth's harbor as "enclosed on every side by hills so steep and lofty that the comparison which leaps into one's mind is that this is the deep crater of some extinct volcano into which the sea has forced an entrance on one side." And he quotes from the report of a Spanish spy who was sent here in 1599 when some deviltry was planned by the Escurial to wipe out the disgrace of the Armada's defeat. "It is not walled," he wrote home of Dartmouth. "The mountains are its walls."

Great headlands with a narrow mouth! A town that is thickly settled on the water level, with houses scattered up the hills! We recall a description by Carlyle of the Paris crowds outside Notre Dame on a day of revolution—a spray of folk that was splattered to the gutters and on the roofs from the moiling sea below. And Dartmouth's white cottages above the town seem like a yeasty foam from the crowded wash of streets beside the harbor.

Dartmouth is not wholly a fishing village, nor is it chiefly a resort for tourists, although several small hotels hang out their signs of food and lodging. Travelers for the most part keep to the highroad from Totnes to Plymouth, and their swift schedule allows them only a week for this southwestern country and no leisure for a journey down the River Dart. But if any motorist can spare an afternoon, we recommend that he hoist himself from his cushions at Totnes, that he have tea at the Seymour Hotel, that he despatch his motor by whatever road suggests itself, that he board a steamer for Dartmouth. After a pleasant hour around the town, he can climb again to his cushions and sleep all the way to Plymouth.

By so slight an expenditure of time, he will see an ancient market, several buildings of half-timbered Tudor front, streets and lanes that clamber on a hill, windows on whose sills black cats stretch themselves. On the quay he will find small hotels where he may quench his American thirst, shops with picture postcards and souvenirs—objects dear to every tourist—and many sailors at their ease. He will discover that Dartmouth preserves an aspect of the past, whereas the mighty Plymouth has enjoyed such prosperity that all old vestiges have been swept away. With still another hour, he can walk or ride to the headlands of Dartmouth and gain an unforgettable view of the English Channel from those cliffs where sailors' wives once watched for sails rising from the south and west.

Mary and I, having four hours before our boat's return to Totnes, first explored the streets of Dartmouth and counted its black cats. The Tudor half-timbering was mostly under scaffolds for repair. We traversed the Butter Walk—an ancient market, as I recall, that suggests the house-fronts of Chester. We stood at the harbor's edge and remembered

verses of Alfred Noyes—his "Knight of the Ocean-sea"—describing the last voyage of Humphrey Gilbert.

> And over us fled the fleet of the stars,
> And, ever in front of us, far or nigh,
> The lanthorn on his cross-tree spars
> Dipped to the Pit or soared to the Sky!
>
> 'Twould sweep to the lights of Charles's Wain,
> As the hills of the deep 'ud mount and flee,
> Then swoop down vanishing cliffs again
> To the thundering gulfs of the Ocean-sea.
>
> We saw it shine as it swooped from the height,
> With ruining breakers on every hand,
> Then—a cry came out of the black mid-night,
> *As near to heaven by sea as by land!*
>
> And the light was out! Like a wind-blown spark,
> All in a moment! and we—and we—
> Prayed for his soul as we swept thro' the dark;
> For he was a Knight of the Ocean-sea.

Resisting the offers of clamorous cabmen, we set out afoot
towards the ocean. Our way led slantwise across the town
and above the harbor, with a wide view at last across the
water and beyond Kingswear to the hills beyond. Still threading our course through woods, our path turned a shoulder
of the cliff and revealed the ocean. Here was a crowd from a
culture-bus, with a guide belaboring his flock with instruction.

We climbed a sharp path and found a bench on the cliff's
edge. A thin marking of smoke may have been an ocean
liner headed for New York; but fishing craft, hull down,
echoed from an older navigation that relied on God and
wind.

Near by were the ruins of a stronghold—the mere stumps

of walls without a roof whose tops were fringed with grass. On a lower level just above the harbor's mouth there is another dismantled fortress that possesses still its walls entire, and this we visited. The building is now a museum and it shows old guns of outworn fashion, deep-splayed windows through whose narrow openings once peeped these brazen muzzles. There is a low squat tower with crenelations and a stone staircase on which the guide told us to mind our heads. I forgot, with results. As the culture-seekers were now knocking at the door, we came away.

On our return to Dartmouth we were thirsty.

"Two Basses," I said, "and a plate of cheese."

The proprietor looked us up and down.

"Sorry," he answered, "but it's after hours. I'd lose my license."

"It is to save two human lives," I suggested.

He softened at our distress. He led us to a back parlor near the kitchen and behind the bar—a room whose only windows looked out stealthily on the stable-yard.

"Two teas," he said with a grin, and he was gone.

He returned with beer, filled two teacups and put the bottles out of sight.

"It is just for safety," he explained. "A peeler might come squinting in the window."

His action so suggested our own sweet land of liberty that we were homesick. As is usual whenever English and Americans meet in such circumstance, we discussed prohibition.

Our boat sounded its whistle, and we climbed aboard. The long shadows of afternoon lay on the Dart as we steamed to Totnes.

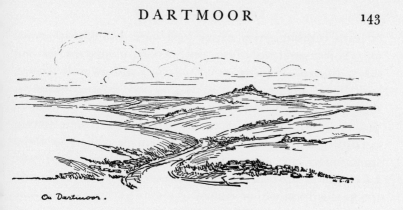

On Dartmoor.

XXIII. DARTMOOR

OUR NEXT excursion discovered to us the Devon moors—
a patch of brown to the north and west of Totnes on any
detailed map. These moors rise abruptly from green river
bottoms that thrust upwards their stubby fingers into the
barren hills above. Down each valley brawls a rocky stream
to grow languid in the lower meadows. There are few roads
through Dartmoor—hardly more than two main highways
which meet at Princetown at the center. The map, it is true,
shows other roads at the margin of this district; but whenever they essay high ground they grow tired and out of
breath, and presently they dwindle into paths and pony
trails which wander as if lost among the ragged tors. Here
and there Dartmoor rises into spots of deepest brown. High
Willhays in the north has an elevation of slightly more than
two thousand feet. In the south Hameldon Ridge is almost
exactly seventeen hundred feet in height. These hill-tops
are, of course, insignificant if we set them against any range
of lofty mountains; but Devon's general table is hardly above
the level of the sea, and its moor, that is so trivial to an
actual yardstick, makes therefore a brave show against the
sky.

In this illusion of immensity, the fancy is a partner of the eye. For Dartmoor is the heart of Celtic England, its last tall island uncaptured by any conquest until the tourist came. Elsewhere plain Saxon and Norman ways of thinking have prevailed against the races they attacked; but here on Dartmoor we find the remnants of belief that prospered at the full when Caesar crossed the Channel. Fancy, therefore, defies mere yardage and finds the tors of Devon more lofty by reason of the superstitious fear that dwells among them.

"Superstition clings to the granite." That is the usual phrase of those who have described this district. And as we see this dark island of gorse and rock rising on the sky-line from the lower plains, we can well believe that this phrase is true. We can know what the "Celtic twilight" is—its customs and beliefs that are not the product of the glaring sun of reason, but lift themselves from mist and shadow. We can understand why a dozen hamlets on Dartmoor claim that the devil is their leading citizen. In these little clusters of lonely living, every old woman is a witch and she needs but a broomstick for her tricks. We can know why every church spire since Christianity was first planted here, has been a target for the electrical storms that hell keeps sending in fiery wrath—why children have been blighted on their way from school, why strong men will not be caught on the open moors at night. In any winter twilight, so it's said, the wind wears a writhing tail and mutters of punishment to come. Dartmoor is so bleak, so unsheltered by any wood, so swept by fog and storm, that prisoners at Princetown at the center, if they escape from its walls, are said to perish with exposure before they can traverse its pony trails to the towns along its margin. To any native, however, their cold bodies have the devil's mark upon them.

The Celts once spread themselves upon the continent of Europe like thick butter on a slice of bread. And when they were worsted by new races, they fled to mountains wherever they could find them. Celtic names and customs still exist in the Pyrenees, unblended by either the French or Spanish. In the hills of Wales, of Ireland and of Scotland they found a stronghold. And here also on these Devon moors they made a stand. If anywhere today there is left a district where magic and witches would seem to prosper and to snap their fingers at our dull progress into reason, that place is Dartmoor.

Any superstitious race will confer supernatural power upon its heroes—a gift of tongues, the knack of healing, an ability to lift a chapel across the mountains. And here in Devon also we find that the county's greatest person, therefore, possessed the faculty of magic. For does not a legend assert that Sir Francis Drake, having licked the Spaniards, offered as an extra boon to make the town of Tavistock a seaport? As the crow flies, Tavistock is thirteen miles from deep water. It stands, moreover, on high land just at the edge of the moorland. But shall such trivial obstacles deter a man who has uncanny strength in his finger-tips? The devil had once planned to drown all Surrey and the churches in its plain, and he would have succeeded except for St. Dunstan, who happened to be walking on the downs with a pair of red-hot tongs. It was only when the devil got this clamped on his nose that he whistled his imps back to hell. But why should we think that Sir Francis would have failed in an equal scheme when his better object lay to the advantage of Devon commerce? We get this legend from Arthur Norway, who is reminded of a conversation between Corporal Trim and Uncle Toby. " 'There happening,' said Trim, 'throughout the whole kingdom of Bohemia to be no seaport town whatever. . . .' 'How the deuce should there, Trim?' cried my Uncle Toby; 'for Bohemia being totally inland, it could have happened no otherwise.' 'It might,' said Trim, 'if it had pleased God.' "

Strange things please God, it seems, on this Devon moorland. Let us listen further to Arthur Norway.

"Yet the man," he continues, "who destroyed the Armada by throwing chips of wood into the sea from Plymouth Hoe, which chips turned to fireships as they touched the water, might have done much, and may do it yet, for it is a mistake to think of Drake as bestowed safely in the shades out of the ken of living people. It needs only a roulade on his old drum to bring him back to the upper world, doubtless with all his magic powers unimpaired; and so it may some day happen that the boon rejected long ago by the men of Tavistock will be received more gratefully, that the sea will come lipping up the Abbey walk, and the ancient bridge with its rich growth of ferns and moss will be crusted over with oarweed and sea shells."

In the witch-infested heath of Macbeth there is a hint of Dartmoor. Dartmoor lies outside of Thomas Hardy's plots, but one will find a touch of its desolation in his Egdon Heath, as he describes it in "The Return of the Native." We must, however, for a just description, draw deeper shadows across the night, toss the country into wilder shapes, and stretch a mild alarm to a shattering calamity of fright.

Dartmoor is Devon's core and intensest self. Elsewhere in the county red fades to pink. In these days of motor travel, when populations are shifted to their holidays on smooth roads, something of its Celtic twilight has disappeared. A traveler will be served beef and cabbage for thirty days through each of the shorter months, and mussy scrambled tarts by way of sweets. Chars-à-bancs will clatter as at Saxon Stratford. He will drink the universal tea of the British Isles, finding a single variant in clotted cream. Anaemic East-Anglian fires will nibble at his bedroom's chilly dampness. Nor will the clouds and sun confess a difference, for they flirt equally against the comfort of a traveler. An untrained ear will detect no difference of language. To the outward senses we have crossed no boundary.

And yet the west is not like its neighbor to the east. The map will show strange place-names that are not easy to an untried tongue. The valleys are of a special snugness; and hills of a bleak wind-swept bareness look towards a horizon without a tree. Nowhere else in England will one sleep so many nights within the roaring of the sea. The fog is of a thicker texture, as if the cliffs and ocean were wrapped in the legends of the past.

And now Dartmoor lies around us, the epitome of Devon. It is likely that it was not always so desolate as we see it now. Lydford, at the edge, possesses the keep of a Norman Castle that was certainly not built to hold a desert under heel. There was once a wall about this town, which would indicate that life was not entirely stagnant. The ancient highways of Dartmoor would seem to prove, moreover, that at one time there was commerce at the center. It is Arthur Norway again who reminds us of this. "For streams of commerce," he says, "do not choose the worst or most exposed roads in preference to the comparatively good and sheltered ones, nor march over quaking bog when they might tread firm ground. . . ." And, he adds, "It was quite possible to cross Devonshire without penetrating Dartmoor." That the moorland's ancient commerce was in tin, we have ample record.

And now, with our lecture done, we bring out the easier lantern slides of travel.

Buckfast Abbey

XXIV. BUCKFAST ABBEY

IN ALMOST any countryside of Britain a tourist may visit
monastic buildings without a roof. Birds are the only chor-
isters of Tintern and of Fountains. Glastonbury's last echoes
sweep in an empty wind. The ghost of Melrose wanders in
its graveyard. The altars of Netley, Valle Crucis and of
Lindisfarne are served with incense by the flowers of June.
Mighty Beaulieu is fringed with the grasses of a silent river.
Destruction everywhere has been the price of religious freedom. If the roofs of St. Albans and of Westminster are still
tight against the rain, it is because the newer faith was content to chant an altered credo to their ancient vaults.

It is at Buckfast only, on this edge of Dartmoor, that a
tourist will see the Roman faith revived after its demolition

to celebrate today its ritual on the site of its former mass. It will be profitable to learn by what strange event this miracle has happened.

The beginnings of Buckfast are not recorded in any charter or document. One authority sets its start in Celtic days—founded by St. Petrock before the year 568. Another writer is of the opinion that Buckfast was founded in the ninth century when Alfred was still the king of England. It was listed in Domesday Book, together with its many fields, its villeins, its plows and the sheep that produced the income of its support. Buckfast prospered through the acute dangers of the Norman Conquest. It suffered under the extortions of King Rufus. Then it disappeared from record.

But better times were near at hand. The first crusade had ended the eleventh century, and its religious zeal had created across Europe a desire to reform the lax discipline of the Benedictines who had become by that time enervated with wealth and easy living. Cluny had been founded in the early tenth century, and it still dazzled Europe with the splendor of its unexhausted faith. But what was of nearer importance to Buckfast was the work of Vitalis of Mortain. After several years of solitary meditation in the forests of Normandy, he founded the Abbey and Congregation of Savigny at about the beginning of the twelfth century; and it was this order, among others, that spread to England in the footsteps of the Conqueror. We find, presently, that Stephen, Count of Mortain and later to be the king of England, conferred Buckfast on the Abbot of Savigny, together with its lands, its plows and sheep.

But in the accumulated fields of Cluny were sprouting weeds that choked it. It was at the village of Citeaux, in the east of France, that another new dawn appeared. For here, early in the twelfth century, Bernard became a monk, to develop, when his piety was ripe, the mighty order of the Cistercians under the primitive and ascetic rule of the Benedictines. The Savignians were swallowed by this new order; and henceforth Buckfast was Cistercian for four hundred years until the Dissolution was ordered by Henry VIII.

What these long centuries were like at Buckfast there are few documents to tell us. Bernard's rule enjoined fasting, flagellation, silence, severe hours of prayer, study, meditation and the service of many masses by day and night. It enjoined hardship and simple living, bodily mortification and ascetic immersion even in the cold of winter. A monk was merely a pilgrim through this world's wicked slough to the celestial heights beyond. It was his chief concern to save his soul from the contamination of society outside his walls and to prepare himself for a safe entrance into heaven.

And yet piety was not enough. There was manual labor in the fields and in the cloister. Cistercian monasteries were usually remote from cities. They were separate from denser living wherever a stream and meadowland were convenient to provide the necessities of life. For they were designed to be self-sustaining and to keep their members from contact with the outside world. They grew their own grain, sheared their sheep and made their woolen garments. They fashioned their sandals, fished their own streams, kept their gardens free from weeds and cropped their grain. They brewed their own beer, made their own flour, wrote their psalters, illuminated their manuscripts in gold by hand, kept the chronicle of the convent's life, taught their novices to sing and read and write. They dispensed charity. Their house was an inn for travelers. It was a church, a school, a factory. Whatever labor a country town performed, that labor fell upon the members of the cloister. The monks constructed new buildings, repaired old walls, planted vines to beautify the house of God. A Cistercian monastery, even at the frontier of civilization, became a center for handicraft and learning.

In February, 1539, all this life ended at Buckfast by the

orders of Henry VIII. Ten monks still in residence were
sent adrift. The Abbey was dismantled. The lead was
stripped from the roofs. The gold relics of the altars were
dispersed and the church bells sold for their weight of
bronze. Buckfast's walls, however, were not destroyed by any
official act. As in the case of so many monastic buildings at
the Dissolution, they were left to be a general quarry for
secular construction; and it was not until the eighteenth
century that they had dwindled to mere foundations and
broken stubs. In 1806, a modern country house was built on
the site of the cloisters and the general property was in
private hands.

And now comes Buckfast's resurrection. It is of such vivid
results that even heretics must lend their admiration. "It
would be idle," writes a Benedictine author, "to try to force
the parallel between the twelfth-century revival of Buckfast
Abbey and the nineteenth-century resurrection of which we
have been the witnesses; yet in both cases we are invited to
trace back the source to the woody recesses of an impressive
solitude. . . . The venerable Père Muard, whose followers
were destined to rebuild the ruins of Buckfast Abbey, had
looked for his abode in the midst of a tangled forest in the
Morvan, not far from Avallon, and pitched his tent under
the shadow of a rocking stone known as 'la Pierre-qui-vire,'
where he heard the call of God and started building his
monastery. . . .

"In this silent solitude," our authority continues, "broken
only by the singing of birds and the rumbling of waters of
a torrent, a fervent community of Benedictine monks served
God in peace till the ruthless hand of a godless government
turned them adrift in 1880. The exiled monks first betook
themselves to Ireland, and it was there that, about two years
later, they learnt of their future Devonshire home being on
the market."

We must cut this good man short. In brief, Buckfast was

purchased by the Benedictines, and the monks came from Ireland and took possession of the country house that marked the old foundations. A temporary church was built, and service was established.

It was not until 1906 that the plan was announced of reconstructing Buckfast to its former grandeur. There was no money for this huge expense, or the promise of any. But "there was Brother Peter, a mason, who knew how to build and could teach others to do likewise. There was sand in the Dart, and an excellent neighbor . . . was only too willing that his sand-pit should be drawn upon for this good purpose. There was a quarry close by where stone was plentiful and cheap."

Buckfast Abbey was not built by contract, but by the monks themselves. The only strictly commercial labor was that of the architects who drew the plans. The manual work was performed entirely by men in Benedictine cowls. They erected the scaffolding and hoisted the material to its place on the growing walls. A monk was sent to Exeter for a few weeks to learn stone-carving; and this seems to be the only outside help until the building was under roof. Buckfast is the only church to be erected in our day under the conditions of the age of faith.

On August 3, 1922, although construction was not completed, High Mass inaugurated worship in the restored church, and a sermon was preached under the text, "Shall these dry bones live?" A ceremony to mark the completion of Buckfast is planned for the spring of 1932.

The design of the building is of transitional Norman and it stands on the foundations of the twelfth century—a majestic crucifix two hundred and forty feet in length. There was still scaffolding against the outer walls and on it we saw Benedictine monks at work.

We were climbing into our motor when the Abbot of Buckfast passed us, on his way perhaps to inspect construction. He is a handsome man, past middle age, with white curly hair, and he smiled pleasantly in our direction and wished us a happy journey. He has been Abbot since 1906, and it is his energy and devotion that have rebuilt Buckfast from the mere stubble of a ruin to this lovely creation of the soul and mind. Holy father, we salute you.

• Holne •

XXV. THERE ARE WITCHES ALL THE WAY TO WIDECOMBE

OUR MOTOR road now led sharply to the moors—a great roof of barren shingles on the top of Devon.

Our first stop was at the village of Holne, just above the gutter of this roof, for it was here that Charles Kingsley was born in the vicarage in the year 1819. But Holne played no part in his life, for he left it as a youth and never returned for residence. It is in northern Devon that we shall find Kingsley in his maturity.

Holne is a solitary village on the bare facing of a hill.

Down its main street there flows a little torrent of clear
water that requires a foot-bridge to each house. A parish
church is so exposed that it must lean against a winter storm.
There are but a dozen houses, and an inn with an old-fash-
ioned tap. It seems that a London artist had once sojourned
at this inn and had drawn a picture of the tap for *Punch*.
The original sketch hung on the wall. To the landlady this
visit was a more valuable memory than any tale of the
novelist's birth in the vicarage. She called our attention to
each tiny accuracy of the picture.

"You can see," she said, "the order of my bottles on the
shelf. And that's my old cat sleeping on the window-sill."

From Holne we climbed again—straight to the ridgepole.
All about were tumbled hills without design. Here were
stored nature's stock of unused mountains, ready for disposal
to any country whose own were wearing out. On every sharp
crest, granite is outcropped, so perhaps the hills of Devon
are also wearing thin.

These tors, as they are called, are of such fantastic shapes
that from a distance they resemble castles that have fallen
into ruin. One might think that an universal war had destroyed both the victor and the vanquished. It is not alone
the inaccessibility of Dartmoor that has guarded its isolation
and its legends; for these fantastic hills breed strange
thoughts and a lack of reason. In any twilight up would pop
a devil's head.

Not all the stony outcrop of Dartmoor is the work of
nature. Man also has had his hand in it. The moorland is
the center of Devon's antiquity, and all of the map is marked
with the monuments of prehistoric life. On this highroad
of ours that hangs so far above the flashing waters of the
River Dart, we shall come presently to what is called the
Blowing House Hut Circle. These artificially piled stones
differ little from the tors of nature. They are a tomb or perhaps a temple. And all about upon the map are the markings

of such remains—monuments that so closely imitate God's work that the eye is plagued to tell where nature laid down her chisel and where man has picked it up.

We now tumbled down a steep road to Dartmeet, where the river's east and west branches join. Near by the present motor bridge is a remnant of flat stones that are piled in a broken footway across the stream. It is called the Cyclopean Bridge; but it hardly merits so large a name, for its level is but a few feet above the water. A local tradition asserts that it is of Roman construction, but this is evidently false. It is, however, a curious survival from days when our present roadway was but a foot-path.

And now our road climbed again among tors, tumuli and stone circles, until in a few miles we came to Widecombe.

This famous village stands in a shallow creasing of lonely moorland. Its best guidebook is Eden Phillpotts' "Widecombe Fair." I had read this story at Totnes in the meadow by the river, so I was crammed with knowledge. The tale is built up from a nursery rhyme.

Tom Pearse, Tom Pearse, lend me thy gray mare,
    All along, down along, out along Lee;
For I want for to go to Widecombe Fair
    With Bill Brewer, Jan Stewer, Peter Gurney, Peter Davy,
        Dan'l
    Whiddon, Harry Hawk, Old Uncle Tom Cobleigh and all.
        Old Uncle Tom Cobleigh and all.

Phillpotts' story deals with such oddments of character as one would expect to find in a land's end of civilization that was haunted by the devil. It is a book that is best read on the spot it describes.

There is a legend in Widecombe that every old woman is a witch. The devil also, as we have said, is supposed to have a special fondness for this village, and to journey there as often as he can be spared from Paris and Chicago.

As most of the devil's exploits of the British Isles center on a church spire, we are prepared to learn that Widecombe's parish building is no exception. Our authority is John Prince, sometime Vicar of Berry Pomeroy. It seems that on a certain far-off Sunday a great darkness gathered at the hour of service. This was followed by fearful thunder and by a flame of lightning that filled the church. And there

Widecombe -

was smoke, says our good old preacher, "and a loathsome smell like brimstone."

Arthur Norway also is sure that Satan was on the job. "It appears that on this very Sunday," he explains, "a rider on a coal-black steed called at the inn at Poundstock and asked his way to Widecombe. The innkeeper's wife directed him, and brought him a glass of ale, which to her vast terror hissed and sputtered as it went down his throat as if it had been running over burning metal. The rider galloped off in the direction she had given; and reaching Widecombe fastened his horse to a pinnacle of the lofty tower and rushed into the church, where service had begun. An unfortunate boy had so far forgotten himself as to fall asleep, and this gave the devil his opportunity. He dashed at the luckless youth, caught him in his claws, and flew with him through the roof to the pinnacle where his horse was fastened, dislodging bricks and beams and the very pinnacle itself in his headlong flight, and so rode away through the air with a roar and rattle of thunder."

This narrative does not satisfy us. Widecombe had been the devil's haunt for a thousand years, and it is ridiculous to think he would ask direction on the road. We shall hear next that he is lost on a journey to Chicago.

There was a hush of noon in Widecombe's empty streets, but it was just as well perhaps to go warily and to sniff for brimstone. We peeked through an open doorway into a classroom where children sat stiffly at their lessons. The teacher was old, but we saw no devil's mark upon her. In the square outside we saw a wrinkled woman, but she had no broomstick. To the casual eye, at least, this was not the season when the devil was about.

It must be that Widecombe is infested by witches only in a winter's storm. We have on occasion stood on a theatre's stage when the curtain is down and the house in front is empty. By the playbill we know that this canvas scene about us is the villain's house; but in daylight the stage is so common and so safe. And this was our impression of Widecombe, with its placid sunlight on the roofs. It was evident that the devil was not yet dressed for his night's performance.

We drank ale at the tavern of Eden Phillpotts' story—an inn a bit more modern than his, with a lunch room for chars-à-bancs added at the rear. In a side street we saw a famous Saxon stone with a trickle of water beneath it that had started noisily to join the Dart in the valley far below.

Our homeward way threaded a high course across the moors, then came down by winding roads to Ashburton. We were at Totnes in time for tea and clotted cream. We had journeyed to the devil's village and had escaped a singeing; but perhaps the world is now so thick with mischief that he neglects his former haunt.

After dinner we found a group of men bowling beside the Dart. We were looking at them across a fence, when they invited us to sit on a bench beside their game. It is of all sports the most fitting to an English village. Across the meadows we saw a four-oared shell skimming with the tide. And now the twilight thickened, and the Totnes tower was but a dim finger in the western sky.

Night was rising from the far-off ridges in the north; and with the coming darkness the devil was perhaps returned to Widecombe on the windy hills. A flaking of cloud sailed high above the rim of moorland touched by the flames of sunset and, as the pattern changed, it seemed for a moment to be a man upon a horse. It was his red majesty galloping towards western fire, bearing in his claws the luckless lad who had slept at service.

Brixham

XXVI. TO BRIXHAM AND BACK
TO TOTNES

WE WENT by public bus to Paignton and Brixham. Paignton is wholly for the summer tourist, with a broad street of small wares to attract his purse, with banks and restaurants, hotels and *movie* theatres, and char-à-bancs offices whose chalked signboards offer bargain tours through Devon. In this off season, these chars-à-bancs stand idle like juggernauts that are living on the dole.

At the foot of Paignton's High Street is a wide beach, a grassy esplanade and a stone parade at the edge of the sand. There is a long pier that offers August cheap amusement. This ocean front is lined with hotels and lodging-houses; and later in the season there will be some animation—children with painted pails, old ladies with gummy-eyed dogs, men and women bathing in a rim of foam or dropping pennies into slots for fortune-telling cards. On the pier there are probably little concert companies whose soubrettes are wearing old.

In May of a backward season, however, Paignton was deserted. A cold wet wind lashed the esplanade and any painted pail would have chattered. If any visitors had arrived so early, their noses would have been out of joint against the windows of these hotels as they prayed nasally for sunlight and a change of wind. All of Paignton can be seen at a glance; and as our glance was disappointing, we came off the beach and took another bus to Brixham on Torbay to the south.

Brixham is not interested in tourists, an ancient town that looks its age and sits in shabby dress, indifferent to callers. It is proud of its gray houses and wrinkled streets. It is a mere huddle of disordered buildings on an inlet of the bay. There is a stone mole that crooks its protecting arm around a crowded harbor where fishing vessels are playing dead-dog in the mud when the tide is out. Sailors stand upon the quay and smoke stubby pipes. Nor is it possible to know from the appearance of a fisherman whether he is out of a job or whether this is his busy day, for in both circumstances his conduct is the same. At most he squints an eye and seems to see a wind that will tell him of the weather. His is the only idleness that is really picturesque. Fishermen, wherever you find them, have a sloppy way of wearing their trousers that delights an artist, and even when they spit they are perfect Rembrandts. When these fishermen retire from the practice of the sea, they still sit on quays all around the world, wherever tourists gather; and they get an easy pension by selling themselves to cameras and to canvas. In southern countries, as in Capri, they tie a red bandanna around their heads and get a double price.

There is a ripe old look about Brixham. It has a line of drinking-shops, tipsy warehouses along the quay that need but a careless shove to send them splashing in the water.

There are everywhere slippery pavements that are blessed with a sense of humor, and everywhere "a very ancient and fish-like smell."

There is a snarl of masts at Brixham, upright when the tide is in, but pointing in absurd diverse directions when the moon is off its job. It is a town of narrow lanes, of flights of crazy steps that are lost among the buildings, of rope and tar, of fishy crates that are packed for London, of sailors' choice plug-tobacco, of ships' compasses, rubber boots, yellow tarpaulins, briar pipes and knitted sweaters.

Brixham was first a pirate harbor, preying on vessels from the coast of Normandy. Into this port was brought the first prize from Spain's Great Armada. William of Orange landed here, and his manufactured footprint still shows in the pavement of the quay. But it is the slimy creatures of the sea that are the proper heroes of Brixham's chronicle. Fish are its diet, its profit and its smell.

From Brixham, William Gifford, as a lad, was sent to sea. He was later an editor. He conducted London's *Quarterly Review* with a ferocity he must have learned upon this quay; and if he spat on the poets of his day, Keats for example, it was a habit he couldn't break. It was said that he looked on authors as a fisherman looks on worms—useful, these writers, to catch a reader, but let the poor devils squirm.

On the bus coming away from Brixham, I was annoyed by a man whom I took to be a drunken sailor. He crowded close to me and kept muttering with thick tongue. I complained to the conductor. But the man had been shell-shocked in the war with Germany. He was one of England's countless victims.

Only one event of this day is left for record—our visit to a dairy where we were instructed in the making of clotted cream. Fresh milk from the cowshed. A two-gallon can into which it is strained and stands for sixteen hours in cool air. A scalding of forty-five minutes above a larger container of boiling water to keep the cream from burning. About eighteen hours to cool. In summer the cream may be cooled by the circulation of cold water about the pan, as this speeds the process and keeps it from souring. If now the surface of the cream is yellow and wrinkled like a Dartmoor witch, it is ready for skimming off. Fat folk will mind their buttons.

The Barbican,
Plymouth —

XXVII. PLYMOUTH

ON THE afternoon of Thursday, May the seventh, we went by public bus to Plymouth. This direct journey forced us to omit Salcombe, its harbor and Bolt Head. It cut also from our travels a visit to the home of James Anthony Froude— "the long veranda running around the low white house, and the study windows giving on the quiet garden." This was a disappointment, for Froude is a favorite of mine.

In an hour from Totnes, we have entered Plymouth's

sprawling suburbs, with occasional views of channeled water and a nest of far-off masts.

We put up at a hotel that overlooks the Hoe. It was of excellent accommodation, but a bit stiff of nose at the office wicket. It prefers old ladies by the month. A young woman, after much thumbing of a large book, gave us finally a room under the roof—a room quite distant from her better clients with their Pomeranians and purple turbans. We looked at the apartment and estimated how far down the bedclothes would take us in case of fire.

"Have you nothing better?" I asked, again at the wicket.

She rang a bell, and an ancient porter appeared from his hiding-place inside the lift.

"Show them 245," she said.

Our new room looked out from a moderate height upon the Hoe and all the shipping of the harbor. We could see the breakwater at the entrance of the Sound and the Channel's white flash of water. Our room had a fireplace. It was laid on, as the English say, with hot and cold. Down the hallway was a bath which we could find with patience, unless we got excited.

Plymouth offers a diary such an embarrassment of wealth that the only difficulty is where to start, or whether, indeed, to start at all—whether to give, rather, our long-suffering readers a cut from class. Plymouth has had its part in every English century that has been nourished by the sea, from the days of the Phoenicians until this morning when a Cunarder dropped its anchor in the Sound. This is enough. We announce this as our text, even if we omit the sermon.

From our hotel windows in the early twilight of the dawn, we saw these enormous steamships from New York, their range of lights streaking the black waters of the outer harbor. For it is at this awkward hour, under a usual schedule, that they arrive. Their time is short, for presently they must lift their anchors and hurry on to Cherbourg in order that their passengers may reach Paris in time for early dinner. They merely sniff the morning air of Plymouth and when the first cock crows on the misty hills, they steal away like guilty spirits.

I once sailed to the continent from Plymouth on an American liner, and it remains in vivid recollection that I boarded the tender while the eastern sky was still unmarked by dawn. The city's harbor was dotted with a row of lamps, like stars that were mustered for the night's last drill. And there were other lights behind, scattered across the town, for the sky had grown too thick with glistening points and had sent emigrants to these dark unsettled shores. When the first soft daylight came, the old city stood upon its hill, and there were greater hills behind where church towers stood against a radiant sky. At this prime hour history lies again inside its cradle and the Plymouth that I saw was a village that sold its tin to Tyre.

Every one who travels has visited Plymouth Hoe. In its fame it is like the Strand, the boulevards of Paris and the open square before St. Peter's. At all of these places we are merely the latest tourist in a vast procession of kings and common folk. The echoes of these feet, whirled out in time's long broadcast, live again in the fancy of any one who stands on these famous spots.

Plymouth Hoe has always been a chief gallery of England's western theatre—a crowded standing-room for those who have watched the ocean drama of the Channel. From this outlook a crowd of villagers saw Frobisher weigh anchor for the Northwest Passage. It beheld expeditions start for Bermuda, for Virginia, for Newfoundland and Massachusetts. The Hoe has been the constant witness of Devon's bravery.

After Sir Francis Drake had obtained from a tree-top of the Isthmus his first view of the Pacific Ocean, it was to Plymouth he returned. We have a record of a certain Sun-

day evening when his ships dropped anchor at the hour of
service. "There remained few or no people with the
preacher," we may read, "all running out to observe the
blessing of God on the dangerous adventures of the captain." And we may be sure that the preacher, unless his
blood was of a faded pink, ran also out of doors to share in
the excitement of the Hoe.

Richard Hawkins recorded how once he sailed from
Plymouth. "The most part of the inhabitants were gathered
together on the Hoe," he wrote.

It was on the Hoe also that housewives met on a certain
famous July morning of the year 1588. "The day wore on,"
writes Froude, "noon passed and nothing had been seen. At
length, towards three in the afternoon, the look-out men on
the hill reported a line of sails on the western horizon, the
two wings first visible, which were gradually seen to unite
as the centre rose over the rim of the sea. . . . It was growing dusk when the Armada opened Plymouth."

The greatest event in England's ocean epic had begun.
One may imagine the chattering of housewives as they
watched the smoking cannon at the harbor's mouth. Then
the battle swept from sight behind the headlands.

Plymouth's present Hoe is a bit too sophisticated. There
is, indeed, a statue of Sir Francis Drake quite near the spot
where once, says legend, he played at bowls. But in a place
where one's thoughts should be heroic, the eye cannot avoid
an amusement pier with a restaurant for tea and clotted
cream. Clotted cream is of course sacred in this western
country, but a slattern waitress chills poetic meditation.
There are, however, many steamers in the harbor, carrying
on England's long tradition of the sea. Of all southwest
harbors, Plymouth only has survived. Shallow water has
ruined all her neighbors.

The dockyard, Eddystone Light, the aquarium—all these

sights of Plymouth we missed, but we did not miss them much.

We found a restaurant that offered spaghetti and Italian wine. Then we went to the Royal Theatre. It is a handsome building that recalls the best traditions of the provincial stage. From our hotel windows we looked down on a winking light that guarded the harbor's mouth.

The Bridge,
Fortuvichiel.

XXVIII. INTO CORNWALL

WEST OF the Tamar, Devon's clotted cream is called Cornish cream. And the villages and headlands have names that are even harder to pronounce.

> By tre, pol and pen,
> You shall know the Cornishmen.

Cornwall boasts of King Arthur and Pendragon, of Merlin, of buried Lyonesse, of Tristram and Iseult, of King Mark. It cherishes a legend that the county was first settled by Brutus—that its history dates from Noah's flood and the Hebrew prophets. Richard Carew, born near Plymouth in 1555, is Cornwall's first great historian. His Survey was dedicated to Sir Walter Raleigh, then still alive. He writes of Brutus and Gogmagog, of the submersion of Lyonesse. He asserts that Noah's flood was responsible for Cornish tin, which was washed to the surface from deeper rock by the waters retreating westward from Mt. Ararat. Sometimes Carew's tongue is in his cheek, but often he is a convert to his own persuasion; and certainly he thought a fact prettier if it were encrusted by moss and legend.

We may listen with profit while this good man describes the commercial advantage of his native duchy. "Though nature hath shouldered out Cornwall into the farthest part of the realm," he writes, "and so besieged it with the ocean, that, as a demi-island in an island, the inhabitants find but one way of issue by land: yet hath she in some good measure countervailed such disadvantage through placing it both near unto and in the trade way between Wales, Ireland, Spain, France and the Netherlands. The nearness helpeth them with a shorter cut, less peril and meaner charge, to vent forth and make return of those commodities which their own or either of those countries do afford: the lying in the way bringeth foreign shipping to claim succour at their harbours when, either outward or homeward bound, they are checked by an east, south or southeast wind: and where the horse walloweth some hairs will still remain."

Cornwall's hills are less rugged than those of Devon, but the bastion of its coast is even stronger. Its fogs are denser and its winds come more briskly from the sea. Something indescribable shows that it is farther off from London. But these differences between Devon and Cornwall are such as one discovers in a family that is sharply marked by likeness.

For a thousand years Cornwall regarded Devon as its buffer against invasion from the east; but now that unarmed trippers are abroad with heavy purses, its fears are reversed. It hopes that this new invasion will remain in its railway carriage through Plymouth and come all the way to Penzance before it spends its money. All locomotives run out from London at top speed, not even slowing down for towns.

But when they have discharged passengers at the Hoe, then they merely amble towards Land's End, halting at every village. Our own train, once across the Tamar, was in no hurry. It seemed to be aping a tourist on holiday and was looking about for a room to let. Later in the season, it will wear white flannels and fetch a painted pail.

At Lostwithiel we left our railway carriage and crossed the platform to a branch line that ambles down to Fowey by the sea. It is a half hour's journey on the bank of a sandy stream that empties as the tide runs out. Each village on its course, as on the Dart and Tamar, is a birthplace of English navigation.

It seems natural that these western ports should have sent ships on uncharted seas. It would be hard to believe that Cathay might be approached from London—and from Liverpool it would be quite absurd. Those mightier harbors do well enough for the export of dirty coal and Lancashire cotton goods; but any seaman who believed in mermaids and golden coasts would choose the magic end of England whose great cliffs are the portal to adventure.

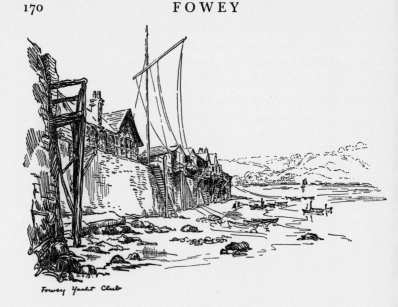

Fowey Yacht Club

XXIX. FOWEY

FOWEY stands upstream about a mile from the ocean. It has been a harbor for pirates against foreign ships and their own retreat when battles were disastrous. Like most of its fellow ports upon this coast, it has great headlands between which a chain was stretched.

No other town in all this district can boast of such narrow streets. The highway from St. Austell takes a hitch in its belt when it reaches Fowey in order that it may wriggle in between the buildings. If a man of moderate girth chance to be on the street when a motor sounds its horn, he will be forced into a doorway. Only now and then does the town open to a tiny square where fat folk may stand securely in any jam of traffic. These lanes are further cramped by the bulging walls of houses that hang above them. They are littered by abutments and doorsteps that jut upon the pavement. No house-owner knows the exact line of his property, and it is the mere guess of streets that find a path as best they may.

Somewhere behind the High Street is the River Fowey, to be seen at intervals through narrow archways and at the foot of crazy flights of steps. These are vistas that all artists seize, so we must add their easels to the litter of the curb. And these houses that bulge forward on the street, bulge forward also on the river. There is economy in this, for narrow foundations give large rooms above. Or shall we say that, like ladies of an older period of dress, they swell from a narrow waist to ripe magnificence above? We have read in our guidebook of a native woman dressing in her bedroom above the river, who suddenly saw the spar of a sailing vessel thrust in her window.

Fowey, like Brixham, smells of fish. It has landing-stages and warehouses, hoists and packing crates, old briar pipes, and yellow tarpaulin and fishermen. Its streets are filled also with idle sailors from the ships that come to this port for china clay—men of every nation, for Fowey's china clay moves in the commerce of the world. We shall see later at the town's dingy little theatre a signboard that is inscribed in English, French, Spanish, Italian, Chinese, Greek, Dutch and German. And any bar-tender of Fowey who is worth his salt knows the names of ale and whiskey in all of these tongues.

But Fowey, unlike Brixham, caters also to the tourist. It has set up shops of knickknacks and colored postcards, brass door-knockers made to the likeness of a pirate ship, and the latest novels of Oppenheim and Edgar Wallace. Small hotels are terraced on the hillside at the edge of town and they look out upon the river and the steep countryside beyond. Across the street from some of these hotels are narrow gardens—just a bench or two, a bit of grass and a pebbled walk— and these gardens are for the private use of lodgers. From them one can see fishing trawlers putting into harbor, or great ships of china clay moving out to sea.

Fowey has an inhabited castle that is known as Place House. From far off one can see its lofty tower rising from the middle of the town, but he can hardly find it when he searches the narrow streets. At most his blind lane will come up against a high wall and end abruptly, and it is only by inquiry that he will learn that it is the wall of Place. Fowey is of denser buildings than Dartmouth, for a narrower valley crowds it in. All streets, except the High Street, lead back from the river and climb to new suburbs on the hills. But these streets are too steep for easy climbing, and most tourists remain in the part below. In any fit of energy they will follow the river to its mouth and climb the headlands—will perhaps drag their golf clubs to windy links and slice far off to sea.

Fowey's origin is obscure. It was transferred to Norman ownership at the Conquest, and there is still older tradition of an Irish saint who was buried here and beckoned afterwards to pilgrims. But although records are scarce, Fowey's early history is apparent to any one who will study its position by the sea. Just as soon as prehistoric man hereabouts had learned to build and sail a ship, Fowey was in existence.

The fame of the town has been bright from the days of Edward I, and Fowey still boasts of a celebrated quarrel with Winchelsea and Rye. It seems that Fowey's ships passed up the Channel and in passing these proud towns "refused to vaile their bonets." This action seems to have been a kind of thumbing of the nose, and out came the Cinque Ports's fleet. Happily, says our historian, Carew, "the Foy men gave them so rough entertainment at their welcome, that they were glad to forsake patch, without bidding farewell."

An evidence of Fowey's importance towards the middle of the fourteenth century is the general muster of ships that

England supplied to Edward III for the siege of Calais. From the list we copy down only such towns as supplied fifteen ships or more:

Fowey	47	Bristol	22	Boston	17
Yarmouth	43	Winchelsea	21	Dover	16
Dartmouth	31	Southampton	21	Hull	16
Plymouth	26	Shoreham	21	Lynne	16
London	25	Looe	20	Margate	15
Sandwich	22	Newcastle	17	Weymouth	15

This catalogue shows more than Fowey's prime importance. It indicates that England's naval strength was chiefly in the southwest counties, with the narrow channel next, and but a scant tonnage from the north. There is no Liverpool on the list—not even a single ship—but this town was then but a harbor of small shipping to the Irish coast, a new port necessitated by the silting of the River Dee that had already forced Chester to be an inland city. Hythe supplied only six ships, Rye but nine, Hastings and Romney only four apiece. It is evident that the Cinque Ports were already declining from their importance as the fourteenth century advanced, in favor of the deeper water of the west.

Fowey once fought Giovanna Doria of Genoa—Genoa that was then the rival of Venice for Mediterranean trade. There is a ballad of this contest, which we quote from the point when the Fowey seamen were making ready for the attack:

> They hoist their sails both top and top,
>   The mizen and all was tried a,
> And every man stood to his lot,
>   Whatever should betide a.
>
> The roaring cannon then were plied,
>   And rub-a-dub went the drum a;
> The braying trumpets loud they cried,
>   To courage both all and some a.

The grappling hooks were brought at length,
   The brown bill and the sword a;
John Dory at length, for all his strength,
   Was clapt fast under board a.

These waters of Cornwall were a dangerous playground for southern ships.

These were great days for Fowey. Its sailors, "unable to bear a low sail in their fresh gale of fortune," skimmed the seas with piracy. And all went well until they made the mistake of cutting off the ears of a messenger sent to them by Edward IV. At this affront the chain was taken from the harbor, and Fowey declined in wealth and power.

We spent five days at Fowey, in a small but excellent hotel that looks out across the harbor from the hillside at the edge of town. During these five days we were the hotel's only patrons, except for several tourists who stopped merely for a night in passing down the coast. To us, therefore, belonged entirely the upholstered chairs against the downstairs fire, the sofa at the window for tea and clotted cream, the iron bench of our little garden across the street.

Although Fowey is a town of unquestioned interest and of romantic beauty, our holidays were marred by fog and rain. We were forever flattening our noses on the windows of our bedroom and squinting at a heavy mist in the hope that it would lift. Occasionally the Cornish hills over Polruan across the river were of distinct outline, but more often a veil of fog shut them out entirely. Fowey's harbor was then a universal gray without a shore. Under a light mist we counted the trawlers and the coastwise vessels, great freighters loaded with china clay, and the tiny ferry boat that was rowed back and forth across the river. We learned by root-of-heart each church tower on the hills, the motors creeping up Polruan's single street to disappear in mist. We watched rain running down the gutters, and tourists, braver than ourselves, in rubber coats, who were out for exercise and wet feet.

With such inclement weather we turned to books and, in particular, to those of Sir Arthur Quiller-Couch—his essays. Quiller-Couch, in addition to being the editor of the "Oxford Book of English Verse" and the author of thirty volumes at the least, is also Fowey's greatest citizen. We could see his house just up the street, quite near our front windows, a cottage whose garden overhangs the harbor. Fowey is such a crowded nest that the building is of necessity jammed against the roadway. This is evidently an embarrassment to him, for now and then a tourist thinks his dwelling to be a hotel and knocks him up at night for a bed and dinner. In one of his essays he complains of finding a tourist "in the pantry searching for a brandy-and-soda. . . . We make it a rule," he adds, "to send out a chair whenever some unknown invader walks into the garden and prepares to make a water-colour sketch of the river." This essay is from the volume entitled "From a Cornish Window." "Of all views," he continues, "I reckon that of a harbour the most fascinating and the most easeful, for it combines perpetual change with perpetual repose. It amuses like a panorama and soothes like an opiate, and when you have realized this you will understand why so many thousands of men around this island appear to spend all their time in watching tidal water."

For five days, as often as the fog settled down on Fowey, I read Quiller-Couch. I took him with me to St. Ives, where I read him every evening while the rain was beating on the windows. He went with me to Boscastle and Clovelly, where I finished another volume during hours of drizzle. He was the solace of a tempest at Porlock, and he endured the showers of Dunster.

We were not, of course, continually housed at Fowey by fog and rain. Each day there were signs that the veil was lifting from the hills, and in a treacherous rift of sunlight we made excursions here and there.

Our first long walk was downstream to the headlands at the harbor's mouth. This took us past Sir Arthur Quiller-Couch's house. We squinted closely at the windows. But if we thought to gaze into his study piled with books, we were disappointed. It was his pantry that we saw, and none of its furnishings suggested genius.

Our road now climbed a hill, where it paused for a moment at an iron bench. Then it ran refreshed in a narrow lane to Readymoney Cove. Here was a yellow beach for swimming. We now clambered up a steep path through woods, rounded the shoulder of the headland and had a wide view of Fowey, of Polruan and all of the harbor. Another turn and we saw the open ocean, streaked with squalls and rainy patches.

Near the top of the headland there stood a lonely monument. It is the tomb of an eccentric man who left a provision in his will that he be buried in such a place as might see the tower of the Fowey church but could not hear its bells.

Beyond the monument we came to a golf course on a sloping meadow at the top of the cliffs. Would it be possible, we asked, to hire clubs and play? With the payment of a fee, the caddy master answered. But he had no clubs that would fit Mary. We were interrupted by an English woman, just off the last green. Mary, she said, might use her clubs on any days but Tuesdays and Thursdays. At my own club at home, there is not one of us who would lend even a broken niblick to a stranger.

Fowey's golf course, as is usual in the British Isles, is cropped by sheep. These ingenious animals know not only how to cut the grass, but also how to rake it in. They even go so far as to spread it with manure. These lesser courses have not the perfection of American links. Their fairways are not of softest turf, nor are the putting-greens of a park-like size or so smoothly rolled. The compensation, however, is a saving of expense, and a moderately poor man can play without neglecting his butcher's bill. British courses are generally open to strangers on the payment of a fee. It is strange that a game that once used the vacant time of shepherds, should be now at such a height of luxury as it is in America, with matched clubs, caddies at union rates, secret cocktails, and striped umbrellas on the terrace.

On our return to the headland, we saw several sailboats zigzagging out to sea in a triangular race. Then suddenly the fog rolled in and they were lost.

For the omission of many excursions roundabout Fowey, rain is our excuse.

Arthur Quiller-Couch has recounted the visit here of a city journalist who spoke condescendingly of his host's house as a "nook"—contrasting its obscurity with the metropolitan areas of suburban London. Quiller-Couch resented that his dwelling was called a "nook." "Its windows," he wrote, "look down upon a harbour wherein, day by day, vessels of every nation and men of large experience are for ever going and coming; and beyond the harbour, upon leagues of open sea, highway of the vastest traffic in the world; whereas from his own far more expensive house my friend sees only a dirty laurel-bush, a high green fence, and the upper half of a suburban lamp-post." Putney gets the worst of it when it trifles with a Cornishman's affection.

Polruan

XXX. WE MEET THE VENUS OF VARIETY

IN OUR wanderings around the streets of Fowey we saw several times the playbill of a theatre.

THE ALL-BRITISH SUPER SHOW

COMEDY	HARMONY	PIANO	MANDOLINS
DRAMA	DANCING	BANJO	XYLOPHONE
SINGING	ACROBATICS	GUITARS	SAXOPHONE

THE FOUR GIBSONS

From the principal theatres of England, Australia, Manila, Japan, Corea, French Indo-China, Siam, Malaya, Java, Burma, India, Germany, Poland, Russia, Italy, France, Belgium, Austria, Czecho-Slovakia.

and

TRIXIE, THE VENUS OF VARIETY

It would have been ridiculous, of course, to sit sluggish beside our fire with Quiller-Couch, when even far-off Siam had acclaimed this accumulated genius. We hurried, therefore, through our beef and boiled potatoes, slighted our stewed rhubarb, and were presently on our way to the thicker town.

We were a bit late in arriving at the theatre, and were given seats in a gallery that was of the gloom that lovers choose. We noticed that for the most part only the rear chairs were taken, and that every pair of lovers had melted to a single shadow. To get to our places we were obliged to cross a shaft of light that was thrown out by a spot-lamp from a round hole in the gallery's back wall. For an instant, therefore, we blocked the flow of this dusty illumination. On the performance of the stage we cast great shadows, as if an eclipse had dimmed the moon. We oozed into our chairs. The rail in front of us was a wobbly thing that teased us to lean on it and to crash through on the heads of those who sat below. For a moment I thought that a South Sea islander sat next to me, but discovered it was an English girl with a wopse of tangled hair. Her neighbor to the rear must have thought he was gazing through a jungle.

It was a variety performance, given by a troupe that suggested those of Leonard Merrick's stories—actors whose lack of talent kept them out of London—or broken players, perhaps, banished by infirmity to stroll among the smaller cities until a cough rings the curtain down.

Leonard Merrick knows England's provincial theatre as no other writer does. We lay a guess that he was himself once an actor on a shabby circuit. For how else could he depict so convincingly the life behind the curtain and the poor diggings of a player, and do it with such mirth and pathos? In his pages one smells the stale odors of a transient lodging-house, the dust and grease-paint of the stage. One realizes the hunger, the privation and the ambitions thwarted—the sallow cheek, the old legs that must caper to the coffin. "Conrad in Quest of His Youth," "When Love Flies Out of the Window," "The Position of Peggy Harper," "The Actor-Manager"—all of these novels deal with the tinsel glitter, the comedy and tragedy of the English provincial stage in its dingier aspect. One of these stories has been prefaced by Sir Arthur Pinero, himself once a shabby actor until good fortune hit him. "It is to Mr. Merrick's obviously first-hand acquaintance with the lower grade theatre," he writes, "that we owe at least two quite remarkable studies of shady theatrical life and character."

An interested student might collect quite a few books that deal with England's obscure stage—its extempore theatre in town halls, its converted barns, its pier pavilions and the tents of county fairs. Now and then he would find a journal, such as that of Edmund Kean; certain early chapters in the life of Sheridan Knowles; the rough experiences of the Kembles on country boards; ten years of a yet unrecognized Sir Henry Irving. Dibdin was once a strolling player of the Channel towns, singing songs of his own composition and of the *Yo Ho* school of poetry. But it will not be in the pages of London's great persons that a student will find chiefly his material. Macready's diary, for instance, skips his early hardships; and Betterton and Garrick seem to have sprung from nothing into fame. Nor can material be found among the submerged players of villages and inns, for failure seldom records itself.

It is in fiction, therefore, that we may best learn of these lean lives—in such stories as Priestley's "Good Companions." The hero of "The Man Who Laughs" was a strolling juggler. There is an echo of the stage in the shabbiness of Alfred Jingle. There is Mr. Vincent Crummles acting once at Plymouth.

Fowey's variety performance was enchanting A big bass in a velvet jacket roared like a lion in a voice that was almost good, but with much sucking of a lozenge between his numbers. A gentleman pianist was of such skill that he could have played the piano, if he had cared to, with the end of his nose—without reducing the melody by a single jot. A lady, gone fat, jiggled like a jelly. A soubrette, except for a missing tooth, was perfect. The tenor's Adam's apple throbbed with passion as he sang "It's You, Baby, That I Am Lovin'." Trixie, the Venus of Variety, however, had stood on her head in so many countries (see the list upon the billboard) that the poor old dear was wearing out.

A cotton hanging was the only scene; but there was a scarlet tidy on the piano which became a lady's scarf when it was needed in a later number. There was also a gilt spindle-legged table, reënforced with iron, on which Trixie danced, bending herself into a hoop with one leg hoisted. This table served also for a drawing-room in Mayfair; and from its drawer, in proper time, the magician lifted out his rabbit. The soubrette was now a cockney street singer asking us to buy her *dafferdills,* and now a lady in a bower; but her missing tooth was a constant badge of her identity.

There were banjos and saxophones, comedy and drama, as the playbill promised. Fowey's theatre rocked with applause; and at the "Co-op" song in particular there was such a stamping of excited feet, that we feared the rickety building would wobble from its foundations and topple into the river that flanked the stage.

And now, when for a last time Trixie had waved her silken leg aloft—that peerless limb, worshiped by Siam and now marked by a stocking's mended run—the show was finished and the audience dispersed. Night had fallen on streets without a light. The only sound in the silent lane were the footsteps of the crowd—footsteps that diminished at each turn, until we walked alone. All windows were dark; but Fowey's old houses bulged forward above the curb, as if curious to see who was up so late.

We were to encounter the members of the variety troupe each time thereafter that we walked through Fowey. Once we saw the big bass sitting at the window of a lodging-house in his same old velvet jacket, gazing through torn lace curtains in a far-off gaze of romantic meditation—poesy somewhat qualified by the toothpick in his mouth. We saw the pianist buying cigarettes. The soubrette we hardly knew in her street clothes, but that was because her mouth was shut. And then she smiled, and we knew her by her constant missing tooth. We discovered Trixie selecting vegetables in the market and putting them into a paper bag. We followed her until at last she tripped up the steps of the big bass's lodging-house. We judged from this that the troupe paid for rooms alone and prepared its own meals.

We debated the propriety of inviting the players to dinner at one of the taverns of the town as an appreciation of its last night's entertainment. Was it not Conrad questing for his youth, in Leonard Merrick's story, who invited to lunch certain ladies of the *Kiss-and-Tell* company, in recognition of their performance on Blithepoint Pier? It was a Chateaubriand, *pommes soufflées,* with all their fixings, that he ordered—"an omelette au Kirsch, with lots of flames." Conrad was inflamed himself with the melody that they had offered him across the footlights.

> What is the use of loving a girl
> When you know she don't want yer to?
> What if she's fair beyond all compare,
> And what if her eyes are blue?

And should we do no less for Trixie and her silken legs?

And now on Sunday afternoon, we noticed that a motor-truck of ancient vintage was stopped beside the stage door of the theatre. Into it were being piled the cotton curtain, the velvet rag that had graced the piano's top, the magician's

table on which Trixie had danced. And there were shabby
bags, containing no doubt the cockney wig, the rabbit and
the pink and yellow tights. The xylophone, the saxophone,
the banjos and mandolins were ranged along the running-
board, each in a cloth wrapper.

The big bass, still in his velvet jacket, was mopping the
sweat of his exertions. The pianist was in front, cranking
the motor.

"Good morning," we said. "Where next?"

"Looe," the B B answered. "And then up along the coast
through the towns with piers."

"And then Siam?" I asked.

He grinned, but did not answer.

And now the lady with the missing tooth appeared at the
stage door with a wopse of garments on her arm.

At last came Trixie.

"Good luck!" we shouted, as the motor coughed and
moved away.

Fowey's theatre, at a careless estimate, holds not more
than the equivalent of twenty-five dollars. There were six
persons in the troupe. Two hundred dollars, at most, were
their combined earnings for the week, without the deduc-
tion of expense. From this one may estimate the profits of
a strolling player.

We glanced in through the stage door. The boards were
empty and in dingy light. Mayfair had disappeared like the
unsubstantial pageant of a dream. The pink rabbit was in
Wonderland with Alice.

The Jonathan Couch House,
- Polperro -

XXXI. POLPERRO

WE WENT up the coast to Polperro. We crossed Fowey's river on a rowboat ferry for a penny fee and then our motor climbed through Polruan by a long steep street that lifted us into thick mist upon the hills. The street, like a Jacob's ladder in a Sunday school, was so narrow that there were awkward moments when wagons or other motors passed, and we must assume that it was designed for donkey travel only. Far below us were the river and the town of Fowey stretched along its shore.

And now a narrow lane wound around the hill-tops, with an occasional view of the ocean across treeless meadows and mighty cliffs. To the north a village and its church crouched in a shallow valley and listened to the wind. On both sides of the road were walls head-high, and so in effect it was a sunken road. On winter days, when ears are nipped, this protected lane must be a comfort to any one who walks or rides in an uncovered wagon. The lane is just wide enough for one-way traffic, with insets now and then for passing. It is called a highway to distinguish it from another passage nearer to the cliffs, which is too narrow for anything on wheels.

The names of villages and headlands hereabouts contain frequently the syllables *pol* or *tre* or *Lan;* and as these syllables spring from no roots of common knowledge (on our street, at least) we shall be forgiven if we look them up to find what they mean. Or perhaps it would be better to make a general list of the syllables on a Celtic map. We are but a freshman in this learning, and we hope we shall not be caught in too many mistakes.

Aber—*a confluence of waters*

Afon—*a river*

Aran—*a high place*

Ard—*a height*

Ben—*a head or mountain*

Bettys—*a chapel*

Bod—*a house*

Bos—*a house*

Briva—*a bridge*

Bryn—*a brow or ridge*

Cader—*a seat*

Caer—*a fortress*

Careg—*a rock*

Coed—*a wood*

Chy—*a house*

Combe—*a bowl-shaped valley*

Cop—*a hollow or cup*

Craig—*a rock or crag*

Cwm—*a bowl-shaped valley*

Dinas—*a hill or castle*

Dol—*a plain*

Dun—*a hill fort*

Drum—*a back or ridge*

Dwfr—*water*

Glyn—*a narrow valley*

Greeb—*a crest*

Gwent—*a plain*

Lan—*a valley*

Laus—*a valley*

Linn—*a deep pool*

Llan—*an enclosure or church*

Looe—*a lake or pool*

Maen or men—*a stone*

Man—*a district*

Nant—*a brook or valley*

Pen—*a head or mountain*

Peel—*a stronghold*

Pol—*a pool*

Porth—*a harbor*

Praa—*a meadow*

Pwll—*a pool*

Re—*a ford*

Rhos—*a moor*

Rhyd—*a ford*

Ros—*a heath*
Ross—*a promontory*
Sarn—*a road*
Traeth—*a beach*
Tre—*a village or house*

Treryn—*a castle*
Ty—*a house*
Ynys—*an island*
Zawn—*a cave or hole*

This list could be profitably pinned inside the hat on any journey into Celtic country.

And now our lane ran downhill and in a wooded valley joined a broad highway from the north. Here was a scattering of summer cottages whose gardens descended to a brawling stream and whose walls were covered with flowers. It was evident that we were near Polperro.

Our motor stopped at the edge of the denser town; for the highroad, as in the case of Fowey, is too cramped among the houses to admit motors with any comfort or safety. Public buses, it is true, manage to squeeze in, but they scrape their fenders at every turn and ruin pedestrians who are caught unawares. Evidently, where buses rush in, even less than angels fear to tread.

It used to be said that Polperro was an unspoiled Clovelly, a picturesque village of ancient charm undiscovered by the traveling world and still possessed by native fishermen. This is no longer entirely true. With the coming of the private motor and the culture-bus, Polperro is now on one of the minor routes of tourists. There are lodging-houses and restaurants, cottages for rent both up the stream and on the cliffs. Old houses of smuggling fame may be entered for a fee, in which antiques are offered fresh from northern factories. An ancient bridge flaunts a Saxon origin and is crowded with trippers. Fishermen will permit themselves to be sketched if you make it worth their time—honest fellows who smell of pilchards. There is not room in Polperro for a large hotel, but small inns hang cards in their windows announcing their accommodations.

Shops are filled with postcards and brass door-knockers.

Making these knockers must be one of the major industries
of England. In the moorland, they are decorated with pixies,
with Sir Francis Drake at Plymouth. In a church town there
is a cathedral at the top. How any American's door, after
its owner's grand excursion, escapes these souvenirs is beyond our comprehension. The door-knockers sold in Polperro specialize in sailing vessels, with pirate flags on the
masts.

In an ancient house said to have been owned in former
days by the family of Sir Arthur Quiller-Couch, there is a
museum. "It will charm the shallow inconsequent tripper,"
says our guidebook, "stimulate the thoughtful and eager,
and prove a gold-mine to the philosopher."

It was a challenge. "Mary," I asked, "are you a shallow
inconsequent tripper?"

"It's worth a sixpence to find out," she replied.

Inside is a smuggler's cupboard and many old documents
both of rough and peaceful days. A sleeping-room above is a
tight little attic with a single narrow window; for sailors
have so much air upon the ocean that they want to be stale
and snug at home.

There are shops for tea and clotted cream, a house on
stilts above the stream because the lot is too small to hold
it. Paths zigzag up the cliffs with wide outlooks. The harbor
is active—the bailing of a boat, the lifting of its sails, its
fish unloaded and on their way to London markets. A tourist sometimes spends the night, but usually as the afternoon
draws in, he climbs to his bus and rattles back to Plymouth
with his arm around a sleepy lady and a raw voice instruct-
ing the countryside that he is seeing Nellie home.

Yet Polperro is not entirely spoiled by daytime trippers.
For in addition to these idling strangers on the stone jetty
of the harbor, there are also idling natives—fishermen wearing the shabby pants that artists love, hitched up now and
then to keep them from falling off. These fishermen some-

times work, I have no doubt, but never with parade and ostentation. They smoke pipes, rather, and gaze for long hours at the ocean. The smoke from their pipes tells them the setting of the wind, and their rheumatic joints are their best barometer. Life for them is the lifting of a sail, the drawing of a net, a sip of gin and peaceful rest.

In the harbor at low tide, trawlers lie in the mud, and they rock back and forth when the water has risen to their battered sides. On each mast-head sits a gull, and a dozen others circle round waiting for his chair when he shall leave it. Gulls sit also in a long row on the top of the warehouse and seem to sleep. This is pretense, for they are merely waiting with one eye open for refuse fish to be thrown upon the water. When this happens there is a scramble as when a kick is blocked in football. The fish is pulled to ribbons in the air. There is squawking until each gull and gullet has its bit. Then the birds retire to the grandstand where they seem to sleep again.

Polperro means St. Peter's Pool. But this safe pool, so idle on a summer afternoon, offers great activity in winter when sudden storms sweep in. For her fishing craft are still outside and the sailors' wives stand on the stone jetty to watch the treacherous progress of the gale. Nor is the usually protected harbor now entirely safe, for great waves toss themselves across the jetty and bump and rattle the boats inside. This is an hour of loud excitement, and sailors tighten their mooring chains and call to one another above the wind and the screeching of the gulls. Belated trawlers, one after another, are swept in dangerously through the cranny of the piers.

Mary was unstrapping her kit of cardboard. "I am going to sketch," she said.

For an hour I walked among the narrow streets until I knew each jutting, each building and every window of brass door-knockers. With one shop-keeper I scraped acquaint-

- Polperro -

ance. He tried at first to sell me a print of the Battle of
Bunker Hill, but I compromised by buying a metal hook.
I had already bought one in Exeter for my pajamas. This
new one of Polperro holds—but why be so domestic?

Even this small purchase in the depression of business so
warmed the shop-keeper's heart that he showed me his entire
house—and one room in particular, from a window of which
it is said that John Wesley once preached to the sailors who
were assembled in the street. "Half of them were smugglers,"
my friend explained, "and the text of his sermon was hell
fire."

The shop-keeper informed me that Polperro is hardly
Cornish, that its origin and early growth were influenced
by excursions from the continent. In his own boyhood a
man of Polperro was scarcely understood at Looe or Fowey.
Hannibal, a Carthaginian name, is still common, and Jago
and Cadenza from Spain. We ourselves observed many
women of swarthy skin.

Few coast towns of England are as picturesque as Polperro.
It crouches in a narrow valley that is merely a deep gash
hacked across the headlands. One street tries to find footing
on a cliff; but the going is too precarious and finally, having
already dwindled to a foot-path, it stops entirely. Somewhere
on this path Hugh Walpole once passed a summer. Polperro's houses seem tumbled from above, like that house of
Frank Stockton's story that was dislodged in rain and went
sliding down the hill.

On the rocks against the ocean there is a chapel of St.
Peter's as a guide to fishermen; yet all this coast abounds
with tales of profitable wreckage by false lights. We remember reading of a certain coast of England, unguarded by a
light, whose beach was strewn by valuable refuse after every
storm. And when a lighthouse was proposed, it met a protest.
It would ruin the prosperity of a near-by village whose live-

lihood was wreckage. It was the theory of vested rights carried to extremes.

After lunch we motored to Looe—another pretty town not quite at a river's mouth and another former nest of pirates. There is deep water here and great ships along the quay. There is also a beach for colored parasols in summer.

On the hills above Fowey, on our return, we were quite lost in fog. The ocean was a void below us. We slipped down Polruan's long hill, shivered in the ferry boat, and were revived by a fire and by tea and clotted cream.

Rain slashed the windows. We crowded close against the hearth. Our umbrella dripped in the hod. "Travelers must be content," said Touchstone.

The Harbor
St Ives

XXXII. TO ST. IVES

ON TUESDAY, May 12th, we went by railway carriage to St. Ives—"kits, cats, sacks and wives." We are informed, however, that the St. Ives of Cornwall is really not the town of the nursery jingle, which comes from a town of the same name northwest of Cambridge.

Just outside Fowey there is a landing dock for china clay, and a ship was lying in its berth, all powdered over as with talc. The laborers were daubed white like circus clowns. Two men in our carriage were discussing china clay and how it fetches vessels here from all around the world; just as tin in ancient times once brought ships from the south and east.

"Housewives," said one of these men, "tried mixing it with flour. But the dough wouldn't rise."

"It looks good for milk chocolate," said the other.

Between Fowey and St. Ives we traveled in a china clay country. On every horizon we saw huge white hills thrown out of quarries and standing ready for export. These great mounds and the abandoned towers of worn-out tin mines are the two most distinctive marks of this district running towards Land's End. Clay is its inland wealth, just as fish is the profit of its coast.

A few miles out of Fowey, not far from Lantyan Wood, we passed near the supposed site of one of King Mark's castles. It was King Mark who sent Tristram to Ireland for Iseult; and it is evident, therefore, that we are coming to the land of Arthur and of buried Lyonesse. I have sat through that beautiful but exhausting opera of Wagner's several times and have always thought that its scene was fairyland—that it was sprinkled, along about eleven o'clock, with the lotus plant. Nor can one understand how the hot love of Tristram and Iseult could have retained its passion in such cool wet meadows as lie beside the River Fowey. These two lovers seem fitted to a southern sky and to a moonlight unspoiled by fog. It is legend, however, that the ship that carried them from Ireland was bound to the stormy harbor of Tintagel; and those bleak waters are after all a better home for tragedy and sorrow. At Fowey, yesterday, I thought I had heard King Mark's singing sailors headed for the tavern below our hotel.

From here to the northern coast of Cornwall one's best guidebook is Malory.

We changed trains at Lostwithiel, at the head of the river's navigation. As there was a half-hour's wait for a westbound train, we walked into the town, passing across a picturesque bridge of stone arches with points in a parapet where one can stand aside for traffic. In an old volume on Cornish bridges, I find that "when Leland visited Lostwithiel in 1539, he found the old stone bridge . . . was nearly choked with sand" and that "Lostwithiel Bridge probably dates from the Indulgence of 1437."

There is a parish church with a lovely spire at Lostwithiel. Once in the civil wars two cavaliers were imprisoned in this church, and they climbed the steeple and pulled the ladder up behind them. The provost marshal tried at first to smoke them out by setting fire to a load of hay. Then he exploded a keg of gunpowder. But the gentlemen on top merely thumbed their noses. Here the anecdote concludes, and we shall never know whether they were hanged.

At Truro we changed trains again and, with an hour to spare, we hired a motor-cab at the station and saw a fragment of the town, with just an outside glimpse of the cathedral while the cab's clock ticked at our expense. The building is newly erected and somewhat raw, but of excellent proportions. A passenger boat was loading in the river and about to start for Falmouth; and if our bags had been with us, we would have gone on a sudden excursion that is not unlike the journey from Totnes to the sea.

Down that stream I had once passed a week-end with friends who had rented a house for the summer season. I recall a broad lawn to the River Fal and an excursion to a stranded ship that had fought at Trafalgar. I remember also that a valet sneaked into my room each morning just at dawn to decide what clothing I should wear. If I found a pair of white flannel trousers laid across a chair, I knew he was forcing me to play tennis after breakfast. No man, of course, can be a hero to his valet, but at least he should be given his choice of neckties.

We changed trains again at the village of St. Erth, and it was towards the end of afternoon when we sighted the wide yellow sands of St. Ives and were presently set down in the terminal station. The end of England, we exclaimed. Only fish can travel farther.

But our first impression of St. Ives was one of disappoint-

ment. We had looked for the kind of dilapidated beauty
that artists love; and instead of finding this at the very out-
set, here we were, seated in a gayly painted hotel motor-
bus among people who had obviously come to this town for
a smart vacation. About us were piled hat boxes, tennis
rackets and golf bags, leather dressing-cases—a general riffraff of fashionable luggage carried by a strange people who
would rather infest themselves with a dozen parcels than
pack one trunk to be carried in the van. There were thin
men who came for exercise, and large ladies with buried
husbands who puffed up the motor's steps and were certainly
looking forward to displaying their fat arms at dinner.

I straightened my tie and smoothed out my travel-battered
hat. "My deah," I said to Mary, "we must conceal our rude
Ohio accent."

And now the motor-bus instead of heading, as we had
hoped, towards St. Ives's dense center, took to a winding
course and turned its back upon the town. Presently St.
Ives's pleasant clutter was far below and we were bouncing
through a country high above the distant sea. And now we
turned into a park on the summit of whose slope sat the
Tregenna Castle Hotel, once a private residence but now
conducted by the railroad for its patrons.

Our fat ladies were lifted down by a major-general in
uniform.

On our travels to this point we had been lodged in empty
hotels that wanted us. The Tregenna Castle, however, was
full. It was only on our promise not to stay until the crowded
week-end that we could obtain a room. No one less than
a duchess could have softened the stiff nose behind the
wicket.

"Has this room a view of the ocean?" I asked.

Whenever it shall happen that a doubtful Christian presents himself to St. Peter with a request for a corner room
and bath on the parlor floor of paradise—a room that over-

looks the Elysian Fields—not till then will a traveler be met by the same vacant stare as now spread across the face of the clerk at the Tregenna Castle.

"All ocean rooms are taken by the season," he answered, "and they are booked from year to year."

We were assigned a room which, in the days of the castle's splendor as a private residence, was doubtless the bedroom of the second pastry-cook. It was at the rear of the building and looked out over the concrete roof of the enormous dining-room. A distant fringe of green trees appeared above false crenelation.

I returned to the wicket.

"Have you nothing better?" I asked.

I was a tramp who complains of broken meat.

"Most certainly not," he answered.

I approached a prosperous porter.

"What is the next best hotel in St. Ives?" I asked.

He was deaf.

I jingled my keys.

Out came his palm.

" 'Cue," he answered.

But still he had no satisfactory reply. There was this and that—we might try them—but he scorned any hotel but his own.

We went back to our room and looked again at the concrete roof. On the wall was a stain that had been made, doubtless, by the aforementioned second pastry-cook. She had left also a few crumbs on the dressing-table.

We got out our tired umbrella and without waiting for dinner started for the town afoot.

We found presently the kind of hotel we wanted, and one that wanted us. Its name was the Pednolva, and it stood at the edge of old St. Ives on a point of rock outside the harbor. This rock was just large enough to hold the building and a narrow rim of garden. At low tide a springboard

The Warren
St. Ives.

stuck out over the rocks and invited suicide. The Pednolva had previously been a private house; but even before that its central structure had been the housing above an ancient tin mine. This oldest part of the building, now the general sitting-room, was circular and it looked out three ways upon the bay and ocean across shallow porches under glass. Each window was splayed through six feet of massive stone wall. We were told that a deep shaft descends from underneath the floor. If a beam had given way, our diary would be finished. We could not discover how old the tin mine was, and we can only hope that Phoenicians quarried here.

In effect the Pednolva was a lighthouse and our evening lamp had uncommon responsibilities. Any storm from the east or north threw spray on the building's windows. Our own bedroom was somewhat around the corner and to the landward of these gales; but a young woman lodger told us later that her room was so noisy with the racket of the waves and wind that she shouted to be heard—that if she left her window open wider than a crack, both Boreas and Neptune climbed into bed with her. She was, luckily, a stiff-nosed person and capable of resisting familiarity even with the candle out.

And now having engaged a room for the following day at eight shillings each, including all meals, with early tea in bed and tea again in the afternoon with clotted cream and slap-cake—a bargain unparalleled throughout our journey—we set out again for dinner and a first glimpse of the town.

The Pednolva is close by a nest of streets that is called the Warren and looks its name. Then came the High Street with its rows of shops. This thoroughfare, after a turn or two, finally wiggled out upon the quay that lines the harbor —wet sand at low tide, a pool when the ocean comes running back. The harbor is guarded by two stone jetties. Along the curving water front there were several shops of trinkets, modest restaurants with blue doors and yellow window-sills, and the station of the life-guard with a great red boat on wheels inside.

A row of dingy buildings had once been warehouses for salted fish, but many of their northern walls were now pierced by sloping windows, and we must assume that masterpieces of rocks and ocean were daily under way. Fishing boats lay in the harbor's sandy mud. A larger coastal vessel was moored along the farther jetty and seemed to be asleep. Gulls wheeled overhead or strutted on the sand and pecked in the shallow pools that the tide had left. There were idle fishermen everywhere, with a scattering of strange beings whose flowing ties proclaimed their occupation if not their livelihood.

There were few tourists but ourselves—none that seemed of the breed of the Tregenna Castle, which would hardly expose its silk ruffles and laundered shirts at this hour when dinner plates were rattling under its vast concrete roof.

We dined on the second floor in a small restaurant whose sign announced that fresh lobster was its specialty. Our table was blue with a yellow border, and our broad window looked upon the ocean. A Persian cat rubbed its back against our chairs and sniffed for fish. On the walls of the room were water-colors, each with its price tag. St. Ives's colony of artists is quite famous, and some of these pictures were of considerable merit—Mary speaking. Only a few of them were offensively modern—myself. At least they were not sick souls crying in distress.

We returned to the Tregenna Castle. Contract and gossip were raging in the lounge as we climbed to bed.

Old Houses
St. Ives.

XXXIII. A WEEK IN A LIGHT-HOUSE

WE SPENT a week of pleasant holidays at the Pednolva, and it proved to be as pleasant as its first promise. There was a bit too much of shepherd's pie for lunch perhaps, but what should one expect for eight shillings, with such delightful lodging in a lighthouse?

The Pednolva was almost empty. There was a young woman waiting for her husband to come off the sea. On any stormy night she glanced apprehensively across the black water; nor could she take comfort in a faint white rim of shoal across the harbor's windy mouth. She had an entertaining little son, who looked out of the window each afternoon at the time when the London train was due, and the trestle it crossed he called a puff-bridge. He was himself a mighty engine around the house, with his arms revolving like driving-shafts and with brassy clangs issuing from his mouth. His mother had once lived in California, and she was, therefore, impatient of English squalls. Her husband was a naval officer, and they had been stationed here and there around the world. They had no permanent home, and she and her son were weathering out a season until her husband's ship should put in at its native port. These naval people are strange driftwood—cosmopolitans who are at home nowhere in the world.

Another lodger was a curiously eccentric man who looked like a cartoon of a German professor. He never mingled with the other lodgers or came into the general sitting-room above the mine shaft. He sat always in the dining-room. As soon as his dishes of any meal were cleared away, it was his custom to reach to the floor beside his chair and fetch up a mass of books and papers. And there he would read and write until it was time for his cloth to be laid again. On the table of the hallway letters lay addressed to him from Leipsic publishers and Greek societies. He cared not a whit about a rainy sky. Day and night we heard the scratching of his pen as he tossed his finished sheets upon the floor.

The Pednolva had a maid of general housework who is typical of England's small hotels. She was busy from dawn, when she made tea for early risers, until she snapped on the lights at nine o'clock in the twilight. Even then there was an aftermath of filling hot-water bottles for cold-footed guests. She smoothed the beds. She waited on table at a trot, shoving around the stewed rhubarb in the very nick of time. She fetched in the hod of coal and went down on her knees to lift out the lumps with her bare hands. She patted pillows in the sitting-room, arranged the chairs for tea, brought in the slap-cake and carried off the empty plates. She polished brasses and whitened door-sills. In a word, like Charles Lamb's old sailor on the *Margate Hoy*, she flamed all day like Ariel around the house. And always with a pleasant smile. If any guest of the Pednolva needed anything, he shouted "Martha," and there she was, appearing out of nowhere—a mere ghost of a little girl with thin legs and arms who was everywhere at once.

We had a cook in a white cap. But we saw him only once, when he climbed out on the rocks below the hotel to capture a lobster that was stranded in a pool. He carried it off, wiggling, to the kitchen. Our shepherd's pie that day had a substitute.

Our landlady sat always in a private sitting-room, busy forever with bills and papers. She had no fondness for Americans, although she was civil to us. During the Great War, it seems, she was in a position to show favors to our soldiers. And she liked them. But afterwards on a visit to New York, a hotel had demanded payment in advance, and this had soured for her the whole western continent. She did not object to Americans in England, but they were different creatures at home. As for prices? She lifted her hands in horror and contrasted her own eight shillings against the extortion of Manhattan.

Smart travelers will choose the glitter of the Tregenna Castle, but I recommend the Pednolva to those to whom contract bridge is not a necessity—to all persons who travel with a single bag and would be likely to enjoy a week in a lighthouse whose windows are beaten by every storm. There is advantage also in being inside the town. St. Ives has a real charm in its narrow streets, and they were just outside our door.

The weather was still raw and uncertain, with sudden squalls, but there was always a fire in the round room and a hod that was full of coal. Nor did the Pednolva lock up its poker. The glass-enclosed verandas offered protection and a choice of stormy seas. Beyond the harbor was St. Ives's thick nest of houses with a tangle of masts and ropes. Each day we made excursions around the town and to the rocks beyond, having first squinted at the clouds and jiggled the hotel's barometer.

much the same. Southwestern England has always loved a man of destiny. It has been the home of lost causes and is dry tinder for a match. The very harbors of all this coast were made for plots and romantic adventure.

"A king who carried an umbrella!" And this as a cause of revolution! It is absurd. Guedalla must have been thinking of France alone and not of his native British islands. An umbrella is the only burden that an English gentleman is permitted to carry on a city street, and it is preposterous to consider it a cause of unrest and dynastic change. The Magna Carta is firm against packages of meat and bundles from one's tailor—even against such slight parcels as might contain a newly-purchased toothbrush. But the constant use of an umbrella is enforced by law. All the kings of England have carried them—not rolled tightly like a walking-stick, but flapping loosely and ready to be lifted. George V is a constitutional monarch to the core; and he would not think of stepping around the corner from Buckingham Palace for a fresh package of *gaspers* without taking his umbrella from its china vase. An umbrella may have started an uprising in fickle France, but it binds England together in a common misery of rain.

A strange character, John Knill, sometime collector of customs at St. Ives, has left his mark on this district. His life has been recorded by Baring-Gould, who angled in every shoal of Cornwall for the odd fish of his collection. John Knill was born in 1733 and having come to wealth and middle age, with thoughts on the after-life, he devised for himself a mausoleum like a slender pyramid on the top of a hill above the town. He also made a will, with a bequest to the town's corporation for providing the cost of a periodic pilgrimage to his tomb. In those circumambulating phrases that lawyers love, it was stipulated that every fifth year, on St. James the Apostle's Day, ten girls under the age of ten and two widows should climb the hill and dance and sing around the pyramid to the music of a fiddler who should wear a white cockade. For every one of these occasions, a pound was laid aside for ribbons. After the hundredth psalm, the children were to sing in chorus a song of his own composition: for it is written that he who pays the fiddler may call the tune.

We can hear these shrill children at his verses.

> Shun the bustle of the bay,
> Hasten, virgins, come away;
> Hasten to the mountain's brow,
> Leave, O leave, S. Ives below.
>
> Haste to breathe a purer air,
> Virgins fair, and pure as fair;
> Fly S. Ives and all her treasures,
> Fly her soft voluptuous pleasures;
> Fly her sons and all their wiles,
> Lushing in their wanton smiles;
> Fly the splendid midnight halls;
> Fly the revels of her balls;
> Fly, O fly the chosen seat,
> Where vanity and fashion meet.
>
> Hither hasten from the ring,
> Round the tomb in chorus sing,
> And on the lofty mountain's brow, aptly dight,
> Just as we should be, all in white,
> Leave all our troubles and our cares below.

St. Ives's soft voluptuous pleasures, its midnight halls where vanity and fashion met, seem to have been entirely in the poet's frenzied eye. A few of her sons may have lushed in wanton wiles, and they are probably still up to their old tricks. As for St. Ives's treasures, they are mostly fish.

An article once appeared in *The Gentleman's Magazine*

describing John Knill's tomb. "On one side, in raised letters
in granite, appear the words 'Hic jacet nil.' It was understood that the 'k' and another 'l' would be added when the
projector should be placed within." John Knill died in London and gave his remains to surgeons for dissection. Here
Lies Nothing, therefore, says the pyramid today.

It was not until the beginning of the twentieth century
that St. Ives attracted artists. But now there are blue doors
on every street, and in every ancient building there are attics
where water-colors flourish. A society of artists holds frequent exhibitions in a converted warehouse. It was our
bad luck to knock at the door on a day after the display
had closed. A man in a flowing tie, however, answered to
our summons. We could see walls of pictures; and unless I
am mistaken, there issued from the doorway a faint odor
of salt and pilchards.

Another great event at St. Ives is the practice of the life-
guard. We observed on the quay one day that a crowd had
gathered at the house of the red boat on wheels. There was
a long delay and then the doors were opened. There was
a mighty shout, which was followed by a half hour of confusion. And now at last a hundred men and boys took hold
of a rope and pulled the boat along the quay. It was finally
launched. Every fisherman of St. Ives was present with his
wife and yelling children. All this had consumed the better
part of an hour and if there had really been a wreck outside the harbor, the last man aboard would have gurgled
three times and gone down forever.

"What would happen," I asked, "if at the time of wreckage all the fishermen were busy? Who would pull the rope?"

"Have no fear of that," an old salt answered; and we
knew that fishermen are never busy.

St. Michael's Mount

XXXV. ST. MICHAEL'S MOUNT

OUR DAY'S objective was Penzance; but the trip by motor
was to include St. Michael's Mount, the south coast as far
as Mousehole, a detour to Land's End, with Penzance for
dinner and the night. A single chapter will be insufficient.

Passing the Tregenna Castle Hotel where long-legged girls
were striding about with golf-bags, we saw the sands of
Carbis Bay and a far-off lighthouse on Godrevy Point whose
blinking eye had peeked in through our window at the
Pednolva.

Our first stop was at Lelant to see its parish church. There
is a path of lilacs and myrtles to the door and in the graveyard a Cornish cross for tombstone. These crosses identify

Cornwall. Often these stones show mileage on a highway.

The old village of Lelant no longer exists. It was buried under sand and only its parish church shows its former site. We have remarked elsewhere on England's changing coast-line—its Channel ports either silted from the sea like Hastings or buried under the ocean, as is the case of ancient Winchelsea. And we shall find in Cornwall and all through this west of England a like destruction—an ocean frontage wavering up and down, now shifting a village inland and again piling salt water on it. Time's laughter is the roaring of the sea. St. Ives was once an island. We shall discover Lyonesse, once on mainland, and now below the ocean until the whirligig shall lift it. Porlock was formerly a port, but now it sits at the inner edge of marsh. We shall cross Sedge-moor, captured within recorded history from the Bristol Channel. When Sir Francis Drake offered to give Tavistock an ocean harbor, he was perhaps counting on the centuries to aid him.

That Lelant's parish church was saved, was due to the foresight of planting rushes on its seaward side as a bulwark against the rising sand; for it is only nature that fights successfully with nature. At Lelant there is a golf course, to which the smart patrons of the Tregenna Castle rattle in a bus for an afternoon of distress and niblicks.

We now motored across the slender waist of Cornwall to its southern shore, between flowering hedges and among trees in blossom. From a point above Marazion we had a first view of St. Michael's Mount. It is from these hills that its church seems to stand the highest, for its stature is dwarfed from the beach near by. It was a Sunday morning, and the bells of service came softly across the water. Far off, St. Michael's Mount is almost a rival of Mont-Saint-Michel, whose greater dimensions dominate Brittany's sandy coast. Both churches stand for religion that holds a sword.

The name of Marazion has been a puzzle to scholars. Isaac

Taylor suggests a theory, only to deny its truth, that Marazion means a hill by the sea and is made up of Phoenician
syllables. Yet he finds some confirmation of this in Cornwall's tin mines and Marazion's proximity for export in those
ancient days when Tyre was of bustling commerce. As a
better guess, he finds the town to be of Hebrew origin,
to be translated as Market Jew. The Britannica, however,
discovers in the name of Market Jew nothing Hebraic. It
says that the original charter of St. Michael's Mount was
granted to Robert, Count of Mortain, at the Conquest, and
that this charter provided that a market be held each Thursday on the mainland. Market Jew, therefore, means no more
than Thursday's Market—Jew being a contraction of *Jeudi.*
In the city of Penzance, just a few miles across the bay,
there is a chief business street that is called Market Jew.

But even if we must desert the company of scholars, we
choose to see in the shallow water by the Mount strange
craft which will presently buffet the storms of the Bay of
Biscay, pass Gibraltar and the last of the Greek islands towards the docks of Tyre. Nor was such a commerce improbable. For the Atlantic is known to have presented no in-
superable difficulty to Phoenician ships, and its merchants
would have preferred convenient Marazion to the ports of
the narrower channel. We shall, therefore, hoist colored
sails at Marazion.

It is easy to find guidebook stuff about St. Michael's
Mount. Arthur Norway gives pages to it. Volumes of "beauties" have its picture. All travelers have it in their diaries.
We are surprised, however, to find that Sir Humphry Davy,
the great chemist and the inventor of the miners' safety
lamp, should have tackled it in verse. "Majestic Michael
rises!" It is that kind of verse; but we have Coleridge's word
that if Sir Humphry "had not been the first chemist, he
would have been the first poet of his age." It is said that

Coleridge used to attend his lectures "to increase his stock of metaphors."

Coleridge had another rhyming friend, W. L. Bowles, who wrote verses about St. Michael's Mount. "Thou only, aged mountain, dost remain!" When Bowles's volume of sonnets was published, Coleridge, as a young man of seventeen, made forty transcriptions of the entire volume and gave them to his friends. Having ourselves an eye on royalty, we look on this as of doubtful help.

It is likely that wherever you find a pointed hill in western England, you will discover a place of ancient pilgrimage and worship—most remotely for Druid rites, and then for Christians when their time had come. The Isle of Avalon at Glastonbury was of Druid use. Druids frequented the Devon tors. They chose the mountains of Wales and the windy tops of Cornwall. Sometimes if no hill offered itself, they built by hand a pointed mound, as in the case of Silbury whose age is attested by a deflection of a Roman road. We are not surprised, therefore, to learn that St. Michael's Mount was another of these Celtic shrines. There is something in all religions that craves the sky; and Gothic spire and eastern minaret alike climb upwards towards the sun.

St. Michael's Mount was an object of Christian pilgrimage as early as the fifth century; but it was after the close of the sixth that it became of special sanctity. The cause was a holy visitation. St. Michael, being already dead by many hundred years, suddenly clambered from his coffin, crossed the English Channel and appeared in person at the Mount. He sat on a crag so that all the countryside could see him. There were already a few hermits living on these wooded slopes; and it was on the hint of the saint's appearance that a monastery was founded. We have no record of the first progress of this establishment, but five hundred years afterwards Edward the Confessor built here a priory of Benedictine monks. Benedictines dearly love a relic; but St. Michael left nothing behind for their case of souvenirs.

If one looks at St. Michael's Mount with an eye that expects to see another Mont-Saint-Michel, he will be disappointed. Its dimensions are those of a pigmy against a giant. The chapel at the top offers no just comparison to the mighty church and its tower across the Channel. Nor is there a picturesque town about the English island's base, with excellent hotels and Madame Poulard's delicious omelettes. There are no such mighty bastions, no terraces hanging above the sea, no shops for Benedictine and afternoon coffee. Mont-Saint-Michel is theatrical, and it might be the setting for a tremendous drama—the church militant, its hero. It is one of the wonders of the world, and Mount St. Michael suffers in comparison. Yet the English island has a beauty of its own and it is worth as many hours as a tourist will choose to give it.

When the tide was out, we crossed the sands for a nearer exploration. On a Sunday morning, however, tourists are allowed to go no farther than the rim of buildings at the island's beach.

I find in my notes that mimosas were in blossom and that blue flowers were growing in the garden hedge, that there are laborers' cottages and a laundry near the sands. I find also that Lord St. Leven is St. Michael's Mount's present owner, that he lives here in retirement, that his wife died recently, that the property will descend, not to his daughters but to a nephew. That is more than I know about my neighbors across the street. This gossip with a boatman cost me a shilling, but authors must not higgle at expense.

I discover again in my diary that a certain visit of King Edward VII is recorded by a footprint on the quay. "Lives of great men all remind us," but we recommend Hollywood's method of soft concrete. Mary Pickford's footprint is outside the Chinese Theatre. St. Peter's bare foot is on the

Appian Way. William's boot is on the quay at Brixham.

And now, having resisted the boatman who wished to take us around the island in his leaky craft, we recrossed the sands and clambered to our motor.

"To Penzance," I said, "for lunch. To whatever hostelry you recommend for tourists who are empty at the belt and overstuffed above the ears."

"A cold cut," our driver answered, "at the Queen's Hotel."

There was a quiet breathing across the sands as if the wind also were asleep.

- Mouse Hole -

XXXVI. LAND'S END

WE LUNCHED beside a window that overlooked Mount's Bay. Then we motored to Newlyn, which is half fish and half artist; and now and then perhaps the product is composite. I asked an old sailor in what quarter of the town the painters lived. Out came his pipe. A finger wagged indecisively across his shoulder. "Up there somewhere," he replied. "I ain't ever been to look."

"And do they paint here on the harbor front?" I asked.

"Do they! They're always mussin' 'round. You can't move without bumpin' on 'em."

Was Giotto so scorned when he covered the Tuscan walls?

The two colonies of Newlyn and St. Ives are rivals. Newlyn has the gentler coast and water that is sheltered from any western storm. Any artist, therefore, of fiercely ruffled hair will disdain Newlyn's quiet charm and choose the rougher headlands of St. Ives, where he will splash wilder colors on his larger canvas.

From Newlyn we kept along the coast to Mousehole. Here is a tavern above the harbor with a veranda over the muddy water inside the pier. As this place offered Mary the best viewpoint for a sketch, we bought ale to pay for our chairs. If Gilbert and Sullivan's "Pirates of Penzance" had ever really existed off the London stage, they would have chosen Mousehole for their base. But Mousehole has had its own pirates. Furthermore, it was sacked and burned in 1595—"the most serious landing of Spaniards," says our historian, "that ever occurred on the shores of England."

Old Carew, the historian of Cornwall, has much to say of this assault. "The three and twentieth of July, 1595," he writes, "soon after the sun was risen and had chased a fog which before kept the sea out of sight, four galleys of the enemy presented themselves upon the coast over against Mousehole and there in a fair bay landed about two hundred men, pikes and shot." It was in vain that the countryside was roused and messengers sent for reënforcement to Drake and Hawkins, "then at Plymouth with a fleet bound for the Indies." The Cornishmen were out-numbered by the Spaniards and badly beaten. But Carew is loyal to the brave traditions of his duchy. "Such sudden surprises," he writes, "work more indignity than damage, and more damage than disgrace." And for the complete acquittal of his cowardly countrymen, he intimated that this disaster was forced by ancient prophecy. For had it not been written in the stars, "how there should land upon the rock of Merlin, those that would burn Paul's Church, Penzance and Newlyn"?

On this warm Sunday afternoon, however, none of Mousehole's old excitements showed. Fishermen stood about in perpetual vacation. Dogs slept on the quay or chased the gulls from the sand. Boats were lying in the mud, and one

of them, a dingy trawler, was named *The Land of Lyonesse.*
Considering that this land went down in storm, it seemed
a bad name for a boat.

And now Mousehole's Sabbath calm was broken by a
blare of music, and the Salvation Army issued from its bar-
racks and stood in a circle on the quay. Nature breeds men
and women for every service, and she has a distinctive brand
of leanness for the Army. There seems always to be a tall
gaunt man especially designed for holding a bass drum
on his stomach. If a fat man should offer himself at the bar-
racks for this purpose, his girth would be measured to be
sure that an extra inch, when augmented by a drum, would
not throw him on his nose.

"Rock of Ages" was taken calmly by the sailors. A few of
them ambled up, but without taking their pipes from their
mouths. Others of them bailed out their boats or issued in
mere curiosity from the tavern, wiping their mouths. When
the hymn was finished, the big horn was shaken and drained.
There was a mumbling of prayer, then the brass went to
work again. Away the Army tramped, marching as to war.
The screeching gulls settled once more into the mud. The
dogs slept again on the quay. There was a wave of movement towards the tavern. Mousehole had come through the
revival without the loss of a single sinner.

The hubbub was over by the time that Mary's sketch was
finished. Remarking only that Mousehole was a pictur-
esquely dirty little town with a fine outlook on the ocean,
we climbed to our motor.

Up the hill was the village of Paul, where there is the
grave of the last woman to speak Cornwall's forgotten language.

THE TOMB OF
DOROTHY PENTREATH
WHO CONVERSED IN ANCIENT CORNISH
DIED 1777

It is hard to think what it would be like to be the last—to have had one crony after another slip away—to share with no one a native language and talk only with a dog or cat.

And now we are traveling to the southwest extremity of England.

Land's End, as an actual and tangible thing, interests me only in moderation. It is a barren point of rock, jutting towards the Scilly Islands, which can be seen dimly on days when the horizon is swept of mist. Lighthouses are scattered here and there upon the ocean, for a continuous procession of vessels moves along this coast. Far-off smoke to the south may come from the funnels of liners running towards New York. At night there must be a fine winking of these many lights. Land's End is a ragged headland where the ocean has torn and frayed the garment of the coast. Some of its rocky pinnacles are cut by abrasion to the likeness of human faces. One of these has been named Dr. Syntax and another Dr. Johnson, and both of them are excellent portraits. These general headlands, although they are of less majesty than those of Tintagel or Boscastle, are worth a visit. Land's End, I repeat, has moderate interest.

But its shortcoming is its fascination for trippers. These tourists of a day sit on all the rocks, they scramble up and down, they buy beer and colored postcards, they spread out their cold lunches under foot. They call loudly to Minnie and to Sarah. They stand on a dangerous point of rock and call to these girl friends of theirs to come and share a broken neck with them. On Dr. Johnson's unprotesting head there are a dozen of them crawling, like flies to be brushed away. They ask little Jackie to keep his fingers out of the jam and to mind the seat of his breeches as Mummie is tired of patching them.

There is a large hotel at Land's End; but it stands baldly in an open meadow, and its chief business is conducted in a monstrous room where lunch is served. Several unpainted shacks are its competition for those who are merely thirsty. The roads towards Land's End are blocked with motors on a holiday. And in the twilight when the picnic is over, huge chars-à-bancs rumble eastwards. Minnie and Sarah have now each a shoulder for a nap.

But if to the actual eye Land's End holds disappointment, there is something here that stirs the fancy. It is not that this is England's last extremity. Nor is it that Land's End's light has so often been a token of arrival on the last night of a journey from New York. Our fancy does not concern itself with the land or any of the lights, but rather with the stretch of ocean at our feet. For beneath those curling waves there lies the buried country of Lyonesse.

Lyonesse is fact, not fancy. For it is attested that there were once broad meadows beyond these cliffs; that these meadows had risen from the sea in geologic times, to sink again beneath the ocean before history commenced its record. All of this district, as far as the Scilly Islands, is another victim of England's changing coast-line.

Legend reports that somewhere hereabouts a road still clambers down the cliff and continues across the beach until its course is lost in water—a road still pointing with its broken finger to the castles of King Mark. Whether that road's short stub can still be found, we have no guess. The device of it was used a few years since by Don Marquis in a play, called "Out of the Sea." It concerned certain old echoes rising from the ocean to affect a modern plot. I am told that the play failed in New York City, but it prospers in my recollection.

Perhaps there was once another such road beneath the Dover headlands that went dry shod to France in the days before England became an island. And there was still another on the Calabrian littoral that crossed the Messina Straits and circled under Etna. Most of it is lost in the Mediterranean, but its course along the Sicilian coast is

left to mark forever the land-bridge between Africa and
Europe. One wonders about these things—whether the shores
of the world will again be changed in the slow upheaval of
the centuries, to show on the bared bottoms of the oceans
the wrecks of prehistoric cities. Perhaps Atlantis will some
day reappear, the grasses of Lyonesse be painted with daisies
in the spring. Noah's flood seems actual, for there have been
a hundred inundations since his ark rested from its cruise.

It is believed, here at Land's End, that sometimes on a
quiet night the shouts of drowning men are heard. And
there is the soft tolling of a church bell as its sunken clapper
is rocked by waves. King Mark perhaps had sat at service
in that church praying for the safety of Iseult in the peril
of the sea.

For these buried meadows whose lights now wink at coastwise shipping, are the land of Tristram. "The sunset bound
of Lyonesse—" Tennyson once wrote:

A land of old upheaven from the abyss
By fire, to sink into the abyss again;
Where fragments of forgotten peoples dwelt,
And the long mountains ended in a coast
Of ever-shifting sand, and far away
The phantom circle of a moaning sea.

Tristram and Iseult, Lynette and Gareth, Dame Lyonesse
and the Castle Perilous besieged by wicked knights—all these
are the persons of our misty drama.

One would like to go apart from the crowd of trippers
to read Malory's tales of Arthur and his Court—to follow
Tristram on his voyage to the King of Ireland where he
met Iseult, to peruse the story of King Mark's marriage
and the tragedy that followed. One speculates on the nature
of the country through which Gareth traveled with Lynette,
what villages they passed, what castles set about with moats.
All of these things are in one's meditation as he stands on

Land's End's crowded rocks. Then there is a slight disturbance across his shoulder and he discovers that a family lunch is being set up at his feet. The sunken bell of Lyonesse, if one could hear it now at noon, would ring for a cold joint, a cheese and a barren salad.

From Land's End we motored to St. Just, on the windswept coast. Here Mary tried to sketch the church in its tiny graveyard; but the attempt roused such an excitement at the windows and such generous offers of assistance that we fled.

For dinner we were back in Penzance at the Queen's, where we took a room for the night. This hotel boasts in its advertisements that it is the finest in all the United Kingdom, but we found its service slow. Only in price did it keep to the terms of its boast.

In the evening we walked on the quay and listened to an outdoor concert of excellent music. All of Penzance was afoot, and boys and girls were arm in arm. A duchess stood at her window in the hotel and looked at us through her lorgnette as we moiled around the band-stand. There was a soft twilight on the ocean, pale colors that faded with the day. Far up the coast stood St. Michael's Mount, its tower on tiptoe to find the sunken sun.

*Market Jew Street
— Penzance —*

XXXVII. BRIDGER'S BOOK-SHOP

AFTER breakfast on the following morning we took our bags to the railway station, left them with the porter, and set out to see Penzance afoot. The principal resort of business is called Market Jew Street, and it is therefore absorbed in sixpences to the entire neglect of a mere Irishman's "Pirates of Penzance." This is the way of most old towns. Even Rome is more interested in selling a tourist fish-skin pearls than in directing him to Trajan's monument. Market Jew Street was laying out its wares at this early hour for town and country patrons.

Mary had run short of pencils and drawing-paper, and

she went by herself to find them. But my eye had been caught by the window of a secondhand book-shop—Bridger's —which proved to be quite the best of its kind until we came to Bath.

Out in front Bridger's displays a table of merely current books, a rack of maps and colored postcards for quick sale; but better shelves run off obscurely into dusk, offering secondhand volumes to those who do not confine their reading to a sheep's path and bone up on fashionable novels to discuss them across a neighbor's soup. You must explore Bridger's—from the leather bindings under glass to the last barrel of broken litter in the attic and the basement. To do this in two hours would be as impossible as seeing Rome on a Cook's excursion.

It is not that Bridger's is of extreme disorder. We have visited many pleasant litters of this kind and speak with authority. We have ransacked Charing Cross Road and are familiar with all of its dark corridors of topsy-turvy learning. In Bath there was once a book-shop, now moved to more commodious quarters, that was built like a rabbit warren—that was not content with a single building but climbed over alleyways in all directions. When you thought you had explored its last room, here was another passage to further nooks where you cracked your head on the beams. And a ladder still invited you to a cave beneath the roof. The treads of every winding staircase were so piled with books that patrons could only go in single file; and if a student bent himself to discover a volume at the bottom, all traffic was suspended until he uncramped his stomach. Murk was made visible by far-spaced dingy lamps.

Where the corridors of this old Bath book-shop wandered into excavations beneath the sidewalk, one wondered whether this might be another labyrinth like that one of ancient Crete. At the end of the afternoon, if you were shopping quite so late, a fearful thought arose that perhaps the last salesman had gone to dinner and that you were locked in for the night. At a dusty window there was still a narrow slit of daylight, but this would presently sink to darkness and calfskin ghosts would creep out from their barrels. You listened for the comfort of footsteps in the rooms above. Unhappily that old Bath book-shop has moved to larger space entirely above the cellar, and it will require another hundred years before these newer rooms are smothered.

Bridger's young lady was at my elbow.

"Have you a shelf of secondhand books on Cornwall and Devon?" I asked.

She pointed to a stairway plastered on both sides with shelves of books.

"Up there," she answered, "a whole room of them."

"And have you a copy of Prince's 'Worthies of Devon'?"

"Perhaps," she replied. "I don't know. Mr. Bridger will be here any minute. Until he comes, you might look around."

It was Cornwall entirely, this room, but a ladder hinted that Devon might be above. My neck was lame and my back was stiff when Mr. Bridger came. I leaned an elbow on the ladder, mopped perspiration and repeated my question.

He looked at me over the top of his glasses, as bookmen do when they are called away from their studies.

"Have you Prince's 'Worthies'?" I asked.

"That's odd," he answered. "I have just bought a library of twelve thousand volumes—mostly a riffraff of old sermons —nobody wants sermons now—but in the lot is Prince, a fine tall volume in calfskin dated 1701."

He fetched the "Worthies" out and smoothed its pages with the fingers of an expert.

"The Reverend John Prince," he said, "was from Devon, the sometime Vicar of Berry Pomeroy, and usually my books are of Cornwall only. One county is enough to stock if one wishes to be thorough. There are very few volumes of the Duchy," he added, "which have not been at one time or another on my shelves."

"You have no history then, I suppose," I asked, "of the Seymour family."

He shook his head.

"No. Nor will you find them in Prince. The Seymours are not really a Devon family, although they have lived there on and off since Tudor days."

I bought the "Worthies," Carew's "Survey of Cornwall," a volume of 1723, at his particular recommendation, Gilpin's "Western Tour," 1798, certain volumes containing old engravings, and a number of other books of Cornish travel and description. It was an excellent haul, and at a low price that would shame any shop at home. We huddled the volumes together, and I gave directions for their carriage to America. There were four great packages on my desk when I arrived home. I recommend Bridger's to any tourist who loves a ladder and a shelf.

On our return to the railway station, we found our bags piled in the window corners of our carriage. A tiny whistle sounded and we were enroute for Tintagel.

The Old Post Office – Tintagel

XXXVIII. TO TINTAGEL

AMERICANS ridicule an English train for the smallness of its locomotive and a whistle that seems to announce fresh fish. But English trains start with an easier motion than ours, and they are not so bumped at the changes of a junction. At Buffalo, for instance, old gentlemen swallow their false teeth. The separate compartments of an English train are pleasanter than our long corridors of seats. There is less confusion in alighting and a shorter haul of luggage to the platform. The windows of an English railway carriage do not require a burglar's jimmy, and they permit a wider view than the cramped outlook from a Pullman. Our trains run in thicker dust and cinders. One either stifles in bad air or is smudged with dirt. Nor are our magnificent terminals as convenient as a modest London station where a line of motor-buses is waiting just across the platform. A traveler arriving at Waterloo will be at his hotel in shorter time than is required in New York to find the cab-stand. Machinery is an Englishman's servant. It is our master in America.

Our trains love back streets—the clutter of dirty yards about the kitchen, a view of unpainted alley fences. If any city has a dingy suburb our railways find it. In a measure this is true of England; but an English town or village as it appears from the railway track, is not as sordid as are most of ours. Of late years, in favored districts an attempt has been made to make our stations attractive; but we are far distant from the primness of an English station with its grass and flowers.

Robert Louis Stevenson had a good word for railways and their uses on a holiday; but he was not writing of the double-jimmied windows of our air-proof Pullmans. Our American sleeping-car was a masterpiece of travel in the days of Franklin stoves and kerosene lamps. But when its inventor died, its continuing ingenuity wilted with his lilies. They build it now of steel instead of wood, but that is only to make it stronger in order that engineers may bump and slap it around the yards. In some twilight of early morning, I shall walk a mile in my pajamas from vestibule to vestibule. I shall climb across the tender. My smoking revolver will tell of justice done.

And why, may we ask, are the compartments of our cross-the-continent trains supplied with an insufficient number of hooks? On a three days' trip one's compartment becomes such an unpleasant clutter. Shall a man's trousers be denied its peg just because his coat has one? Except for a kind of rat-catching device at the corner of the walls and a shelf too high for comfort—except for these and a towel rack— there is no place to stow away his luggage. The steamship has advanced from hardship to luxury, but our sleeping-cars are still built on the model of the Civil War. Mr. Pullman's ingenuity ran out evidently after he had made little brackets to hold a table and had shoved a nickel-plated cuspidor into each compartment.

Were we dictator of these things, we would not burn coal.

And in the resultant cleanness we would construct a parade on the top of each train—a breezy sitting-place where a traveler could enjoy the view. We would build up the sides of it with glass to break the wind. Here lunches could be served with fizzing drinks when America becomes normal. There is nothing preposterous in this. Our hotels use their roofs for dinner and entertainment. In any decent weather one's food is of better taste under the freedom of the sky. Arcturus winks aloft. The moon lends its silver to the night. Who would choose a motor for a journey when the Alleghenies or the Rockies would unroll in a flying panorama as a tourist sits at ease without the chance of blow-out?

It is just as well to have this spleen out of our system in order that we may smile again.

We left Penzance in a rift of sunlight through heavy clouds. All the valleys and hills of Cornwall were clad in the softest green of springtime. The recent rain still sparkled on the fields and flowering hedges, on the varnished ivy of old walls and on any leaf that fluttered in the wind.

Near Marazion we turned from the coast and had our last glimpse of St. Michael's Mount, guarding eternally this shore of Phoenician commerce. We ran through St. Erth, St. Austell and Lostwithiel—old friends now by reason of our frequent passage. At Bodmin Road we alighted, as our train was bound for London. At Wadebridge we changed again. It was a typical journey for any one who goes cross-country in England. London is every locomotive's mecca; and to proceed across the grain of travel is like climbing fences where no street is cut. At Wadebridge we had an excellent lunch of ham and eggs in a dingy restaurant after such preparation as was provided by yellow soap and a last week's towel.

Here is an old bridge of many shallow arches; and we walked to its middle for a view up and down the River Camel—a thirsty camel in a sandy channel. We shall meet this stream again at Camelford, where we alight for Tintagel. One hopes vainly that it is King Arthur's Camelot. We are still, however, in the land of Merlin and his magic.

Arthur Norway, our frequent cicerone, is, we infer, a native of Wadebridge; and as no man can so lovingly describe a town as one who was born therein, we must quote from his page. "It is as the tide is flowing," he writes, "that I like to think of the old town with its granite bridge of many arches. For, when the first signs of the coming flood sweep round the sandy bed from out the foldings of the hills, a cool salt wind runs up in advance, and almost before one has felt its freshness or tasted the briny odour on one's lips, the first wavelets are lipping already around the ancient buttresses."

Arthur Norway is merely preparing the reader for the introduction of a certain white rabbit of magic powers that once frequented the near-by church of Egloshayle. For there is a legend that any one who strikes this rabbit will meet with sudden death; and all this is attested by the chronicle of a stranger who jeered that this was false. To make good his boasts, he drained several brave cups in a tavern, then loaded his gun and started out at midnight. When the taproom lights were lost in the distance, he whistled to keep his courage hot. Then he sat waiting in the churchyard.

Several of his companions had lingered at their drink; but as time went on and he did not return, they set out at last to find him. "They ran up and down," writes Arthur Norway, "calling his name; there was no reply. He was not in the lane, nor on the high road, nor on the marsh, where under the bright moonlight the motion of a water hen could have been seen with ease. At last one of the searchers . . . found him lying dead, with one barrel of his gun discharged, and the contents buried in his body. That happened many years ago," Arthur Norway concludes, "but still the stranger may be seen leaning over the low wall, pointing an ancient flint-lock at some object which moves quickly in the long grass."

Legends of this sort infest all of these Cornish towns and are evidence of general superstition. When modern writers repeat them—even when their tongues are inside their cheeks —it is with a kind of relish that seems to hope they may be true.

As we were waiting for our north-bound train at Wade-bridge, several cars of cabbages were pushed by us to a siding. You may guess what emotions this stirred in us. We had now been in England about thirty days—sixty meals, excluding breakfasts, and at each of those meals we had been crammed with cabbage. The very plumbing of our digestions was green with cabbage. We dreamed of it in nightmare. And here before us, clearly in our power, was a whole trainload of this pernicious fruit—millions of cabbages to poison once again the British stomach. Should I run forward while the cars were still moving, throw the switch and send the cars crashing to destruction through the open rails in order that tourists might be spared thereafter their daily loaf? A monument would be erected to me somewhere. *Hic jacet homo Americano qui*—wrecked six cars of cabbages.

But my pious villainy delayed too long, with the result that we ate pressed cabbage for another month and until we climbed the gangplank of our Atlantic steamer. "A little cold-slaw?" said our steward of the *Majestic*. "Very tasty, very nice indeed!" "Baked potatoes," was my answer.

Our course towards Tintagel now followed a slope of tree-less hills that rose on the east to a lonely moor without a house or any road. To the west there was an occasional glimpse of the ocean. We passed the old Delabole quarry, where men have quarried slate since the days of Arthur. I leaned from our carriage window when we stopped, hoping to see the bottom of this tremendous hole. A pigmy car was drawn upon a chain and creeping up the farther side, but I could see no flooring of the vast abyss.

We alighted at Camelford station, which is a mile outside the village. We had hoped for a public bus to convey us eight miles to Tintagel, but there was none in sight. The station porter, however, knew a man in a cottage down the road who owned a motor, and off he ran to hire it for our use.

Our train moved on, leaving us in a silence that was broken only by the wind. About us were miles of treeless country, with fantastic tors breaking the horizon to the east. As far as we could see there was no house, only a steeple arising from a valley to show where Camelford was hiding from the wind—a steeple that seemed to stand in vain on tiptoe and look on abandoned country for the sinners its Sunday hymn might save.

Up rattled the motor and we jounced on winding roads through shallow valleys towards the sea. It was a country outcropped with slate. It was tea-time when we came to Tintagel and to the King Arthur's Castle Hotel, standing at the edge of mighty cliffs in a broil of wind and fog.

"A room with a view and a bath," I said.

A Cottage,
Tintagel.

XXXIX. TINTAGEL

SIR THOMAS MALORY'S "Morte d'Arthur" has several
references to Tintagel. In an early chapter of Book I we
are instructed that King Arthur was born here in the old
castle whose ruins are still extant. The story is not wholly
nice.

It seems that Uther Pendragon, King of the British Isles,
lusted for Igraine, the Duke of Tintagel's wife. Having no
success in his bad persuasion, presently he set down his army
before this castle at a time when the duke was away at
battle. But Tintagel's walls were thick and high and, like
their mistress, they did not yield to assault. Whereupon
Pendragon summoned Merlin to his aid—Merlin, a consulting engineer, as we might say, in all matters of love and
war. Merlin, thus solicited, cooked up a customary broth
of magic by which Pendragon was converted to the likeness
of Igraine's husband. It was in this masquerading costume
that Pendragon was admitted to the castle and to the bed-

room of Igraine. We may have our own suspicions of her morals, but Malory stands firm that she was innocent and that she thought the man to be her husband returned suddenly from war. Nothing is more common in old tales than ladies who mistake their husbands in the dark; and we are not one to cast a stone.

Now it happened on this same night that the Duke of Tintagel was killed in battle. The news of this calamity arriving after breakfast must have somewhat confused Igraine. We must suppose that Pendragon had departed before daybreak; for presently a messenger came from the camp below the cliff offering marriage to the lady now that she was a widow. And in all haste, so the legend says, "they were married in the morning with great mirth and joy." Hollywood papers will please copy.

Tintagel is reputed also to have been a stronghold of King Mark of Cornwall, and it enters therefore the tragic story of Tristram and Iseult. In his narration of these lovers, Malory throws us in great perplexity, for his separate chapters are scattered through a thousand pages. In Swinburne we find the story told with less confusion.

> About the middle music of the spring
> Came from the castled shore of Ireland's king
> A fair ship stoutly sailing, eastward bound
> And south by Wales and all its wonders round
> To the loud rocks and ringing reaches home
> That take the wild wrath of the Cornish foam,
> Pass Lyonesse, unswallowed of the tides
> And high Carlion that now the steep sea hides
> To the wind-hollowed heights and gusty bays
> Of sheer Tintagel, fair with famous days.

Tristram, the nephew of King Mark of Cornwall, had been sent to Ireland, as everybody knows, to fetch home to his uncle, Iseult, the daughter of the Irish king, to be his wife. But then, as now, it was a risky business to send a daughter to a foreign husband, and it needed thought. Luckily, Iseult's mother was skilled both in magic and in domestic relations. She prepared, therefore, as a wedding gift to King Mark, a golden bottle of wine "to charm their marriage unison." All might have gone well if a storm had not arisen on the journey and Tristram had not seized an oar to help the sailors. For now, as the wind died down, Tristram was tired and thirsty. Iseult, therefore, got out the bottle and pulled its golden hasp. Tristram drank like any seaman, and even Iseult herself took a sip. Whereupon

> Their heads neared, and their hands were drawn in one,
> And they saw dark, though still the unsunken sun
> Far through fine rain shot fire into the south;
> And their four lips became one burning mouth.

The ruins of Tintagel as we saw them from our hotel window, although they suggested Igraine and Pendragon, did not seem to fit Tristram and Iseult. Perhaps we think of tragic romance as a product of the south, of warm days and moonlight, of soft Italian music and of stars that ride in a heaven free of clouds. But Tintagel's ruin sits on a stormy cliff of wind and fog. It suits a rougher plot of siege and battle. Its light is a beacon to a harsher death than that of Tristram and Iseult.

It was from Tintagel that King Arthur issued to fight that last battle of his in which he was mortally wounded. It was from Tintagel also that Morgain carried him dying to the Isle of Avalon, the place of departed spirits—bearing him through the air as by a valkyrie's magic.

Did King Arthur really exist? Was there such a man, or is his whole life merely a nursery tale? The Britannica, that dear old soul, has an answer ready for us. "The truth," it says, "thus appears to be that, while there was never a *King* Arthur, there was a noted chieftain and general of that name. If we say that he carried on a successful war against the Saxons, was probably betrayed by his wife and a near kinsman, and fell in battle, we have stated all which can be claimed as an historical nucleus for his legend." These legends, the Britannica continues, arose in the twelfth century, because English national pride demanded something as glorious as the Charlemagne cycle of traditions. The twelfth century was a crusading age and it, therefore, "represented the personages and events of the sixth in the garb and under the conditions" of its own time. Arthur, so to speak, like some Hamlets today, was in modern dress; and a crusading age, busy with the foundations of the great cathedrals, invested England's ancient crudity with a piety and an architectural grandeur that were its own. The Hamlet of Shakespeare's bankside was in modern dress—the Tudor. Palestine of apostolic days, when the Renaissance painted it on the walls of Florence and of Venice, was in modern dress —Italian. No great creative age higgles at the mere breaking of fact if it can gain thereby a broad effect. And so powerfully does it lay its genius on the shadowy forms of half-forgotten periods and men that it re-creates them new. King Arthur, therefore, comes to us today clad in the pious garments of men who traveled to the Holy Land, who built Cluny and the Cistercian houses, who compiled the mighty Papal doctrines. And for this reason we shall not marvel that a petty chieftain of a petty island is dressed in silk and bows his head in prayer. And perhaps this is fitting for such a shadowy figure. The age of piety (the twelfth and thirteenth centuries) seems to us today as more remote than the hard cynicism of ancient Rome. Ruined Tintagel seems of greater antiquity than the Roman walls of York; while the Coliseum, so like a modern stadium for football, is almost our contemporary.

Passing from legend and speculation, we learn that the first castle of record on these rocks was probably erected in pre-Saxon days. No vestiges of this building now remain. Under the Norman earls of Cornwall, Tintagel was rebuilt, but it stood in ruins in the middle of the sixteenth century when Leland paid a visit here. Outside of this meager record, "Tintagel," as Carew observes, "hath kept long silence in our stories." Nor should history's neglect entirely grieve us, for the castle's better chronicle rests with Tristram and Iseult, with King Arthur and with all the battles that are still fought upon a nursery floor.

The hotel at Tintagel, although comfortable, is an absurdity. It has a pretentious likeness to a castle with towers and battlements. And it is too big and too bleakly placed. It stands on a headland across a deep and narrow valley from Arthur's ruins—a headland that would be better to the eye had it been left empty. It is only when one's back is towards the hotel that the coast of Cornwall is unspoiled. And there must have been a time, perhaps forty years ago, when the ruin on its cliff sent a thrill dancing down the spine. The town of Trevenna, nearly a mile inland from the rocks, had the good taste not to intrude its modern life on a spot where Iseult had lived.

Yet the hotel has some material advantage—food that is better than the average, a great lounge with windows to the sea, balconies and baths, tepid radiators and open fires. Thomas Burke, in his book on the English inn, commends it. "You enter the hall of a castle," he writes, "and I think if any knight of the Round Table were to enter it he would recognize it as the hall of a castle of his age. A little tidier perhaps, but otherwise what he was accustomed to see." I doubt it. No one better than an old shepherd blind in one eye could make such a great mistake. He might say it looked like a hotel on the Strand or the smoking-room of a good-sized steamship, but nothing nearer.

But Sir Henry Irving liked it and he was once a patron here. When his holidays were finished and he was departing for his season at the Lyceum Theatre, he is said to have remarked that when the time came for his retirement from the stage, he would engage rooms at Tintagel to linger out his remaining days. Sir Henry had once acted King Arthur in London. We wonder if on this Cornish coast he cried out that his varlets should pour oil from these modern concrete crenelations.

On our present visit the hotel was not at its best. It was too early in the season for a rush of patrons and, of a consequence, the house was in an upheaval of spring cleaning with carpets up. Arthurian breezes leaked in through the French windows of the lounge. Three or four tourists cannot bring back successfully the jolly hospitality of the feudal ages, and we had our choice of fifty empty chairs.

There was a fireplace in our bedroom; but the coal, instead of burning, massed itself into a crust of clinkers. Our balcony would have been pleasant on any sunny day, but now a cold wind spattered rain upon it and shook our windows. I suppose that Iseult's window-casements were not really tight and that they also rattled in a storm. Malory does not mention these slight inconveniences of mediaeval living that the English still inherit.

> Magic casements, opening on the foam
> Of perilous sea in faëry lands forlorn.

It sounds quite nice, but one must reach for aspirin.

After tea and clotted cream, after shivering a half hour before our clinkers, we went outdoors to get warm and to see before dinner the ruins of King Arthur's Castle. We slithered down a steep hill to the valley and stood before a stone cottage near the sea and beneath the further cliff. An old woman stood at the door.

"Get your key to the castle," she said. "It's only a sixpence. Postcards, photos and souvenirs, tea or *rawsbry*, if you want it. 'Cue."

A key, of course, is quite absurd. There is nothing to steal inside the enclosure of the broken walls, but this rental of keys is the old woman's livelihood. She has at least a dozen of them, and each tourist is required to promise that he will lock the door behind him and so prevent a fellow-traveler

King Arthur's Castle

from getting inside without the payment of the fee. Nor is there any castle—nothing more than an outline of shattered walls without a roof, one of whose walls blocks the path on the precipitous side of the headland and offers a door for entrance.

It is a dizzy path to the top of the cliff and when the stones are slippery with rain, not wholly without danger. As a tourist nears the top, he wishes that nature had contrived him to advance gracefully on all fours.

And now we were safe on level ground within a hollow square of ruined walls composed of unsurfaced rubble. A further path climbs across a meadow to the summit of the headland. And here are foundations of cruciform shape that must once have held a chapel. It is the situation and the outlook that are majestic, for the ruins are no more imposing than those of demolished farm buildings. There are also foundations on an adjacent headland—a spur of rock that once joined itself to the headland where we stand before it was severed by earthquake or slow abrasion. There is a legend that the two halves of the castle were once connected by a high-flung bridge, but now they are severed by an open cut of terrific depth.

Below Tintagel's rock there is a small inlet but half protected from the ocean. Here landed Iseult. Here also, says one legend, the infant Arthur was found on the stony beach. We could see the foaming water from the cliff.

There is a feeling of terror on Tintagel. Since these ancient buildings were destroyed, it seems certain that no one has passed the night here in the exposure of the wind. And although the surface of the rock is of several acres, it seems a dizzy place. Perhaps one is thinking of the narrow path that he must clamber down. As a child I once scrambled to the ridgepole of a neighbor's barn. It was a safe straddle against the chimney, but the slope of the shingles and the end of the ladder rising above the gutter were quite enough to give me shivers. One recalls such an experience on Tintagel.

And now the wind was rising in a squall of rain. We pushed open the castle's door and the gale rushed past us. I muttered something, and Mary asked me what. Then we hugged the wall. There was wet scum on the stones as we descended.

Once safe in the valley, Mary asked me again what I had said.

"I was singing," I answered, " 'Nearer, My God, to Thee.' "

Red Riding-hood's grandmother came out to get her key. Her wicked wrinkles, however, were wholly on the surface. For when we had spent a shilling for postcards and had praised her ginger-beer, she ceased to look like the villain of a nursery story. We are confused. It was the wolf that was the villain, and she certainly did not look like an ugly wolf when we asked for second bottles.

She did not know how many generations of her family had been the key-holders of Arthur's ruins. She remembered as a tiny girl—"and there wasn't any motors then"—that her mother had the key, and she supposed that her grandmother had it before that. She pointed to her prize possession—a framed photograph of Queen Victoria and all of her royal family. In the picture Prince Edward was still a young man, and a bouncing little fellow with a hoop must have been our own King George. In the midst of widespread skirts and all this brood, sat the queen, looking as if she were just about to crow again, and that another little chicken would join the group.

"The old queen, that's her," said the keeper of the keys. "She came here in 1854."

"And did you give her the key?" I asked.

"Me? You're jokin', mister. I ain't that old. It's rheumatiz that's got me bent." Whereupon she fell to computing her years in the terms of a Michaelmas to come. "Did you say *rawsbry*," she added, "or ginger-beer?"

"*Rawsbry.*"

She drew the cork and continued:

"Only last week an old lady came to the Castle that was eighty-three."

"I'm sure you had to boost her on the path."

"Not a bit of it. She was as spry as me."

"Aren't you afraid to live here alone?" Mary asked.

"Who's goin' to bite me?" she replied.

Who, indeed?

We sipped our beer and let her ramble on.

"After all my years here," she continued, "it would seem stuffy sleepin' in the village. I don't leave this valley not more'n once a week, when I need green groceries and things like that. And I never go into town until I've locked the Castle for the night."

"You don't mean to tell us," Mary answered, "that you climb that path every evening to make certain the door is locked."

"You're foolin', missis. Course, I don't. I just don't give out more keys after seven o'clock. When I've counted my keys and know that all of them is safe back to me, then I know that the Castle can take care of herself till mornin'."

We climbed up the side of the valley to see the mainland half of Tintagel's ruin. An old man was dumping the contents of a rubbish cart from the edge of the precipice. His pick and shovel were lying on the grass beside a half-buried wall.

"What are you digging?" we asked.

He stopped and wiped his sweat, then leaned on his shovel like Hamlet's first grave-digger. The question was a poser. He had been hired to dig and not to think. He paused. "For treasure, I suppose," he finally answered.

"And do you find it?" I persisted.

"Not as yet I don't. But I'm always lookin'."

We put our question to the foreman of the work. He had orders, he said, to dig to the footings of the walls and to the stone flags of the floor. Already he had laid bare the stumpy walls of several rooms. When the work had progressed further there was to be an expert down from London to determine the age and uses of the buildings.

The foreman remembered a time when what was now but a stub of wall had stood in its entire length at the edge of the rock. And then one night there had been a crash, and cliff and wall had fallen to the ocean four hundred feet below.

We walked up the valley towards the town. Another old man stood waiting on the path.

"Perhaps you'll buy a postcard," he said.

"We've hundreds of them."

"But this is most particular. It's about me. I'm Charles Hambly."

"Pleased to meet you."

He held out a card on which was a picture of a ship dashing against rocks.

It seems that many years before when the man was young a vessel had been wrecked near here. It pounded in the surf while all of Tintagel was gathered on the height above. The only way to save the two survivors of the crew was by letting down a rope-ladder to them. It was Charles Hambly who carried them up the face of the cliffs to safety. It was a miracle of bravery and endurance, for one of the men was helpless with a fractured leg. A medal was struck in Hambly's honor. And now, past work of any kind, he sells the postcards that show his heroic act.

The village of Tintagel, or Trevenna as it is named on the map, consists of but a single street that dwindles at each end into treeless country. The chief sight for tourists is a building, now vacant but once the post-office, that is famous for its antiquity, its beauty and its sagging ridgepole. On a former visit here I was inside this house. We offer to playwrights, as a scene for a plot of smuggling, the large hall with its great fireplace, its splayed windows and a balcony across the end. Luggers were once anchored in Tintagel's little harbor, and tubs of illicit rum were rolled up the steep path to the village and to this house.

At Tintagel are the headquarters of a society that calls itself "The Fellowship of the Knights of the Round Table of

King Arthur." It is housed in a substantial building and there are meetings here. "Arthur," its pamphlet starts, "is a world-wide asset, and it is fitting that at Tintagel, the place where he was born, something should be in existence which will be a centre to which the thoughts of people can turn and from which the necessary inspiration can be disseminated to enable the ideals associated with his name to be a living force for all time."

After two nights at Tintagel we went by motor to Boscastle, only a few miles up the coast, and took a room at the Wellington Hotel.

-Boscastle-

XL. BOSCASTLE

BOSCASTLE is not a village of the moor, for it hides in a wooded valley. It has no broad prospect from the devil to the sunrise such as you find on the roof of Cornwall. Nor is it a village of the sea, for it only scatters down a highroad and has spent itself before it comes upon the ocean. Its valley is of some capacity above, but it narrows to a gorge that is barely wide enough for the egress of its runnel. There is, it is true, a rounded basin inside the high cliffs; but it is the product of storms' abrasion and too cramped for any vessel under sail. In a western wind, the Atlantic's great waves carom from the entrance rocks and sweep across it with tremendous uproar. No chain would be needed here to keep foreign pirates out. Just above low water in this basin there is a stone jetty, behind which a trawler might lie safely imprisoned in the mud. But how it got in, except in calm weather, or out again through the boiling water at the entrance, is a query with a doubtful answer. It is like a ship in a seaman's bottle.

Less than half a mile from the ocean, a stone bridge carries the highway across the stream and on its northerly course to the Bristol Channel; and here by this bridge stands the Wellington Hotel. Boscastle is sprinkled on the hillside to the south—a row of modest cottages with lawns and gardens descending to the stream. It is the kind of village in which one keeps looking for the center, to find presently that the last house is behind him.

The Wellington's nearest neighbor, across the lawn, is an abandoned mill with great water-wheels that are out of use and green with moss. The stream that we have mentioned flows noisily beside the grass, bearing to the ocean the gossip of moors and upland. There are outcropped rocks above the valley, but in this snug hollow there are several shops and houses.

We found our hotel to be excellent. I would mention especially a small parlor with a low ceiling, an open fire and easy chairs, a case of books, a table of current London papers—altogether such a room as comforts a rainy evening. There was almost a year of old *Punches*—the one periodical of my acquaintance that age cannot wither. Nor was it unpleasant at such a land's end as Boscastle to review last winter's London fashions in the pages of some *Queen's Own Magazine*. One gets to know the little Princess Elizabeth so intimately in these pages. She is England's pet, and communists would think twice before disturbing her succession to the throne. There is also something rather jolly in the absurdity of her Majesty's old hats. We have ourselves never read the Magna Carta, but we have no doubt but that it stipulates that the royal family must sit before a public camera once a week, and that the ladies shall wear always their purple turbans.

We would mention also a number of excellent prints in the hallways, together with framed mottoes of all sorts. I copied down one of these in my notebook. Its publication may lose me here and there a Methodist reader.

> Cold water is the best of drinks,
>   So all the poets sing;
> But who am I that I
>   Should have the best of anything?
> Let princes revel at the pump,
>   Peers at the pond make free;
> But whiskey, beer or even wine
>   Is good enough for me.

After reading that I pulled a bell-rope that tinkles in the bar.

Thomas Hardy laid at Boscastle the plot of his "Pair of Blue Eyes," and it was here also that Hardy, still a young architect and without a novel to his credit, met his first wife when she was living in the vicarage of St. Juliot near by. He had been sent to make drawings of the parish church as a preliminary to its restoration—the same errand that he used afterwards when writing his story. Hardy and his hero had, both of them, pockets that bulged with unpublished verses. These two narratives, one real and the other ficti-tious, had whetted our curiosity to see the great headlands they described. For had not Elfride Swancourt in the story saved her lover's life by tying her undergarments into a knotted rope which she lowered to him from the top of the cliff? Jaeger they were, my dears, three-quarter length.

Description never really snapped a likeness. No matter how faithfully it tries to depict each tree and outline, a tourist can never entirely recognize the scene whose description he has read. The pages, even of the most careful novelists, are never able to present a particular quality that shows a certain spot to be different from others that are similar; and adjectives are always a useless lumber. Writers know this limitation of theirs and they therefore offer a landscape, not as nature made it, but as seen darkly through the window of a mood. Hardy's Egdon Heath, as an example, is not merely a Dorset moor. Like the moon, it is a mirror of strange lights—a mirror even of eclipse and shadow when a dark slide is placed across the lantern. Most good descriptions are subjective—the effect of majesty, of storm, of distance or of sunlight on the one who writes. A cliff is terrific, dizzy and awful when it inspires terror and dizziness and awe; and when we say that morning paints the meadows with delight, it is our own delight we chronicle.

In Hardy, therefore, we must not look for a series of actual photographs of Boscastle. A camera is a most excellent machine, but it is not a substitute for genius.

After tea we climbed to the top of the rocks.

The coast of Boscastle is as rugged as any of Cornwall. As far as the eye can see there is foam along the bases of these cliffs. Waves come running from the storm to seek a cranny for protection. They explode upon the reefs and in any crevice that they find. One might think that the ocean, mindful how once it had cracked off Lyonesse, was now at work on another victim. Nor is this fanciful. A great scar shows in the exposed rock above the pool at the stream's mouth—an unscabbed sore running upwards to the meadows several hundred feet above. Nor is this the only witness of destruction. Waves from the outer ocean have forced a passage below water and under the great headland. At mid-tide, the inner opening of this passage is exposed and water explodes from it on the pool with the noise of cannon. At high tide, there is a strange confusion in the pool, but no report. Time's drama of land and ocean is, therefore, in process on this stage. The headland where we stand some day will be an island. It will be another rock, divorced from the mainland, like that of Tintagel.

To the south and west we could discern in the mist of afternoon the outline of King Arthur's Castle Hotel, its modern pretense now softened to a fairy tower. Nearer was the station of the coast-guard. To the north and east the rocks were scalloped towards the Hartland Light, where the shore turns into the Bristol Channel.

> From Padstow Point to Hartland Light
> Is a watery grave by day or night.

Far beyond a line of spray that was breaking on the reefs, were solitary vessels in penciling of smoke. Lonely birds were wheeling in the air—choughs, we must suppose. Legend affirms that the soul of King Arthur reposes in one of these birds; and as no sailor knows which one, he will permit none of them to be molested. There is something in this story that suggests the unknown soldier's tomb. It was a scene of impressive loneliness, as if this were the world's last point of land—as if civilization had turned back from fog and wind to easier living in the valleys.

Landwards from the cliffs were cottages in Boscastle's hollow, with barren hills as a high horizon to the east.

But if one thinks he is quite by himself upon the headland, he will be deceived. Let him look sharply at the rocks around him and he will see many persons walking here and there, their colors and outlines almost lost against the parti-colored stone. He will observe them sitting with books or gazing at the sea, strolling on paths so steep they seem in danger. Now and then, behind a bowlder there will be a bit of love. Yet with all these half-concealed companions, one's spirits seem alone.

These terrific rocks are marked by fire—the same black

vein one sees on the coast of Capri, where hell is still close
beneath the surface. It was in an upheaval of burning stone
that Cornwall first appeared above the sea, and now its worn-
out craters are buried under stormy water. The rock's strata
are warped and broken where the headlands snapped and

Forrabury Church
Boscastle

writhed in fire. No other coast hears such angry music of a
storm or is wrapped in fog of such a ghostly texture. Nowhere else is one so remote from the common thought that
prospers in a village or in a safe valley that does not hear
the sea.

One of Boscastle's cottages near its pool is evidently used
only in the summer season and by a man of thrifty humor.
He has cut a rowboat in two. The stern of it is a seat in his
hillside garden; while the boat's prow, set up on end, is a

shelter on his lawn. There is a touch in this too practical and shrewd. Like an old horse out of harness at last, the boat also deserves a pasture and a quiet age.

We climbed above the great scar of the headland where the ocean's fist had landed—where the cliff still staggers and listens for the count of ten. We followed a path to the coast-guard's station. Here was the same line of cliffs extending both north and south, but seen from a higher level than before. It was nature's pageant from a loftier gallery. We were informed later that during the Great War with Germany this station warned English ships of submarine attack. In peaceful times the coast-guard's work is light, and on our visit the station was deserted.

We returned to our hotel across the open heathland. Our map showed the village of Forrabury to be near. At first we could see nothing ahead but a meadow of endless horizon, and then at last a church tower popped in sight. Still below the church there was a village seated in a hollow, with clouds above to tell the direction of the wind.

Forrabury's church has no peal of bells. And there is a legend to account for this omission. It seems that once upon a time the parish ordered bells to be cast in London and to be despatched to them by sea. It was a season when bad weather was expected, but the ship traveled in a lucky breeze and came at last to Cornwall and to a point within view of its destination. The pilot, thankful to escape from storm, offered a prayer. The skipper, however, informed him with an oath that his was the skill instead of God's.

> Thank God, thou whining knave! on land,
> But thank, at sea, the steersman's hand.

At this, all of a sudden and out of nowhere, a tempest appeared and lashed the vessel to the rocks. All but the good pilot were drowned. On a still night the Forrabury bells are still heard tolling beneath the water.

We spent the evening with old *Punches*. I fell at last into
a talk with a graduate of Cambridge, here on a few days'
relaxation. He described to me a life-drill he had once seen—
a rope thrown from the cliffs to the rescue of an imaginary
steamer pounding at the base. Down the rope a harness is
slid, and with luck the crew are drawn, one by one, to safety.
It seemed a perilous thing, especially when the man was
five hundred feet above the water and was being scraped
against the rocks by the uncertain movements of the vessel.
There are white reefs all along this coast, and their boiling
water laughs at mischief. Neptune, when he lived among
the sunny Aegean Islands, was doubtless a god of pleasant
temper; but since he moved his lodgings to the foggy north
Atlantic, his disposition has been sullen.

My Cambridge acquaintance travels with a hammer and
taps at rocks. He confirmed my guess that all this coast
shows volcanic origin.

No other village of our trip—no range of cliffs, no hotel
perhaps—stands more pleasantly in our recollection than
this. And yet we do not recommend the Wellington to tourists. One must be content under a low ceiling and beside a
narrow fire; amused by an ancient bathtub of Phoenician
tin that sits always in the draught of a leaky window. One
must enjoy not only a row of Holbein prints along the hallway, but have an equal zest for a wiggling stair-rail and a
pitcher of water for washing. One must find enjoyment in
all these things before he will get a full relish from the
Wellington Hotel.

Above the harbor
- Clovelly -

XLI. CLOVELLY

THE LAD who drove us north to Clovelly knew America
from Zane Grey. Usually, English boys know us from *talkies*.
I met once on a Surrey road a ragged little fellow carrying
a basket of blueberries. The dome of the Crystal Palace
showed just above the hills, but it was only on the rarest
holidays that he had seen London's streets. But he knew all
about Chicago gangsters and the New York sky-line. America
was to him the home of delightfully outrageous crime and
wealth and of Max Sennett's bathing beauties. Any man
just as soon as he had made his dough—I quote his very
words—lived in a marble house with a marble staircase with
marble figures on a marble landing. He drove a fast motor—

usually off a precipice, but with little damage to himself. Elizabethan sailors used to sit in English taverns and talk about America. It is the same tale modernized that the *talkie* brings to England now. And if we object to its inaccuracy, we must remember that Francis Drake did not stick entirely to facts in his accounts of red men and scalps, of fonts of youth and easy treasure.

The lad who drove our motor north, instructed less fiercely by Zane Grey, informed us that Devon resembled Oregon. Both were mountainous, both had an ocean, both were of tremendous size. It was his ambition to live in America's great northwest. Every cowboy there carried a six-shooter and killed an elephant for breakfast. Ohio was no more than a doormat to adventure.

After a few steep hills, our road found easier going at some distance from the sea. We were, therefore, close to Bude before we ran again within sight of water. Bude is modern in appearance—monotonous rows of huddled houses where, doubtless at low rental, city folk can afford a cheap summer near the sea. And now, in about an hour, our road has abutted into Devon's north-coast highway. To the left, at a distance of six miles, is Hartland Light at the extremity of the Bristol Channel—to the east and north, Clovelly. We have a glimpse of the estate of the Hamlyn family, the owner of the village; and presently we have entered a vast parking space where there is a long shed for the storage of motors. This is our terminal, for Clovelly stands beneath this upper table on a road that is too steep for wheel traffic. We went down afoot, and our bags were put on sleds to be jolted on the flight of cobbles.

There was a time many years ago when it was permitted a traveler to discover Clovelly and to boast of its charm and unique location to persons who had never heard of this village. Tourists were obliged then to catch an inconveniently early steamer out of Bristol, or to be dragged by sweat-

ing horses across the hills from Ilfracombe. After a rough
sea passage, cramped across the rail, or a rougher journey
on heavy roads, Clovelly was a great discovery and it justified
the most extreme eloquence.

Motors have changed all this, and Clovelly is now in the
common rut of travel. Itineraries of Mr. Cook or of the
American Express will have, with few exceptions, Clovelly
on their schedules—arrival before noon, an hour for sights
along the stairway and at the harbor, another hour for cold
beef and clotted cream, then a motor-coach to Tintagel for
the night. The parking space holds several hundred cars,
and it is an index to the crowds that journey here in the season. During this summer haul of land-fish, every house is
a restaurant and a tea-room. Every shop that was once a
private parlor offers maps and guidebooks, brass door-
knockers, colored postcards and gay crockery as gifts to "dear
ones" left at home. And in anticipation of this custom, for
a whole month in advance every window of the village has
its sign of rooms to let.

Clovelly during August is as thick with people as are the
platforms of a New York subway after the evening whistle
has been blown. This throng will last from the arrival of
the chars-à-bancs at ten o'clock in the morning until they
pull out for Ilfracombe and Bristol at the end of the afternoon. As a part of the crowd goes by steamship, there are,
therefore, two receding tides at five o'clock—one puffing
towards the parking space above, the other oozing to the
harbor. It is only when these human floods have drained
away that Clovelly has room to be itself. For a few hours
now it can count its profits and reënforce from storage the
wares behind its windows.

There are, therefore, two Clovellys to be described—
Clovelly at its circus hour and again when the crowd is ab-
sent. I have myself visited the first of these Clovellys in
August from a crowded Bristol steamer and have fought my

way to a counter for a sandwich. I have had elbows in my sides all day. And now on this present cold and rainy afternoon of May, I shall describe a Clovelly that is as yet bare of its August trippers, that squints at the sky and hopes for sunny weather to bring its summer profit. Even in the downpour, when there is a runnel in the street and woollies are a necessity, it is this deserted Clovelly that I prefer.

But Clovelly, even now, does not wear well. Its first appearance is its best. To a stranger, as he climbs down the path from his motor, Clovelly offers all its charm. It seems then to be a village in which he would wish to spend his entire summer; and already his fancy is selecting a pretty cottage and offering generous terms. For the houses are all so lovely and at each chimney there is the tiniest veil of smoke—not thick enough to soil the village, but enough to suggest dinner and a comfortable chair before a fire. Nor is there anywhere in England a street so steep and so quick to arouse a traveler's wonder.

Perhaps Clovelly's beauty is too obvious. Fowey's attractiveness is not, for one must seek it through a dozen elusive lanes. Polperro too smells on the surface unpleasantly of fish; and its charm, therefore, when found, is the better relished. Clovelly, on the contrary, like a lady in party silk, is overconscious of its beauty, and it sits with too broad a smile awaiting commendation.

Or it may be that Clovelly, even when her trippers have departed for the night, retains too distinctly their remembrance. Some flavor of their presence would remain even if the village took down its signs of clotted cream, dragged in its racks of postcards, its weighing machines and the tables of brass knockers. One would still be aware of empty chairs and tables, and even crumbs. He might find tea-cloths drying on a line. Or at the door of a pretty cottage where perhaps an old cat sleeps, he would still hear the rattling of forks and spoons in a wash-pan—a warning voice crying to the kitchen that tomorrow is Saturday and that a larger beef be cut. Trippers, no doubt, have left their echoes in the village; and they also cast their shadow on tomorrow.

I suspect there are no real fisherfolk left in Clovelly, and that the old fellows who lounge upon the pier and offer boats for hire are artificially salted for tourists' satisfaction. I suspect that they are the parasitic husbands of better employed housewives who are using the comparative vacancy of evening to skim off clotted cream for tomorrow's rush. In brief, I have no doubt but that Clovelly's smell of fish issues out of cans. One old house, it is true, was pointed out to us as the dwelling of a retired sea-captain; but that house seemed to be the only one in all the village that had not been converted each August into a tea-room.

There is usually a disappointment in famous places. They are so seldom what you expect. Neighboring buildings intrude upon them and they are infested with modern life. Or they are spoiled by crowds. A poet's house, as an instance, should sound with the droning of bees and be lapped in solitude; but there will be a great bus at the door and a chatter of voices in his study. A ruin should really be a ruin and not a postcard shop. Nor should a guide lift an instructive finger in a famous church. Clovelly's pests are its crowds and its counters of clotted cream.

Although of vast antiquity, it has no such glittering history as Fowey or Brixham. Clovelly's ships never ventured to the Northwest Passage or landed colonies in Massachusetts. Old Hakluyt turns up his nose at Clovelly, for it sent none of its trawlers to the siege of Calais or with Drake against the Spanish. For Clovelly's harbor is but a tiny break in the cliff and it is protected from storm merely by a curving jetty. Here, therefore, piracy must have been of a dirtier definition—a piracy that was content to prey on English ships outward bound from Bristol—pirates who fought with other pirates from Lundy's Isle near by, but who did not dare to lift a sail against a Spanish galleon.

Fowey, Polperro and Brixham were the residence of sailors whose practice was still on the open sea. Clovelly, as I choose to think, was a place to which old pirates retired when they had made their pile and were growing stiff with age. These bearded rascals now enjoyed an easy life on shore—a cottage on the cliff, a view of the Bristol Channel to remind them of their past, a tavern for hot grog on winter nights. Half the legs of Clovelly were made of timber, hooks served for hands, and there were bandages across missing eyes.

I read a play once whose scene was laid in Clovelly and whose plot dealt with just such pirates. Patch-Eye, the duke and the captain were earning a decent living by wrecking ships against the headland with false lights. Their plans, however, on a last occasion, were tripped by a new apprentice who proved to be—ridiculous!—the Prince of Wales. In the final act he pulled off his false pigtail, laid the wicked pirates by the heels, and engaged himself to marry his laundress's pretty daughter who was now discovered to be a long-lost duchess. The soft-hearted author reformed his villains, when already the nooses were on their necks. He lined them up behind the footlights for hot grog and a final drinking chorus. We can hear them as the curtain falls:

> Old Pew had a jerk with a long-handled dirk—
> His choice was a jab in the dark—
> And Morgan's crew, 'twixt me and you,
> Considered a rope a lark.
> But a prettier end, I repeat and contend—
> And I've sailed on every sea—
> Is a plunge off the side in the foamin' tide.
> It tickles a sailor like me.

Clovelly is undeniably old; for no men this side of antiquity would have conceived it possible to build a village

so steeply on a slippery hill. Its origin must be contemporary
with the pinnacled towns that hang giddily above the French
Riviera and the Italian cities that straddle the Apennines.
It was conferred by the Conqueror "on Matilda, his consort."
It belonged to a certain Sir John Cary in the early years of
Richard II. Its first stone piers were built in the first part
of the eighteenth century and have been several times repaired and lengthened. It was in our own lifetime that
Clovelly was discovered by the tourists. It is now the possession of a certain Mrs. Hamlyn, who is also the owner of the
Hobby Drive, which is the town's best gateway from the
east. No motors are permitted on this three-mile drive along
the cliffs and it is, therefore, unspoiled by traffic.

Clovelly's cottages were formerly all white. But an artist
once came on a visit to Mrs. Hamlyn, and he suggested a
few pink walls and some of blue. Several buckets of color,
therefore, now spot the staircase that is called a street.

At the New Inn we were given a room that overlooked this
staircase—a thoroughfare at such a slant that any doorway is
at the roof level of its next neighbor towards the harbor.
The room was so small that when our bags were open we
straddled them to wash. One clambered over a footboard
into bed. The view from our window was cramped by near-
by walls and did not find the sea. This was in the hotel's
annex; for now that the report of Clovelly's beauty has
spread to Akron, the New Inn has gobbled buildings here
and there for extra space. Greed has a monstrous appetite,
and the New Inn stands on both sides of the street.

We climbed down to the harbor and had tea and clotted
cream at the Red Lion Hotel. The proprietor served us.

"Scones?" he asked.

"And *rawsbrys*."

He inquired if we had ever visited the Corcoran Gallery
in Washington.

We had.

"Then," he answered, "you have seen the portrait of my father."

It seems that James Hook when painting his "Luff, Boy," used him as a model for the little lad at the stern of the boat. "Little boy, Richard Pengilly," says Clovelly's guidebook, "in the *Cockran* gallery, still alive."

"The old man's dead now," said our proprietor, as he poured our tea. He lamented the wet weather and the lateness of the season, but hoped for better patronage in July.

"The Red Lion's sleepy when it rains," he said, "but in a month this room will be crowded and I'll be serving beer and tea all along the corridor and out in front."

"You are convenient to the steamers," I replied. "A first drink and a last."

"Yes," he answered, "but it's not them that counts. They bring folks only by the hundreds. They come in buses by the thousands. And there is this about it too that hurts. If it's rough on the Channel, the passengers ain't got no stomachs to eat or drink. They just want to sit on the pier and be let alone. That's what I tell the missis, and I ought to be gettin' lower rent. You're stayin' at the New Inn? All right. They get 'em there right off the buses, and buses are always thirsty."

He stood at the window and pointed to the water.

"There's Bideford Bay," he said. "It kicks up with a bit of wind. Not so pleasant when it makes you squiffy. Perhaps you've read a poem by Charles Kingsley that is called 'The Three Fishers': 'For men must work, and women must weep, and there's little to earn, and many to keep.' It tells about three fishermen who were drowned off Bideford, just up the coast. 'Three corpses lay out on the shining sands'—that's the kind of gloomy poem it is, and I suspect that it don't do business any too much good. You can't make money out of a tap when folks feel that way about it."

"Hardly."

"Another pot of tea?"

"No, thanks."

" 'Cue!"

We sat on the jetty and saw Lundy's Island dimly through the mist.

> Lundy high, sign of dry,
> Lundy plain, sign of rain,
> Lundy low, sign of snow.

Lundy was a bit low, so we turned up our collars.

Then we hired donkeys. They were asleep. They looked up with that same grieved eye that their betters open when the alarm-clock strikes. We prodded them to the upper town. To me a donkey is an ideal mount—for a horse is too sportive and much too tall. I like a low beast, so that my feet can drag both sides.

In a rift of clear sky we walked on the Hobby Drive—sheer beauty—and visited the parish church on the Hamlyn estate. Just above Clovelly there is a little public park with a vista to the Channel that is cut from dense woods. It must be that in summer this park is too much a picnic ground for trippers with box lunches, for our guidebook prints verses by A. A. Milne as a warning against the leaving of litter.

If you go a-picnicking and throw your scraps about,
You'll never see the little folk go running in and out,
And if you leave your orange peel all littered on the grass,
You'll never go to Fairyland or see the fairies pass.

> For empty tins and tangled strings
> And paper bags are not the things
> To scatter where a linnet sings.

So if you go a-picnicking, remember you're a guest
Of all the tiny people, and you'll really find it's best
To leave their ball-room tidy and to clear away the mess,
And perhaps you'll see a fairy in her newest dancing dress.

But paper bags and broken combs
Will really wreck the pixie homes,
And frighten all the tiny gnomes.

But if you go a-picnicking and you are elfinwise,
You'll maybe hear with fairy ears and see with goblin eyes.
The little folk will welcome you, and they will open wide
The hidden doors of Fairyland, and you will pass inside.
And, maybe, see a baby jay
White cradled in a cherry spray,
Although it is Bank Holiday.

And now, in a return of rain, we hurried to our hotel.

Whatever Clovelly is in sunlight, it frets one in a downpour. There is really no place to go. Climbing a stairway is not enough, and one needs a roof above it.

We secured at last two easy chairs beside the open fire in the lounge. This was a task that required watchfulness and persistence; for there were only two really comfortable chairs in the room that commanded a full share of heat. Our novitiate was spent on a piano bench—pure ornament—against the furthest wall. From this we advanced to a hard window-seat in a draught, and thence to creaking willow-bottomed chairs that stamped their pattern. It was only when hope had almost vanished that we seized on a moment of vacancy and took our happy places by the fire. Other less fortunate tourists would now, from time to time, put their cold noses inside the room and they would look at us with envy; but we seemed to read, ignorant of their pathetic shivers. Time's whirligig fetches its revenge. We had ourselves on several occasions stood banished in the suburbs of the hearthrug.

Rain was beating on the windows, but there was still traffic in the street. A sled of coal-bags came slithering down the steep incline to a bin that was near the harbor; and from it a lump got loose and bounced along the cobbles in advance with a merry air that defied the weather. It would presently jounce upward through a window and wreck a pot of tea. One sled held a load of vegetables—green cabbages, of course—another sled was conveying a bed and a sodden mattress. Still another sled of miscellaneous household furniture almost escaped its keeper to perform its journey quite alone.

Now and then donkeys passed on slippery hoofs, flicking rain from their tall ears. They carried congealed tourists from their motors at the stairway's top—tourists who would presently come whimpering for our chairs beside the fire— who would whirl a bit on a revolving stool and tap their cold feet, then depart upstairs to change for dinner.

But we were deaf to their suggestive glances. Not for all the sodden world beyond our rain-splashed windows would we surrender our soft cushions by the fire.

- Barnstaple -

XLII. TOWARDS LYNMOUTH

WE HAD planned to spend several days at Clovelly in order that time might wear off its tourist surface into a more genuine metal underneath. If we had had a pleasant bedroom with any outlook from the window, or space to stand without straddling, we might have been content, as at Fowey, to await a sunny day. As for last night's fire, it seemed on the following morning that it was held by others in perpetual lease.

So we suddenly changed our plans at eleven o'clock. The hotel porter informed us that a bus was leaving presently for Barnstaple and that it connected with the Toy Railroad whose tiny train would set us down at Lynton not later than the middle of the afternoon. Nothing of this was true. We might have guessed it from the early British aspect of the greasy sheet that he consulted. When the porter of an English country inn essays the exacting task of ascertaining the schedule of trains or buses, he is performing a labor for which nature did not intend him. For even approximate correctness, a tourist will lay his problem on the desk the night before; for a porter keeps no information in ready cash, and he must have an hour to fumble in a book.

"The bus connects at Barnstaple for the Toy Railroad," our Clovelly porter repeated glibly. "Yes, sir, right in the station, sir. 'Cue."

Our bags were put on a sled and dragged with us up the hill. Presently a great bus came lumbering into the parking space.

"Barnstaple?" I asked.

"Bideford," the conductor answered.

"But the Barnstaple bus is due," I persisted.

"There ain't any—not from here."

"What about the Toy Railroad to Lynton?"

"Maybe it's running, and maybe it ain't."

"How do I get to Barnstaple?"

The conductor shouted, "Bill! Does a bus run from Bideford to Barnstaple?"

"The gent will have to inquire when he gets there."

"But our porter—" I persisted.

But the bus was starting and we clambered up.

In many of these buses a square cardboard of advertising is placed at the middle of each window just at the level of the eye. There is, therefore, a blind spot in the center of each landscape. In the midst of the Devon hills a tourist is advised by the cardboard to drink *Bovo* at bedtime if he wishes to sleep. If he glances across the bus to the windows against the sea, he is counseled to sip *Buvo* for his blood. And ahead of him, where the driver sits, is *Bevo* for jaded nerves. In America we build a separate and expensive signboard to spoil each view. The English, more thriftily, pack a dozen of them on a bus and wreck the countryside with comparatively little cost.

We came to Bideford. We sat in a waiting-room that smelled vaguely of peanuts. They specialized here in Barnstaple buses and were quite glib. The Toy Railroad, however, was too far off.

We hailed another bus.

"Do you connect at Barnstaple with the trains for Lynton and Lynmouth," I asked.

"George," shouted the conductor, "are the Toy trains running?"

"I don't know," was the answer. "They can tell him at the station."

"Do we go to the station?"

"No, we don't."

"But our porter—" I started, but the bus had started too.

We wavered unsteadily along a narrow aisle and collapsed into an empty seat. *"Bevo,"* I read against the hills, *"Bevo, Bevo, Bevo* for fatigue." The placard was on every window. Perhaps the British public is tired, is tired, is tired, is tired of buses.

At Barnstaple we hired a boy to break his back for a shilling. Down the street he staggered with our bags to the railway station. We had planned to be at Lynmouth in time for a heavy tea; and here we were, without lunch, when already the afternoon was half gone and we had more than two hours of travel before us. A man is dangerous on an empty stomach. On our last bus I had dozed for a few minutes and I had strangled our porter in a nightmare. Nor did a cup of tea and a few stale crackers restore my temper.

Lynton's Toy Railway deserves its fame. Its track winds so pleasantly through lovely country that presently my sourness vanished. Now and then there was a village huddled from the wind, and a white road that would be an intermittent companion to our destination. We were beyond a view of the Bristol Channel, but a high ridge marked its position.

Lynton sits on the cliff, Lynmouth at the level of the sea. We chose the harbor village. They are but a rolling stone apart, but there is no road between them that is safe for motors. We were forced, therefore, to travel several miles further up the valley into moorland before we could find a break and descend to Lynmouth.

It was dinner time when we pulled up to the door of the Lyn Valley Hotel.

"A double room with an open fire," I said.

The Quay,
Lynmouth

XLIII. LYNTON AND LYNMOUTH

IN GLASGOW there is, or used to be, a railway station on
two levels. From one of these platforms trains ran north,
and from the other, south. There is a similar arrangement
in the contiguous villages of Lynmouth and Lynton. Devon's
coast road from the east ends at Lynmouth on the level of
the tide. Its westward highway starts at Lynton, four hundred feet above.

Walkers from the lower town to the one on top may climb
a zig-zag path and rest on frequent benches or they may ride
in a cable-car for a penny. The cable road's equipment consists of two enormous water tubs with covered platforms on
them. The lighter tub goes up, while the full tub comes
down. The only power appliances are a bunghole at the top

and a spigot at the bottom. Taking one's morning tub at Lynmouth is a term of locomotion.

Lynmouth is favored by travelers who prefer a beach of colored stones, fishing boats and the near-by sound of waves, and a certain snugness beneath the cliffs. It offers the arrival of the Bristol steamer. There is a parade along the sea, with a coping for a tourist's dangling legs.

Lynton is the choice of those who prefer a wide outlook. On clear nights the lights of Wales dot the far-off northern coast. Sunsets burn the headland to the east—a purple flame of blended rock and gorse and heather. One can walk on the facing of the Channel cliffs or farther afield across the tree-less moors. He will see wild ponies threading a hill-top against the sky or, on a day of hunting, hear the cry of hounds. One shivers a bit as he thinks of being lost here when night is coming on.

Usually a traveler prefers the village he knows the better. If luck, on a first visit, has cast him into Lynton, it is there he returns for his succeeding holidays, satisfied with what he has already enjoyed. And this is also true of Lynmouth. Travelers, moreover, are so true to their first love that they band themselves into opposite cliques of adoration, and each of them underrates the village that is not its choice. The fact is that both towns are perfect in their different ways. To some persons, scenery is a background, and these will choose Lynton. To others Nature shows itself best in detail, and these will lodge at Lynmouth.

In Lynmouth there are only a few shops. Lynton has a long street of pretty merchandise. Lynmouth has had no space to grow. Lynton sprawls southward into a tiny suburb. In hotels there is no real choice between the towns. At Lynton you sit for tea in a garden whose foot falls sharply to the sea four hundred feet below. At Lynmouth you eat your clotted cream beside the singing waters of the Lyn and are content with a narrow outlook. If one cares little for moorland, he will prefer this snug protection. Except at the coming of the Bristol steamer, Lynmouth is quieter than Lynton and has fewer chars-à-bancs to fret it. But the book-shop and the better merchants are at Lynton. It is there also that one goes to the *movie*—in a dingy room, up one flight. They are not first runs, but old reels at a bargain. In any climax, the screen goes white. Lynton and Lynmouth should not be mere lodgings for the night. Each day of several weeks can show a fresh discovery.

A few miles down the coast is Lee Abbey—a private residence that is now an excellent hotel. A ridge of wooded rock shields it from the Channel. One can issue from the trees to a barren headland. Occasional placards of warning in the woods ask a stranger to mind his step, for several by-paths end so abruptly at the precipice concealed in bushes that further advance would be destruction. And as one might expect in a region so romantic, there is a legend here of a lady who was crossed in love and jumped. We leaned forward timidly and saw the glistening water almost a thousand feet below. One may proceed on sheep trails anywhere above Lynton until they lead nowhere and are lost. He may sit on a pinnacle above the Valley of the Rocks and drop an apple into the funnel of a passing Clovelly steamer.

From Lynmouth one may follow a wayward path above a noisy stream, and in a mile or two he will come to Watersmeet. Here are rival tea gardens, one on each side of the brawling river. They have already been advertising themselves by means of boasting placards, and chiefly at a foot-bridge which we passed a bit farther down the valley. To cross or not! Both banks had their persuasion in three-foot letters. And if a man be not content to fatten himself on cream at either of these gardens, then is he fit for stratagem and spoils.

Behind our hotel at Lynmouth there was a narrow glen with a winding path that climbed to God-knows-where. We had approached this glen as if it were a common picnic ground, but we found it of rarest beauty. It was almost semitropical in its density of foliage, and in the evening twilight the path seemed lost in leafy tunnels. It scrambled on the stones and crossed the stream on high-flung rustic bridges. It went on all-fours up steep inclines. It dived into darkness and again consorted with the tree-tops. There was something fanciful in this, as if creatures lived here whose forms were not of our common world—as if green twilight were of a softer texture than open valleys know. And there was almost a touch of fright; for the night might descend in a sudden gloom and hold one a prisoner here.

Countisbury Headland juts into the Channel just up the coast from Lynmouth. Its huge curve might be the back of some great creature escaped from chaos. It is a long climb and it is steep. The road is cut against the headlands and has an unobstructed view. Lundy's Isle, far out at sea, marks the entrance of the Channel. A northern smudge of land is Wales. There is smoke of frequent ships.

If one follows the Countisbury Hill a few miles farther towards Porlock and peers down into each hollow of the rocky shore many hundred feet below, he will presently see the very scar and beach where Stevenson placed the Admiral Benbow Inn of his "Treasure Island"—the very path on which Blind Pew came tapping in the night. It is a chapter so exciting that one shudders even in daylight on the safe road above.

Few books have had their origins so carefully recorded as has "Treasure Island." We know that its genesis was a wholly fictitious map that Stevenson once drew. We are informed of the story's progress from day to day until at last the sheets went off to London to be printed. But Stevenson never gave a precise location to the Admiral Benbow Inn, nor told where he got the couplet of verses that was bellowed so often by old Bill Bones.

Fifteen Men on the Dead Man's Chest—
Yo-ho-ho and a bottle of rum!

We used to think that the dead man was killed by this tremendous weight. Then we were informed that the chest was
not pulmonary, but was none other than old Bill Bones' sea-
box on which his traitorous companions were squatting before they divided the loot.

Both of these theories are untrue. We are now instructed
that the Dead Man's Chest was a sunken reef in the Carib-
bean Sea on which pirates' boats sometimes smashed. These
fifteen pirates had evidently been washed up after a bad
time in the water.

Where Stevenson got his couplet about this reef, we do
not know; or whether it was of his own composition. But a
few years ago, an American poet, Young Ewing Allison,
built it up to several stanzas. We quote the poem entire, as
we find it in an anthology called "Songs of Men." It is a
description of the aftermath of mutiny.

Fifteen men on the Dead Man's Chest—
Drink and the devil had done for the rest—
    The mate was fixed by the bo's'n's pike,
    The bo's'n brained with a marlinspike,
    And Cookey's throat was marked belike.
        It had been gripped
        By fingers ten;
        And there they lay,
        All good, dead men,
Like break-o'-day in a boozing ken—
    Yo-ho-ho and a bottle of rum!

Fifteen men of a whole ship's list—
Dead and be-damned and the rest gone whist!—
    The skipper lay with his nob in gore
    Where the scullion's ax his cheek had shore—

And the scullion he was stabbed times four.
    And there they lay,
        And the soggy skies
        Dripped all day long
        In up-staring eyes—
At murk sunset and at foul sunrise—
    Yo-ho-ho and a bottle of rum!

Fifteen men of 'em stiff and stark—
Ten of the crew had the murder mark—
    'Twas a cutlass swipe, or an ounce of lead,
    Or a yawning hole in a battered head,—
    And the scuppers glut with a rotting red.
        And there they lay—
            Aye, damn my eyes!—
        All lookouts clapped
        On paradise—
All souls bound just contrariwise—
    Yo-ho-ho and a bottle of rum!

Fifteen men of 'em good and true—
Every man-Jack could ha' sailed with Old Pew—
    There was chest on chest full of Spanish gold,
    With a ton of plate in the middle hold,
    And the cabins, riot of loot untold.
        And they lay there
            That had took the plum,
        With sightless glare
        And their lips struck dumb,
While we shared all by the rule of thumb—
    Yo-ho-ho and a bottle of rum!

More was seen through the sternlight screen—
Chartings ondoubt where a woman had been—
    A flimsy shift on a bunker cot,
    With a thin dirk slot through the bosom-spot,

And the lace stiff-dry in a purplish blot . . .
Or was she wench,
Or some shuddering maid
That dared the knife
And that took the blade?
My God! She was stuff for a plucky jade;
Yo-ho-ho and a bottle of rum!

Fifteen men on the Dead Man's Chest—
Drink and the devil had done for the rest—
We wrapped 'em all in a mains'l tight,
With twice ten turns of a hawser's bight,
And we heaved 'em over and out of sight—
With a yo-heave-ho!
And a fare-you-well!
And a sullen plunge
In the sullen swell,
Ten fathoms deep on the road to hell!
Yo-ho-ho and a bottle of rum!

But we have an even greater poet to deal with here at Lynmouth.

Shelley lived in Lynmouth for several summer months in the year 1812. He had been drawn to Dublin in the previous winter by his revolutionary desire to do his part for home rule. He made speeches on O'Connell's platform, and had published several pamphlets of a doubtfully seditious nature. It was his respectable name that Ireland wanted more than his eloquence; for Shelley was too pacific to suit leaders of revolt. He was presently snubbed and he crossed to Wales.

After searching for a cottage for himself and his wife, and being in some embarrassment about a guarantee of rental money, the Shelleys left Wales, crossed into Devon, with a hope of finding a suitable house at Ilfracombe. It was on descending Countisbury Hill "on foot or horseback" that they first saw Lynmouth—"then some thirty cottages," says Dowden, his biographer, "rose-clad and myrtle-clad, nestling at the foot of the hills. It was enough. Why should they wander farther if by good fortune one of these straw-thatched cottages might be theirs?"

We must not think of Shelley during this brief residence at Lynmouth as England's famous poet, nor hope to find that in this sheltered fairyland were written the "Skylark" or the "West Wind." Shelley this summer was hardly twenty years of age. He was known to a very few persons as the author of several obscurely published and unread novels. To his father's family he was rather a nuisance—a rebel against all tradition except his quarterly allowance. To a few more persons, chiefly in Dublin, he was regarded as a young aristocrat with prospects but little cash and of doctrines that were too mild for Ireland.

Shelley spent his summer writing—seditious pamphlets, chiefly, although his biographer finds just a hint of processes towards Queen Mab and of several lesser poems.

But outbursts against the English constitution during these days of Irish discontent were getting their authors into trouble. A London publisher had been sentenced to several months' imprisonment for the indiscretions of one of his contributors; and the government was disposed to crush sedition. Shelley devised, therefore, the notion of enclosing anonymous copies of his pamphlets in bottles, setting them adrift in the Bristol Channel in order that the tides might scatter their revolutionary seeds along the coast. His "Declaration of Rights" was too big for a bottle, so Shelley "constructed a little box, covered with bladder, well resined and waxed to keep out the water, with lead below to maintain it in an upright position, and a tiny mast and sail above to attract attention at sea. . . . Accordingly," Dowden continues, "we discover Shelley—a boyish figure—in the August days . . . pushing certain small boxes, each with its mast and sail, from the rocks; or watching from his boat a little flotilla of dark green bottles, tightly corked, which rise and sink as the waves sway them seawards."

In these trivialities of revolution, Shelley was at first merely an object of curiosity or derision to the villagers. Then it happened that one of his pamphlets was washed ashore and was read by a government agent. An inquiry discovered Shelley to have been its author, and a warrant was issued for his arrest. Hastily leaving his Lynmouth cottage, he and his wife escaped across to Wales.

Shelley seems to have passed little time at Lynmouth in poetic meditation. The wind on the cliffs above the town was not yet the "breath of Autumn's being," but was only a trivial revolutionary breeze from the French Bastille that

had echoed out of Ireland. The guillotine's Rights of Man
were toy ships that he had fitted with a silly sail.

Yet this coast must have had some part in his education.
The Valley of the Rocks was a favorite haunt. It was Shelley's habit to scrawl pictures on the flyleaves of his books,
and thereafter through his life, he drew the "points, spires
and pinnacles of rocks and crags as recollections and memorials of the fascinating spot." From Lynmouth he wrote
to Godwin: "Mountains certainly of not less perpendicular
elevation than a thousand feet are broken abruptly into
valleys of indescribable fertility and grandeur. The climate
is so mild that myrtles of an immense size twine up our
cottage, and roses blow in the open air all winter." Devon's
mild majesty would grow some day to be the terrific ridges
of the Caucasus. Yet Devon was but a prologue.

One regrets at Lynmouth that the Bristol Channel did
not seize the imagination of Shelley as the Italian shore
would later seize it. It was on the morning of March 12,
1818, that Shelley saw England for the last time. He was a
man with genius still unripe. For four years, until his death,
Italy would be his home. Every one of his poems of any
special consequence came from below the Alps. It was in the
southern world that he beheld

> . . . a pumice isle in Baiae's bay,
> And saw in sleep old palaces and towers
> Quivering within the wave's intenser day.

The "Ode to the West Wind" was written beside the Arno,
and its leaves of "hectic red" are all from Tuscan woods.
The "Cenci" was composed at Rome and near Leghorn:
"Prometheus Unbound" at Este, Rome and Florence; the
marvelous poems of 1820 when he was in residence at Florence, Pisa and Leghorn. A Scotch singer stays at home and
endures a drizzle. It is thrift, perhaps. Irish genius expands

in London. The English poets thrive best in Italian exile.

We spent a pleasant week at Lynmouth. Our hotel was excellent, with little parlors, each with its open fire. Our proprietress was so eager for our comfort that after an occasion when we had dined out, she inquired whether our absence had been due to dissatisfaction. We had, in fact, gone to Lynton by tub for a change of fare. Lobster, hinted the waitress. But it came to us straight from a round tin and showed the marks of its entombment. After this foul supper we went to the *movie*. Mary was still holding her last cracker as we entered, and the usher thought it was her ticket and tried to take it from her.

On cold evenings, Mary re-read "Lorna Doone" and I fell asleep on "Westward Ho!" This novel is best when drawn from a Sunday-school lending library. "Lorna Doone" is in every shop of Lynton and in every variety of edition, from pocket size to ooze leather for the piano top among the family portraits.

Sunday, May 24th, was Whitsun. For several weeks we had seen Whitsun on every hoarding and on every handbill in railway stations, with its offers of cheap rates by boat and train and bus. It is a universal holiday. Shops advertise new clothes for Whitsun. *Bevo* warns against fatigue on Whitsun and suggests a teaspoonful night and morning. Leather stores have bargains of luggage. Hat dealers have special bonnets. Whitsun is in the calendar like Christmas.

And now Whitsun's boats and chars-à-bancs had come. Restaurants that yesterday were empty, now were crowded. The tub railroad had every platform filled. Obsequious land-lords were today of harassed incivility. There was a scramble to Watersmeet for clotted cream. The beach was searched for pretty stones. The witch's cavern in the Valley of the Rocks had its circle of admirers, each pinnacle its pair of legs. Benches groaned in the cliff-side path. The *movie* theatre was filled by lovers whose soft nothings would be resumed in the evening chars-à-bancs.

And then, towards night, peace again settled on the village. Waves lipped softly up the beach.

- Watermouth -

XLIV. DOWN THE COAST

WHEN THE Whitsun crowd had been absorbed again in city traffic, we went on an excursion down the coast. Our motor was an old sedan that preserved from its better days a cracked vase of wilted flowers. And when artificial roses are dropping petals they are real antiques. Our motor coughed at starting and was weary on the first hill, but our driver said it had a sturdy little engine.

We climbed the valley of the Lyn above Watersmeet, then descended Biddaway Hill to Barbrook—pretty names, these. In yesterday's uproar this junction had been a racket of motors and its traffic officer had been as busy as a one-armed juggler. But now the highways were empty. For a few miles our road followed the Toy Railroad, then branched northwest to the hills above Sandy Bay. And here Mary sketched the distant sea.

At Watermouth, a castle stands beside the road—not a ruined pile, but the dwelling of its present owner. It has crenelations, but we must suppose that they are merely decorations that stayed in fashion after their use was gone. I explored the beach of a little harbor, while Mary sketched again. She was busy at the roadside when a lordly man came striding up with hunting dogs and invited her to work inside his garden. "No?" he said. "Then be careful not to be clipped off by a motor." Near Watermouth is laid the plot of a novel by Marie Corelli. We found it dull and forget its title. And now the highroad climbed again to high rocks above the Channel and we saw Ilfracombe ahead.

Ilfracombe is the tourist's capital of northern Devon—the terminus of trains from London and the starting point of local buses. It is a sprawling city of many hotels and lodging-houses, of monotonous lodgings, of restaurants and band-stands. It lies in a scoop of bare granite, with a great rock between it and open water. This rock is encircled by an esplanade, from which an occasional path scrambles up its ragged slope to suggest picnic lunches taken out of paper bags. Ilfracombe's pleasure pavilion is on that part of the esplanade that is protected from the sea.

We have remarked in our chapter on Dawlish that a pavilion in France is a place of merriment, of dancing, music and gambling. This one at Ilfracombe was but a barren floor enclosed in glass. It may be joyous in the summer months (we doubt it) but now, in May, it was of hollow cheek and bothered with a cough. It was in Xanadu, not in Ilfracombe, that Kubla Khan his stately pleasure dome decreed. Under today's dark clouds, with rain whipping from the sea, Ilfracombe's pavilion windows wept.

Perhaps this is just as well, for the English do not like indoor amusements. If cooped by bad weather their noses are flat on the window as they look for a change of wind. "Ilfracombe," says our guidebook, "makes justifiable claim to be-

ing the premier watering-place of North Devon. For variety
of scenery, magnificent cliffs, seascapes, picturesque walks,
and marine and water excursions, it has few rivals in the
kingdom." There is nothing in this about pavilions. It is
exercise it offers. It is a walking-stick and heavy boots that
endear Ilfracombe to English travelers.

We had tea; not to allay thirst, but because we thought
that hot water, if poured along the pipes, would lift the
chill.

We motored to Barnstaple. While Mary sketched a bridge,
I walked in a park beside the river. There was a cricket
match going forward with tea-and-muffin leisure.

Barnstaple figures in Kingsley's "Westward Ho!" Arthur
Norway slights the town. "I could never find anything in
Barnstaple," he writes, "which repaid the trouble of going
there." He confesses that it sent ships to assist Drake against
the Spanish, then trots through without another word. To
my eye it seemed a pretty town, quaintly set beside a broad
and shallow river.

Norway has better things to say of Bideford, where we
motored next—anecdotes of witchcraft and of Kingsley. But
as he slighted Barnstaple, our favorite of these two towns,
we shall in revenge slight Bideford. We motored without a
halt to Westward Ho!

This small town is but a single street of hotels and modern
dwellings. It is absurdly new, and it took its name from
Kingsley's novel. This surprised me, for I had thought that
Kingsley borrowed his title from the town. Westward Ho! is
famous chiefly for its golf course. It is thinking of niblicks,
not of primitive adventure on the ocean. For the past week
we had been reading of the progress of the British Amateur
Tournament, and how its results would affect the selection
of the team to cross the Atlantic. But we came too late, as
its final rounds had finished on Whitsun. We had tea, how-

ever, at the club-house, having first inquired timidly of the
steward if this were permitted. It was against a strict ruling
(" 'Cue") but in the case of strangers from across the ocean
an exception was sometimes made.

Our table stood at a window with a full view of the links.
The room, though bare and of cheap construction, was comfortable and served its purpose. The grass is nibbled by

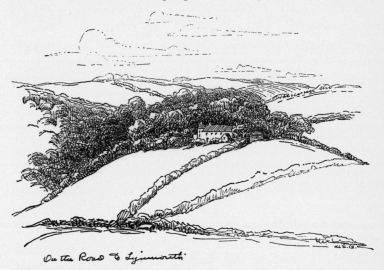

On the Road to Lynmouth.

sheep. The eighteen holes are encompassed and crossed by
patches of barren waste, whose sand and sedge-grass are haz-
ards enough.

Westward Ho!, Bideford and Appledore! There is rather
a magic in these names, and we regret that a visit here somewhat dispels the charm. It is a region of sluggish harbors
and flat sand.

And now came a sudden seizure of our motor. It was on
the hills above Barnstaple on our homeward course that our
old sedan smothered and stopped. Our driver pulled in turn
at all his gadgets. He lifted the hood and peered with an
air of wisdom at its mystery of plumbing. Then he stood

off and scratched his head. It was the blinkin' spark plugs, he
said—or it might be that the carburetor "had gone blooey."
Our motor seemed to need ether and a knife. Again our
driver pulled his gadgets. He rattled anything that could
be jiggled by his dirty fingers. He tried kicking at a tire in
the hopes that this might rouse the engine.

We were several miles from any town, on lonely hills,
with but a solitary dwelling far across the valley. From its
one chimney there was an ironic hint of supper. The sun
was running to the west. Our motor's faded magnificence
taunted us—the soft cushions of its ancient grandeur, the
cracked vase where artificial flowers had bloomed. At these
last sad rites there were festered lilies.

"What's to be done?" I asked. "It's ten miles up hill to
Lynton, so we can't push it. I'm told that these moors are
cold, once the sun has set."

I was interrupted by the coming of another motor, the
first that had passed us for several miles. Our driver hailed
it.

"You wait here," he said. "I'll go back to Barnstaple for
help."

The ship's captain had deserted in the only lifeboat.

We sat inside our motor among the silent hills. Not so
much as a moan issued from the engine and we knew that
its suffering had ceased. A long valley mounted into meadowland that was marked in a checkerboard of walls and colored
grain. Our lonely chimney's penciling of smoke rose un-
twisted in the calm of twilight—a ribbon such as might proceed from a widow's shepherd's pie. There was stillness, and
the day waited for the night.

And now, when already darkness was settling in the valley, our new motor came. It was a bus—a bus for twenty
people—with a roaring engine. Our driver, not finding a private motor, had stumbled on a char-à-bancs that was return-

ing empty to Lynton. *Bevo, Bevo, Bevo, Bevo*—for fatigue, fatigue, fatigue, fatigue.

Our landlady had saved our dinner. There was a fire in our bedroom and our chilly spirits thawed.

Oare Church —

XLV. A SENTIMENTAL DAY WITH LORNA DOONE

WE HAD found Lynmouth a delightful village—of cold wet weather, for the most part, but with enough brief sunlight to give us a taste of summer. Neither here nor elsewhere on our travels, it is true, had we found the scene or climate that persuades one to linger from week to week; but perhaps the lotus thrives only in the south. I had discovered once that sleepy drug at Taormina on a coast where a tourist throws away his watch—where he dreams in ancient cloisters protected from the world. A booking-office in Taormina is an absurdity, for who wants a ticket when he has once arrived? In the gardens of the San Domenico there is no time or schedule. But Lynmouth has none of this drowsy persuasion. Devon's pharmacy lacks anaesthesia even in August; and certainly its shelf is bare of lotus when the fingers and nose are cold. Yet Lynmouth is lovely to the eye, and suits better our northern blood than the almond countries of the south.

But our week was up. It was our plan to go by motor to Porlock—not by the direct road along the coast, but by a circle across the moors for a glimpse of Oare and Badgeworthy Water. We were careful to hire a stalwart motor.

We climbed Countisbury Hill to an incomparable view—the Channel to the north, and to the south an endless stretch of treeless upland that seemed too large for England's tiny island. This apparent contradiction is in the mind of every traveler in these waste spaces of the west. And how does it happen, he wonders, that through all the three thousand years of British history such infrequent settlement has lodged in this wide land? The cause is an unfertile soil and a bleak exposure. Wind is here man's special foe, and it is only in the valleys that he can escape the winter's gales. Nor can the eye easily find these villages that have crept to shelter.

It was in Oare's parish church, as all readers will recall, that Lorna was shot by Carver Doone. And as romance is always a crowded shrine, we shall not be surprised to find at the church door a pile of volumes each filled with tourists' names. "The sound of a shot rang through the church, and those eyes were dim with death," says an exciting chapter. After so exquisite a situation—Lorna in John Ridd's strong arms before the altar—it seems almost too bad that she recovered. But Blackmore may have been thinking of *talkie* rights and a necessarily happy ending.

The home of Exmoor's present master of the foxhounds

is adjacent to the village of Oare, and I put inquiries to our driver about hunting. The driver's name was Ridd. It is a common name in the moorland, he said, and he made no claim to kinship with the fictitious John Ridd of Blackmore's story.

"Do country folk ride free?" I asked.

"Those who are poor, yes," he answered. "There is no compulsion of payment. But those who ride regularly and can afford it, are asked to contribute. If a man gives as much as a hundred pounds a year, he is given an honorary office in the pack and is permitted to wear a scarlet coat."

"How much does it cost the master of the hounds?" I asked.

"For foxhounds, as much as six thousand pounds a year. For staghounds, more."

The master of the Exmoor pack keeps a dozen hunters and about thirty dogs. From kennels in the distance I heard their yelping.

There arose the sound of a cuckoo clock. I listened until it had sounded twelve.

"It's noon," I said.

"It's a cuckoo," our driver answered.

The stroke kept up to forty-seven, and I knew that he was right. Not even an English clock could be so wrong.

It is only a few miles from Oare Church to Badgeworthy Water—or Baggery, as it is pronounced. As this stream plays its part in Blackmore's story, it is also a tourists' mecca. A simple cottage at the foot of the valley has been enlarged to a barnlike room for feeding a hundred persons. There is a gate at the roadside, exacting a fee from those who wish to explore the upper reaches of the stream. About three miles up Badgeworthy Water is the Valley of the Doones, a barren pocket scooped out of the upper moorland. In Lorna Doone's time, Badgeworthy Water marked a no man's land between the peaceful settlements near Oare and the

wilder district of the outlaws. It was while strolling along
this stream that John Ridd discovered the Waterslide that
was the outpost of their stronghold.

We paid our fee and passed the gate.

(It is best to read Blackmore vaguely, like a tale from fairyland. His geography is not precise. He describes the Waterslide as less than Niagara, it is true, but a dangerous bit
of footing where John Ridd almost broke his neck. In reality
it is a bowlder of no great size, with a trickle of water over
it and a pool beneath of just size enough to drown a puppy.
We fear also that Blackmore has overpainted the Valley of
the Doones, its precipitous sides, its remoteness and security
from attack. Its slopes are as gentle as those of a city park.
It has a remnant of old foundations, probably those of a
farmhouse, and it was from these that Blackmore constructed
the stronghold of the Doones. A lonely dwelling stands
within the valley and a pretty girl was hanging out the wash.

We are not denying the existence of these outlaws. They
were real enough—a wild clan that existed as late as the ending of the seventeenth century, as the story says. And if
Blackmore chooses to throw in Lorna as an extra measure,
we would be ungracious to deny him the privilege. As an
Italian once reminded us, he is a fool who asks in Verona
whether Juliet once lived.

When one is hungry it is a long walk to the Waterslide.
Most tourists content themselves with a half mile of Badgeworthy Water and return hastily for lunch. A bleak beauty,
however, makes the journey to the top worth the time ex-
pended. We saw no trippers—no one but a boy and girl.
She was dressed in knee breeches with bare legs, and when
we came on them suddenly, hidden in ecstasy behind a rock,
it was evident that romance of another kind had brought
them to this secluded spot.

Next to us at lunch sat a lodging-house keeper from
Ilfracombe. We would have known her profession even if

she had not confessed it—a square jaw of nature's special modeling, designed to rent out lodgings and ask for a deposit in advance—an eye that stiffens at complaints of chilly rooms and shepherd's pie. She had eaten but a slice of beef and the piece of dry lettuce that the English call a salad, when a bill for three shillings was put beside her plate.

"Three shillings!" she exclaimed. "Some folks have nerve. My eye! [*That eye which we have mentioned.*] I wish I could get half as much in my tea-room."

She hoped to see us again and left her card with us.

She turned at the door.

"Drop in on me in Ilfracombe one day," she said. "I've bedrooms with an ocean view at two guineas a week, exceptin' wash."

This lunch-room and the fee at the valley's gate yield no doubt a greater revenue than all the wool and mutton of the district; so perhaps our friend from Ilfracombe was right.

We now crossed the high moors, where our barometer measured a height of more than fourteen hundred feet above the sea. We passed piles of peat waiting removal to the towns. Then a fog was blown upon us, and in a gray blanket we speeded on.

The face of Exmoor, says our eloquent guidebook, is the face of eternity; and like time and the ocean, it has no history. It is a "bare rolling waste very like the sea, with its long heaving monotony of gray water, without a voice, without life, and without human habitation; for there is only the sound of wind and of running water, only the life of a rare black cock or curlew, a rarer pony or herd of deer, only far off, lost in the rolling bald downs, a shepherd's hut for dwelling."

Exmoor discovers to us no Roman occupation, but it offers evidence of sparse Celtic living. Its recorded history does not stretch behind the Conquest.

And now at the foot of a long hill our road found Simonsbath. This town is the capital of this district; and there is a story of a certain Mr. Knight who once purchased Exmoor from the king for the vain project of bringing it to a state of cultivation. Beyond Simonsbath there was further rugged country until, under Dunkery Beacon, we were traversing a green valley with Dunster at its foot. We shall return later to this pleasant town, but our destination is now the Ship Inn at Porlock around the corner of the coast.

We were in time for tea and clotted cream. All this day we have been in Somerset, for Devon is behind us.

I seem to have read somewhere in Coleridge's diaries or letters that his morning's quota of poetic meditation was once interrupted by the arrival on business of "a man from Porlock." The Man from Porlock. It stands as the very title of all the distractions that beset an author. It is the telephone, the bond-salesman, the housemaid with a dusting rag, all rolled to one. It is the general intrusion of the world upon a student's time. Some day, if no one anticipates me in the effort, I shall use this man from Porlock as the subject of an essay whereby to show my spleen for the broken hours I have endured. And now we are in the town of Porlock from which this nuisance issued.

*The Ship Inn
- Porlock -*

XLVI. PORLOCK

WE HAD hoped to find the Ship Inn of Porlock listed by
Thomas Burke as one of the oldest hotels of England. Burke
has been at great pains to enumerate the several inns that
claim to be the oldest. His list is worth quotation. "Only
one or two of these stand as they were built," writes Burke,
"but all of them have at least portions of the original."

THE FIGHTING COCKS, *St. Alban's*	795
THE FOUNTAIN, *Canterbury*	1029
THE BELL, *Finedon*	1042
THE OSTRICH, *Colnbrook*	1106
THE ANGEL, *Grantham*	1213
THE ANGEL, *Blyth*	1270
THE GEORGE AND DRAGON, *Speldhurst*	1270
THE MAID'S HEAD, *Norwich*	1287
THE GREEN MAN, *Erdlington*	1306
THE GEORGE, *Salisbury*	1320
THE SARACEN'S HEAD, *Newark*	1341

THE SEVEN STARS, *Manchester*	1356
THE CROWN, *Chiddingfold*	1383
THE CROWN, *Norton St. Philip*	1397
THE NEW INN, *Gloucester*	1430
THE SPREAD EAGLE, *Midhurst*	1430
THE KING'S HEAD, *Aylesbury*	1445
THE RED LION, *Colchester*	1470
THE GEORGE, *Glastonbury*	1475
THE LION, *Buckden*	1477
THE GEORGE, *Southwark*	1554
THE BULL, *Long Melford*	1580
THE GEORGE, *Winchcombe*	1583

Of this list only the Southwark Inn is in London, for the
capital city has been too prosperous to save its relics. The
oldest of the list might have gossiped of Charlemagne's new
empire. All but the last three were in use before America
was discovered. Every tourist gauges the age of Europe by
the sailing of Columbus. This comparison and our horn-
rimmed glasses betray American birth.

But the Ship Inn, even if it has no place among Britain's
prime greybeards, has, nevertheless, an appearance of age
and wrinkles. Its walls are stooped. Like most Englishmen
of advanced years, it is rheumatic. But it is not so proud
of its infirmity as to offer a stiff nose to travelers, as is sometimes the case of inns more famous.

The Ship Inn is modest in all respects but one. It boasts
of Robert Southey, who spent here the night of August 9,
1799, and composed a sonnet. " 'Twas my lot," he wrote,

> To view the lonely, lingering close of day
> Making my sonnet by the ale-house fire
> While Idleness and Solitude inspire
> Dull rhymes to pass the duller hours away.

If we were in charge of the Ship Inn's advertising we
would not use this poem. "Dull rhymes to pass the duller
hours away" does not impress us as an effective selling slo-

gan. There must have been at some time or other in the inn a jolly poet who clinked a cannikin.

It seems that Southey and his wife had been on a visit to the Coleridges at Nether Stowey in the near-by Quantocks, where the two verse-makers had collaborated in something called "The Devil's Thoughts." It was Southey who described their method of joint production.

> There while the one was shaving
> Would he the song begin,
> And the other when he heard it at breakfast,
> In ready accord joined in.

No, the Ship Hotel could have done better. It could have used Coleridge and Wordsworth in its advertising. There is, of course, nothing jolly about either of these poets. Neither of them, even after a couple of snifters, climbed to the table and put the jorum about. But at least they were great poets, which Southey was not, and they both at one time or another sojourned here.

In the spring of 1798 Coleridge, Wordsworth and his sister walked down the Devon coast, and we cannot doubt but that they passed through Porlock and spent the night at the Ship. They must have spent the night; for just to the west of the town is a three-mile hill that would require the freshness of a morning's start. Coleridge was a bit stout [*Who says so? We do.*] and there was never yet a fat man who could tackle such a hill except after a full night's rest. This walking trip produced consequences much greater than any of Southey's mediocre sonnets, for it gave rise to the "Lyrical Ballads"—a volume that contained "The Ancient Mariner" and the "Lines Above Tintern Abbey"—a collection that opened a new century of poetry.

We can fancy Dorothy and these two men in the Ship's small lounge. Coleridge had a bad stomach and he frequently took a drop or so of laudanum in a noggin of

brandy. And, as Hazlitt says, he enjoyed a drink called "flip."
Coleridge smoked; and as he did nothing by halves, we may
assume that the room was blue. There was good conversation that night. Coleridge was England's greatest talker, and
men were lucky if they sat at his feet and listened. There
were "two centers of intellectual light in England," wrote
Leslie Stephen, "one flashing out from Jeremy Bentham to
illumine such dull things as 'the greatest happiness of the
greatest number,' and the other from Coleridge, who commanded as his general subject the whole metaphysical uni-
verse." There were, it is true, jealous persons who said he
talked too much—that his words were like water running
from a tap. And Leigh Hunt remarked that Coleridge's argu-
ments were perfect if one granted that they started from no
premise and went to no conclusion.

But Dorothy was a good listener, and her brother a man
of silent meditation. On that memorable night at the Ship
Hotel there was no writing of "dull rhymes to pass the duller
hours away." It was after midnight, we may be sure, that
candles crept through the crazy corridors to bed.

The Ship Hotel looks its age. Its ceilings are low, the
hallways and rooms are small. A narrow staircase hides in
the dark and if you make a wrong turning you are in the
kitchen, where the cook thinks you are no better than a
flirt. There is the snuggest of taps, with a wooden bench
along the wall for village gossips. Nothing is large except
the great fireplace and Southey's easy-chair.

Porlock is situated at the western end of Somerset, at
the foot of almost the steepest hill in England. It is so haz-
ardous in wet weather that a toll road has been built in a
circuit to avoid its gradient. As our motor had come on a
still wider circle through the moors, we set out afoot to see
this famous Porlock Hill.

A traffic officer of the motor association sits at the first
steep ascent. He remains through all the usual hours of

travel to assist in any mishap. We stopped to talk with him. He was a jolly fellow. Like an undertaker, whose business depends on calamity, he saw death with cheerful philosophy. He showed us snapshots of recent casualties—a car upside down in a deep gutter, another climbing a tree. It was evident that his best photographs were those of direst mishap.

"And how many were killed?" I asked, as I looked at a picture of a motor that had turned turtle.

Disappointment showed on his face.

"Only a broken leg," he answered. "But here's one that cracked five ribs. Here's another where the poor devil died in *hagony*. Only sixpence. 'Cue."

A light rain was falling, and the hill was beaded with water and oil. A descending motor swayed at the turn, then righted itself and glided down to safety. Another motor sizzled up in low gear.

"Why don't they go around by the toll road?" I asked.

"It's too *hexpensive*. It's horrible *hexpensive* for big cars filled with passengers. Last Whitsun we had a parade of chars-à-bancs." His voice sobered in disappointment. "And not a smash from mornin' till night."

"What make of car climbs best?" I asked.

It was the kind of question that cigarette-makers put to their blindfolded clients.

He considered for a moment. He shifted his weight to his other leg, as if that side held his brain's mightier lobe and it needed strong support. He looked like a doctor who balances the probability of appendicitis against mere gas.

"Well," he said at length, "by and large, the Ford."

My chest expanded with patriotic pride. Here was authority speaking. He referred to Henry Ford as Sir Henry.

And now the rain increased to violence and we trotted back to our hotel.

Electrical storms are rare in England, but we were no

sooner in shelter than one of these infrequent tempests
burst on Porlock. In a few minutes the street before our
door was flooded across the gutter and above the sill. The
torrent had gathered on the three miles of Porlock Hill
and its inundation rushed upon us. In the worst of this a
motor-cycle with a side-car stopped and a man and woman
scurried to protection. The tub where she had sat was over-
flowing. Both of them were dripping like sponges. And then
of a sudden the woman fainted. She was carried to the tap,
laid out on the bench and given brandy until she regained
consciousness.

It was merely fright, for the English are terrified by lightning. The storm, though violent, was no worse than we have
once a week through August in Ohio. Once in London I
slept during an electrical storm, to be told in the morning
that every servant of the house had dressed when the lightning was at its worst and that they had stood in terror in
the hallways. England, so used to a steady drizzle, marvels
at a downpour. One must suppose that its skies are too leaky
to store a deluge. In a half hour the rain had abated, the
tub of the side-car was sponged dry, and the man and woman
departed on their travels.

Porlock is another of England's coast towns that has been
silted inland by a changing sea. Below its High Street there
is a wide stretch of low-lying meadow that was once covered by the tide; and, we infer, that the Ship Inn took its
name when it was a resort of sailors and near their ships.
Porlock's harbor is now at Porlock Weir, several miles away.

Porlock's recorded history starts in the year 918, with an
invasion by the Danes, who had been spreading ruin along
the Bristol Channel. Porlock, however, says our informant,
"gave them so warm a reception that the greater part were
cut to pieces; and those few who escaped alive were obliged
to retire with great precipitation to their ships." In Porlock

church there are stones that are marked by fire—a record, perhaps, of an assault by Harold in the year 1052.

We stayed in Porlock only for a day, and then for the night of May 28 we went to Dunster.

Dunster Castle.

XLVII. DUNSTER

DUNSTER lies off the coast highroad by a quarter of a mile. This wide pavement from Bath and London has a center streak of paint to hold motors to their proper sides. It sweeps around the foot of a hill quite near the town and rushes to the west. A secondary thoroughfare does, indeed, cross Dunster's market place, but it has only the villages of Exmoor strung on its narrower thread. Because of its retired position, Dunster's High Street has a semblance of the past.

Its generous width invites cottagers to stand about and talk.
It is a street on which old ladies meet at the butcher's door
and exchange the rheumatism of one for the goiter of the
other. And camomile is argued against sassafras.

Above one end of the street you see Dunster Castle standing in a wooded park. At the other end, squarely in the
middle of the cobbles, is an Elizabethan yarn-market—a
hexagonal band-stand kind of building, but with a charm

Dunster Cottages

of outline. Shops are closely set. There are no trees, yet this
very bareness induces friendly gossip from door to door.
As Dunster is somewhat out of the stream of tourists, its
shops show few windows of brass knockers and postcards.
They are evidently supported by native buyers, and they
take their shillings from their neighbors rather than a foreign coin from strangers. This makes for milder manners; for
towns that are too thick with trippers assume the brusque-
ness of a county fair.

Around the corner from the High Street is the parish
church. This foundation is of Norman origin and it still
shows remnants of the eleventh century, which, however, are

quite smothered in later types of architecture. Dunster's cell, at its inception, was Benedictine and it was an offshoot of the Priory of Bath. Its old garden and monastic walls may still be seen. Against the village street, but inside the church enclosure, is a building of Tudor appearance. In its original state, this was the dwelling of the parish priest. In the window there is now a sign of teas and clotted cream. In the High Street near by there is a building called "The Nunnery," for no evident reason, as no convent of women is recorded hereabouts.

Dunster Castle is comparatively modern—part Tudor and part of the eighteenth century—but it was built to replace a fortress erected at the Conquest. This first castle was besieged by King Stephen in his Barons' Wars, when a certain Lord Mohun "was busy laying waste the whole countryside." There was a Lord Mohun many hundreds of years later who attempted to abduct Mrs. Bracegirdle as she issued from Covent Garden Theatre—an adventure mentioned in "Henry Esmond." The Mohuns, therefore, as acquaintances of Thackeray, are old friends of ours.

The great days of Dunster Castle were in the civil wars, when the Luttrells—its owners to this present day—stood hotly for parliament and resisted the king's army. For this allegiance they lost their title. In the chronicles of Dunster we run on William Prynne, another old friend to any student of this period. Prynne wrote a book called "Histrio-Mastix," directed against stage-plays; and for slander against Charles I and the queen had his ears cut off. He was a vicious old puritan—a nuisance even to Oliver Cromwell. Prynne was imprisoned at Dunster Castle and used his enforced leisure in arranging the muniments of the Luttrell family. Luttrell Castle is closed to tourists, although a part of the gardens are open on certain days. It was quite by accident that we got over a fence at the foot of the gardens and saw a bit of them without a fee.

We narrowly missed a letter of introduction to Dunster's exalted family. "I wish I had known you were going there," was written to Mary by an English lady. "I would have given you a note to my dear old friends." It was a happy escape, as my ruffled tweeds would have made a bad impression on the butler.

The best of Dunster is not its High Street, although that

Old Mill—
Dunster—

is charming, or its church or castle. If one will follow a road that eventually leads to Exmoor until he comes to the town's last house, he will find, by asking questions of any one he meets, an old mill beside a stream that comes brawling from the hills. This mill is now used as a public laundry, but its dirty business is conducted with discretion inside its walls and offers the lane outside no hint of soiled apparel. The mill wheels are out of use and green with moss; and here is a little garden beside the noisy stream. It is a spot where even a bearded man might write a sonnet without shame. It is a damp, dripping, green hollow carved from the hillside and the arching trees. The grass is always beaded here, and water forever in a hurry.

And hereabouts, on another lane, is a nest of thatched cottages with a foot-bridge that was built for donkeys packed with wool. The River Avill slides below on glistening pebbles. The water shines in sunlight and holds the trees in wavering shadow.

We stayed at the Luttrell Arms, which is the equal of any English country hotel that I happen to have found on many trips through many parts of England. I am aware that it is customary to put Broadway's Lyggon Arms at the top; but this famous inn is too crowded with motors, and its quaintness is too conscious of itself. I stayed there once in a little attic below the roof; and it was small comfort that there was Jacobean furniture in the better bedrooms I could not get. I used that room later in a story as a scene of violence; and I am reminded by this of a talk with Earl Derr Biggers in which he informed me that he got even with an overcharge in London by using that hotel for a murder in the *talkies*.

We liked the Luttrell Arms. Were this book of mine to be bought by a hundred thousand travelers, I would suppress my enthusiasm, for it would be a shame to have their accumulated motors soil its quietness. Just among the few of us I drop a hint—put Dunster on your schedule into Devon. Ask the young woman at the wicket of the Luttrell Arms to take you to the Tudor kitchen that is now a parlor, then out to the garden where half-buried embankments beyond the wall mark a battle of the civil wars.

During our visit a younger son of the English King came for breakfast to the Luttrell Arms, on a trip of inspection to a near-by army station. We missed him, for that morning we were late at kippers. We saw his empty dishes on a table in the common dining-room, and we thrilled at the crumbs he left.

We spent only two nights at Dunster, and then our journey began again. We are now headed through Somerset towards Bath.

Cleeve Abbey gate -

XLVIII. ACROSS SOMERSET

THE HORIZON of every journey for these several weeks had been rimmed with barren heath. Every night's lodging had heard the ocean pounding at its door. St. Ives, Penzance, Tintagel, Lynmouth, had looked on stormy water. Fowey and Boscastle, although sheltered by headlands, had heard the washing of the tides. But now we leave all this. Hence-

forth, all the way to Bath, except for the slight Quantocks
and the Chilterns, our road will lead through meadows that
are drained by ditches and are hardly above the level of
the sea.

On May 30th, we piled our luggage in a motor for the
last stage of our trip—to Glastonbury, to Wells and Bath,
to our steamer at Southampton. We shall pause today at
Cleeve Abbey, and then at Nether Stowey.

Few travelers go to Cleeve. One wonders why some of
England's ruins are so famous and others so neglected. Kenilworth is crowded, yet Tamworth's rusty key unlocks a finer
castle. Tintern, Melrose and Fountains are on every tourist's route and deserve their fame, but Beaulieu's empty
Abbey is quite as beautiful. Stonehenge is thick with chars-
à-bancs, yet Avebury holds a larger Druid mystery and its
cromlechs stand forgotten in the meadows. The Maiden Castle's lonely upland is for sheep alone. There is no tripper
at Bodiam down in Kent. These preferences are not confined to ruins. Every one has gone to Blenheim, yet Arundel
Castle is set in a lovely park beside a lake and its lawns are
quite deserted. There are crowds at Hampton Court, none
at Knole House. Broadway honks with motors, but at Dunster there is silence. The Cheshire Caves and the Devil's
Dyke are thronged, but Silbury rises from a lonely plain
and holds forgotten centuries in fee. We can account for
some of these preferences by proximity and easy access—
and by advertising. Sir Walter Scott made Kenilworth a
noisy center, and after that a journey there was habit. Or
perhaps the tourist agencies are sly. They send their clients
only to hackneyed places and save the rest for future ex-
ploitation.

We make no assertion that Cleeve Abbey is as beautiful
as Fountains. No spot is, this side of dreamland. At Fountains there is magic, whether in storm or sunlight. There
is no lake at Cleeve where nature might paint the summer

clouds. Cleeve's ruins, however, are enough to halt even a
jaded tourist for an hour. Its cicerone, moreover, has never
learned a distressing patter. He can be interrupted without
going back to chapter one. He has instructive theories as to
the state of Cleeve's original walls and their uses.

Cleeve Abbey was founded under Cistercian rule towards
the close of the twelfth century. In 1537 a king's receiver
was sent here to determine "whether to dissolve it," and he
was so touched by "seventeen priests of honest life who keep
hospitality" that he recommended that Cleeve be spared.
Perhaps this receiver was influenced by the legend above the
Abbey's door:

> Patens porta esto,
> Nulli claudaris honesto.

"Let our gate never be closed to honest men," we translate
from our rusty Latin. It was not long, however, before Henry
the Eighth and Thomas Cromwell coveted the lead on the
roof and the gold vessels of the altar. "The house fell in that
very spring."

Of Cleeve's hospitality towards all honest men there is
evidence in a great gate-house still standing, for it was in
this building that the Abbey's guests were lodged. In those
days of infrequent inns, any traveler if caught by night
within the sound of Angelus or compline bell, had only
to knock for a bed and dinner.

There are ruined cloisters at Cleeve—a refectory, a dormi-
tory, a chapter-house, a common room, cellars and kitchens.
The church is entirely gone, but its site is marked by a
stub of foundations in a meadow beside the cloister. All
of Cleeve's glass is knocked away, its walls are ragged, its
mullions shattered, its pavements piled with broken decorations. Even those few roofs that yet are left show evidence
of pillage. "Pay your visit to Cleeve," writes our historian,
Edward Hutton, "and hurry away lest it remain too long in

your heart and make you out of love with your own day.
These old places which men built for God's delight and for
love, and because there was something in the world which
is no longer to be found, or not in any satisfying quantity,
keep something about them which may easily drive us mad,
fill us with misery and unavailing regret."

This is a bit too strong. We would rather quote Charles
Lamb when he visited an old home of his that had been
destroyed: "Had I seen those brick-and-mortar knaves at
their process of destruction, at the plucking of every pannel
I should have felt the varlets at my heart." Nor is Hutton's
contempt entirely justified. "God's delight" may possibly be
as strong today in a modern hospital where the poor receive relief without pay. It may even reside in wireless sets
and the cure of diphtheria, in central heating and anaesthesia. And if Babe Ruth bulks larger than St. Bernard, base-
ball, at least, is better than extermination by the Danes or
bubonic plague.

As far as sheer beauty is concerned, Cleeve was no doubt
lovelier before its roofs had fallen in; but there is a drop
of comfort in knowing that in those old days no stranger
would have been admitted to the cloisters. He would have
been kept strictly inside the guest house, lest this contact
of the outside world soil a piety within. Cleeve, at the top
of its undestroyed beauty, existed chiefly for those who had
taken its vows.

A Catholic historian has written that the thirteenth was
the greatest of all centuries. He cites the building of the
cathedrals, the founding of the universities, the signing of
the Magna Carta, the origins of representative government,
"something like constitutional guarantees throughout the
west of Europe," the education of the masses. His four hundred pages discuss art and piety. He affirms that the greatest beauty contrived by man lay in the shadows of the cathedral vaults enriched with colored glass—and that it is in faith,

and not in reason, that man has scaled his noblest heights, in emotion rather than in intellect. But his definition neglects a cruel dogma, suffering and filth, persecution and judicial murder, hard denials, privation and starved living. His argument omits the loneliness of a world that had no traveled roads in winter, the pain that had no cure, death from insufficient causes.

Yet something today, no doubt, is lost. Our new progress is too scornful of its legacy, too content to build itself anew on green foundations. Something of that faith that died with Cleeves would enrich our lives today. Reason constructed the great ships on the ocean, but faith built Chartres and Fountains. An ancient shrine, in these present antiseptic days, is but the end of a holiday excursion and a place for a picnic lunch.

— Alfoxden —

XLIX. NETHER STOWEY

WE CIRCLED the Quantocks to the north, traversed a wooded park and came to the manor-house of Alfoxden. It was here that Wordsworth lived for a brief season while Coleridge was residing at Nether Stowey, about three miles distant across the hills. Alfoxden is a fine big country-house designed for a heavy purse—too large, we think, to have suited entirely a poet who would presently live contented in a Grasmere cottage. We have William Hazlitt's word, however, that Wordsworth got it rent free; with another contrary story that his rent was often in arrears. The woods around Alfoxden must have given him good matter for his verse. At our arrival a small boy was swinging on a gate; but our inquiry about Wordsworth met with a vacant stare. For the present we shall push on to Nether Stowey, where Coleridge lived for a part of the years 1797 and 1798. These two poetic neighbors can be discussed together.

Nether Stowey was a disappointment—a long barren street of close-set cottages with monotonous unbroken roof-lines merging like a child's example of perspective. "Dear gutter of Stowey" it was once described. It was a most unlikely town for a poet to select. Another street and several paths led upwards to the south towards the Quantocks; but except on their higher reaches, where extensive country might be in prospect, neither the town nor its immediate district seemed to have an ounce of stimulus.

It may have been this negation that commended Nether Stowey to Coleridge—a town where he might study in retirement without distraction and regain his health; for in his letters we find a reference to neuralgia, a blister under his right ear and "twenty-five drops of laudanum every five hours." Not so long before this, moreover, there had been an unsuccessful love-passage with a certain Mary Evans; and although in love's first rebound Coleridge had married Sarah Fricker, perhaps the old wound still needed time and country air to heal.

But the immediate cause in the selection of Stowey was Thomas Poole, a tanner by profession and a friend who had come to Coleridge's assistance several times in financial stress. It was to Poole that Coleridge had written about the blister and the laudanum, together with inquiries about Nether Stowey as a place to live. We find Coleridge, still in residence near Bristol, seeking "a horse of tolerable meekness" on which to ride to Stowey to visit Poole. On his return there were more letters asking him to look about and learn what could be leased. Although Poole's comment on a certain wayside cottage had little but "evil to say of its accommodations," Coleridge was interested.

It seems that there was an attached garden, and this was a strong persuasion. "Literature," he told Poole, "though I shall never abandon it, will always be a secondary object with me. . . . I would rather be an expert, self-sustaining gardener than a Milton, if I could not unite both." Authors are queer birds. They are forever expressing a preference for romantic cabbages. And all persons of distinction seem to be looking forward to a farm and quiet living. Was it not a Roman emperor who deserted his throne and went off across the Adriatic to find a plot of ground where he might hoe in peace? And if his cottage there contained five hundred rooms, it merely shows his eagerness to do it right. We can quote from another letter of Coleridge written about this time. "My farm will be a garden of one acre and a half, in which I mean to raise vegetables and corn [*cabbages, beyond a doubt!*] for myself and wife, and feed a couple of snouted and grunting cousins from the refuse. My evenings I shall devote to literature, and by reviews in the Magazine and other shilling-scavengering, shall probably gain £40 a year. . . . I am not fit for *public life;* yet the light shall stream to a far distance from the taper in my cottage window." It was in the last days of the year 1796 that Coleridge, his wife and infant son moved to cramped rooms at Nether Stowey.

Several weeks ago in our travels, we parted company with Coleridge at Ottery St. Mary, when he was a lad of nine years of age and was leaving for Charterhouse School in

London. At Nether Stowey we encounter him as a man of
twenty-four, not as yet famous, it is true, but known at least
to Charles Lamb, to Robert Southey, to William Hazlitt
and the Wordsworths as a prodigy of learning in which
strange flames of genius burned. For had he not recently
commissioned a friend in London to buy him the works
of "Jamblichus, Proclus, Porphyry, the Emperor Julian,
Sidonius Apollinaris, and Plotinus—a little Neo-Platonic

—Nether Stowey—

library"? Was there not also a flash of thought in those long
evenings with Lamb and Wordsworth that promised a miracle to come?

After several years at Charterhouse with Charles Lamb,
Coleridge had gone to Cambridge, had offered marriage to
Mary Evans to be repulsed, had incurred debts that made
his college residence an embarrassment, had enlisted for a
brief term as a dragoon in the English army, had bought
his discharge with the money of his friends, had returned
to Cambridge, had visited Oxford, where he met Southey.
A dragoon! A mounted soldier! That reference to a "horse
of tolerable meekness" shows the absurdity of Coleridge's
military service.

It was in discussion with Southey that Pantisocracy was devised—a kind of communistic Brook Farm to be started on the banks of the Susquehanna in Pennsylvania. This location was selected because the name was pretty in English ears and it was so far distant that no one could know of its defects. Had not Rousseau selected the American Indian for his treatises on Utopia—the Iroquois being too remote for anything but romantic gossip to filter back? Although now engaged to Sarah Fricker, Coleridge retreated to London —perhaps to brood on Mary Evans. Southey, engaged to Sarah's sister, followed him and brought him back to Bristol to be married. Coleridge and his wife took a cottage at Clevedon, near Bristol, and we soon find him and Southey engaged in a joint editorship of a new paper, *The Watchman,* which lasted, however, only a few weeks.

After that came residence at Nether Stowey.

William and Dorothy Wordsworth had met Coleridge in Bristol in the brief days of *The Watchman* and being mightily impressed with his learning and genius, they came to visit the Coleridges in their new home in Stowey. This admiration still increasing, they presently rented Alfoxden to be near their friend. *Friend,* for Sarah seems not to have counted. She was a bit too domestic, we fear, too ready to work on Mondays at the wash. A necessary person, Sarah, but not addicted to nightingales and nature's frenzy.

Coleridge "is a wonderful man," wrote Dorothy Wordsworth. "His conversation teems with soul, mind and spirit. . . . At first I thought him very plain, that is for about three minutes: he is pale, thin, has a wide mouth, thick lips, and not very good teeth, longish, loose-growing, half-curling, rough black hair. But if you hear him speak for five minutes, you think no more of them. His eye is large and full, and not very dark, but grey—such an eye as would receive from a heavy soul the dullest expression; but it speaks every emotion of his animated mind."

Thin! We had forgotten this. We must amend our former comment about his fatness on Porlock Hill.

Dorothy's diary repeats many times her walks with Coleridge in the woods. One wonders where Sarah was all this time. We discover, however, that on one occasion when a caller came from London he found Sarah alone in the house with a tub of week's washing. Life awards both nightingales and yellow soap. Dorothy's diary turns our sympathy somewhat towards the laundry. And we shall not forget that it was Sarah who mended Samuel's socks.

The triangular relationship with the Wordsworths is sketched in a life of Coleridge by J. Dykes Campbell. "They saw as much of one another as if the width of a street instead of a pair of coombs had separated their several abodes. It was a rich and fruitful time for all three—seed-time at once and harvest; and its happy influences spread far beyond their own individual selves. The gulf-stream which rose in the Quantocks warmed and is still warming distant shores. Although Dorothy Wordsworth produced nothing directly, her influence on both men was of the highest importance. . . . The best work of both poets was done, alike by the Quantocks and by the Lakes, under the direct influence of her companionship."

Samuel's socks and Sarah's soap! We must not forget them entirely.

"So stupendous," writes Edmund Gosse, "was the importance of the verse written on the Quantocks in 1797 and 1798, that if Wordsworth and Coleridge had died at the close of the latter year, we should, indeed, have lost a great deal of valuable poetry, especially of Wordsworth's; but the direction taken by literature would scarcely have been modified in the slightest degree." How rapid was the change of poetry's scope and purpose in the next succeeding years can be learned from a comparison between Gray and Shelley—a cold perfection that has turned to flame.

Charles Lamb heard about "the farm," wrote humorously, "What does your worship know about farming?" but came to visit with his sister Mary. Coleridge refers to the Lambs in "This Lime-tree Bower My Prison."

> My gentle-hearted Charles! for thou hast pined
> And hungered after Nature, many a year,
> In the great City pent, winning thy way
> With sad yet patient soul, through evil and pain
> And strange calamity!

This reference to himself irritated Lamb. He liked London, and he had never "hungered after nature." He was happiest in the crowds of the Strand. He wasn't a "sad yet patient soul." He was a wit, and he sat up late and drank. Nor was he inclined to pity himself for the "strange calamity" of his sister's intermittent insanity. And "gentle-hearted Charles" rubbed him particularly the wrong way. "In the next edition . . ." he wrote to Coleridge, "please to . . . substitute 'drunken-dog . . . stuttering,' or any other epithet which truly and properly belongs to the gentleman in question."

Mary Lamb having had a return of insanity a few months after this visit, Coleridge suggested that she come to live with them at Stowey during her convalescence. Lamb declined the invitation. "You would almost make her dance within an inch of the precipice," he wrote. "She must be with duller fancies and cooler intellects. I know a young man of this description, who has suited her these twenty years, and may live to do so still, if we are one day restored to each other."

In April, 1798, William Hazlitt, already a worshiper of Coleridge, came to Stowey. This visit is recorded in his essay "My First Acquaintance with Poets." Hazlitt walked to Stowey and was taken almost at once to Alfoxden. "I slept that night," he writes, "in an old room with blue hangings." William Wordsworth was from home at the time of this visit, but Hazlitt met him later at Stowey and comments on his "brown fustian jacket and striped pantaloons." Instantly, he adds, Wordsworth "began to make havoc of the half of a Cheshire cheese." We may be sure about this cheese. Hazlitt was always meticulous as regards food. No English writer has furnished such exhaustive lists of viands encountered in his travels. Of this particular visit to Stowey, he mentioned "tea, toast, eggs and honey" on one occasion; a quaff of flip on another; and on a third "some excellent rashers of fried bacon and eggs."

We may learn from Hazlitt that "Wordsworth always wrote . . . walking up and down a straight gravel-walk, or in some spot where the continuity of his verse met with no collateral interruption." Coleridge, on the contrary, "liked to compose in walking over uneven ground or breaking through the straggling branches of a copse-wood." Hazlitt spent three weeks with Coleridge—a visit that included a walk down the coast to Lynton, a long day's march with feet keeping time "to the echoes of Coleridge's tongue." "I observed," he continues, "that he continually crossed me on the way by shifting from one side of the foot-path to the other. This struck me as an odd movement; but I did not at that time connect it with any instability of purpose or voluntary change of principle, as I have done since."

Coleridge had been in correspondence with John Thelwall. Thelwall was a disciple of French revolutionary doctrine, was a member of a notorious Society of the Friends of the People, had uttered seditious speeches and had written inflammatory pamphlets. He had been confined in the Tower of London for a brief period in the year 1794. Thelwall was still under espionage when he came to visit Coleridge at Nether Stowey, and here he was suspected of fresh plots. His visit is recorded by Coleridge. "We were once sitting in a beautiful recess in the Quantocks, when I said to him, 'Citizen John, this is a fine place to talk treason in!' 'Nay, Citizen Samuel,' he replied, 'it is rather a place to make a man forget that there is any necessity for treason.' " Thelwall became intimate with Wordsworth, who was himself still warm with the doctrines of the rights of man. The owner of Alfoxden objected and declined to renew the lease. It was in the midst of this unpleasant friction that Coleridge tired of Stowey and departed with his wife to Germany for the study of philosophy. German metaphysic, henceforth, was to cloud the Pierian pool that had bubbled in the Quantocks.

Coleridge's house at Nether Stowey was a disappointment —no rose-clad walls or any vista across a garden—no evidence even of pigs and cabbages. Its front windows looked on a narrow barren street and a nonconformist chapel across the way. The house had only two rooms downstairs that we might see, with a hint of a present tenant's kitchen at the rear. One of these rooms was a museum, but still with a great fireplace that must have been a comfort on a chilly night. On the walls there were photographs of Coleridge and of all his friends; and there was a case of books and a register for tourists who had paid a sixpence at the door.

Upstairs we could find two bedrooms only. We can only guess where every one slept—the three Coleridges, the Wordsworths, the Lambs, Charles Loyd (a paying guest), William Hazlitt and John Thelwall. Even if they came in the most convenient rotation, there must have been nights when every corner of both rooms had its pile of animated blankets. There was once a lime tree in the garden, but it has gone and the garden with it. The brook mentioned in several letters has disappeared.

We had intended to spend the night at Nether Stowey and to climb the Quantocks in the morning to discover what precious quality of wind had blown "The Ancient Mariner" this way. But the inn's appearance had no invitation and the town no charm. After leaving Coleridge's house,

we walked for a half mile into higher country and found a
pretty view above the chimneys to the north; but pretty
views are common in western England.

We had lunch at Bridgewater in a dirty little restaurant.
And here we saw a church of lofty spires. Then we crossed
ditch-drained meadows which were flooded by the ocean in
ancient times. Far to the south was the field of Sedgemoor—
the last chapter but one in the life of Monmouth. And now
from our motor we saw the sharp point of Glastonbury Tor.
Presently we arrived at the town and at the George.

"A double room with an open fire"—a chorus that has
ended so many of our days of travel.

-Glastonbury Abbey-

L. GLASTONBURY

GLASTONBURY has been called "the cradle of Christ in
Britain, the foundation and the root of our happiness and
our civilization." And in support of this tall assertion, legend
makes out a pretty case. For it tells us that Joseph of Arimathea, having obtained the body of the Christ, brought its

blood to England—blood that nourished a holy thorn whose offshoots are living to this day. This westward journey must have happened, if at all, in the second half of the first century. All of Europe, all of the world, was still pagan. There was no organization that could be called a Christian church, merely a group of worshipers hiding from the law in Roman catacombs—at most a few lonely figures spreading the new gospel from its center. Granting this, the altar of Glastonbury may have been Christianity's first shrine, really its first church, a first cross to signalize openly the martyrdom of Christ.

Rome's military conquest of the first century was pagan; and England, except for a legendary Glastonbury, stayed pagan through Roman rule and during the first breakdown that followed the departure of its legions. It was a country in which Woden fought with Mars. When St. Augustine came to England in 597 and Canterbury became a Christian shrine, one wonders how much of Glastonbury was left. It seems improbable that it could have endured the black ages of the Saxons and Jutes, or that St. Augustine could have found more than a ruined church of wattles whose meaning the natives could not guess. It seems more gracious, however, to accept legend and to believe that Glastonbury provides us a continual thread of Christian thought from apostolic days to the present time. Tennyson believed this, at least for poetic use. "From old books I know," he wrote

> That Joseph came of old to Glastonbury,
> And there the heathen Prince, Arviragus,
> Gave him an isle of marsh whereon to build;
> And there he built with wattles from the marsh
> A little lonely church. . . .

But Glastonbury was famous even before the reputed coming of Joseph of Arimathea, and his altar was not the first shrine to be worshiped here. Glastonbury Tor, just outside the town, rises five hundred feet above marshy ground. It was once a tall island on a shallow coast washed by the tides of the Bristol Channel. Under Celtic ritual, it was an island of the blessed, a place of departed spirits, akin to the Valhalla of the north. Pilgrimages today still gather on this windy top of Avalon; and pilgrims trudged up its steep sides a thousand years, maybe, before Julius Caesar landed under Dover's cliffs. Any sharp hill-top, as we have already hinted, must be suspected as a seat of Celtic worship, and here at Avalon the evidence seems sure. Man, in his exaltation, has always sought a nearness to the clouds.

Glastonbury's first actual history resides in a charter of the year 704, in which there is reference to a wooden church. This building was swept away by fire in 1184, to be replaced by Henry II—a structure, in turn, whose ruin today is called the "Chapel of St. Joseph."

It is said that St. Patrick is buried at Glastonbury, and Edmund the Elder, Edgar and Edmund Ironsides. Here was the grave of King Arthur, who departed from Tintagel to fight a last battle against his enemies. To Glastonbury was carried the body of Guinevere "all a summer's day from Amesbury" to be placed beside him. At Glastonbury were interred the bones of St. Beda and of St. David of Wales.

And St. Dunstan, when it came his turn to die, was carried to this shrine above the marsh. This was appropriate, for it was Dunstan who chased the devil out of Glastonbury. Dunstan was always chasing devils—one in particular, we remember, down in Sussex who was digging the Devil's Dyke to drown the churches of the Weald. The Sussex devil, in trying to save his nose from Dunstan's red-hot tongs, leaped in fright across the hills, with Dunstan pelting after. It was only by the narrowest squeak that his Majesty escaped a blister on his nose, for he had barely time to thrust it into the springs of Tunbridge Wells. To this very day, their waters taste of sulphur. As for the devil at Glastonbury, he

came to Dunstan "in an eventide in the likeness of a woman,
as he was busy to make a chalice." Unluckily for the devil
there was no near-by spring to save him, and Dunstan got
his hot tongs so firmly fixed upon his nose that never afterwards "the devil had lust to tempt him."

Glastonbury's history is confusing. There are references
to Norman charters, the names of bishops, the listing of
new buildings, fires and their destruction, travelers' tales on
the state of the Abbey at their several visits. The monastery
was dissolved in 1539. Its doom was written in Thomas
Cromwell's own hand, with instructions that its abbot be
tried and hanged, that the evidence be well sorted to exclude
any chance of acquittal. The abbot, on this prearranged condemnation, was dragged on a hurdle from Wells to Glastonbury and was hanged on Tor Hill. The king's receivers took
the valuable lead from the Abbey's roof, stole the vestments
and utensils of the altar, knocked down the roofs and vault-
ings, and left the stumps of the walls to be the usual quarry
for secular construction. But even such desecration did not
destroy Glastonbury's shrine. The ruins are still today a
mecca for Catholics and Protestants alike. We are ourselves
to see this afternoon a procession of priests with a singing
congregation at its heels.

We were given an excellent room at the George Hotel.
The four-post beds were partly modern, but everything else
was old—the half-timbering and plaster of the walls, the fireplace, floors and window mullions. The plumbing, especially, was genuinely Tudor.

Thomas Burke, in his list of ancient English inns, assigns
the year 1475 as the origin of the George Hotel. Its age,
however, impressed him less than certain cheese-cakes he
once ate there. "Whenever I see the word 'cheese-cakes,' " he
writes, "I think at once of the George, at Glastonbury. I
ought to think of it," he continues, "without any such mean
aid: it has so many facets to touch and stir the mind. I

ought to remember it by its stone hall, its stone staircase, its deep, recessed lounge, its mullioned windows, its Penitents' bench, and the queer snuggeries of its hall that have the appearance of chapels in a cathedral . . . but I think of cheese-cakes."

Most of us, if we were honest, would confess that we associate hotels with food. And towns with food. An artichoke will bring back Paris, an omelette fetch Mont-Saint-Michel. And for yourself, dear reader, has not a certain delicious sauce marked for you these many years some French resort?

But English writers are especially susceptible to good food. We can trace Dickens all around England by his honest beef and mutton. The persons of English novels sit indefinitely at dinner. Essayists are always eating. We might learn on what Hazlitt dined through a dozen volumes. It is a "boiled scrag-end of mutton and hot potatoes" at Winterslow—"a partridge getting ready" on another night. We find him again calling for "eggs and a rasher, a rabbit smothered in onions." "It was on the tenth of April, 1798," he writes once more, that he sat down "at the inn at Llangollen over a bottle of sherry and a cold chicken." On the evening that he first talked with Coleridge, "I remember," he wrote, "the leg of Welsh mutton and the turnips on the table." In his peerless essay "On a Sun Dial," he breaks off from a disquisition on eternity to remark on the odor of bacon. "On Going a Journey" refers succulently to "a dish of sweet-breads."

We can discover in Hazlitt no mention of the George at Glastonbury. This hotel was doubtless too famous and too stiff in price for one who traveled with so lean a purse. He liked hostelries more modest. His lodgings at Winterslow were cramped and mean. His inn at Llangollen is of small pretense. "How fine it is," he once wrote, "to enter some old town . . . and then after inquiring for the best entertainment that the place affords, to 'take one's ease at one's inn.'" There is nothing in this about wiring ahead for a porcelain tub or a bedroom with stone mullions.

There are two chief sights at Glastonbury—the ruins of the Abbey and the Glastonbury Tor. Of the Abbey there is left just enough of the walls to show the outlines of many buildings; and enough extra foundations, almost level with the grass, to indicate where other buildings once existed. The ruins are tended with loving care. The sunlit interior of the church, now without a roof, is planted with grass that is dotted with daisies and blue flowers for which I have no name.

One can explore these outlines of the Abbey's buildings and conjecture which of them marks the convent's kitchen, its refectory or sacristy. He can pry about in cellarways and confirm his guesses by the placards on the fallen walls. Or he can find a bench which commands a general view. Both ways have their advantage. It is merely a question whether one prefers a dozen hasty snap-shots for his doubtful recollection or a more enduring time-exposure.

Other abbey ruins are more beautiful than those of Glastonbury—Fountains, for example—but there is enough beauty here for any reasonable eye; and it is joined to such splendid traditions as to make Glastonbury the most crowded mecca of pilgrimage in England. Nor did a hundred trippers or the honking of their motors in the street outside entirely soil the peacefulness of these wide lawns and crumbling walls.

Towards the end of the afternoon, as we were taking tea in our Elizabethan bedroom in front of our Norman fire, we heard the music of a band. Looking out of the window, we saw a procession of pilgrims coming down the street and from the hill. In front was the brassy hymn. Behind the music was a company of priests in their robes of office, open-mouthed like cherubim in song. And then there followed a huge throng—a thousand, at least, of men, women and

children, with monk-like creatures at the side to keep them
two by two.

Our waiter had entered with more toast and Somerset's
imitation of Devon's clotted cream.

"What's it all about?" I asked.

"It's the Roman Catholics," he answered, with just that
curling of the lip that denotes a heretic. "Next week there
is to be a pilgrimage of the Church of England."

"To the same shrine?" Mary asked.

"Yes," he answered. "At the top of Avalon. Beside the
tower."

"And I suppose if both processions went up together," I
continued, "there would be a bit of a mix-up."

"Two lumps?" our waiter asked.

The hymn died slowly in the distance, to be replaced
by the monotonous tramp of feet. And presently even this
died off to leave silence in the street. We went back to our
clotted cream beside our Norman fire. In fifteen minutes
there was a roar of chars-à-bancs—a dozen of them. They
contained the pilgrims departing home to Bath and Bristol
and other cities to the north. No wife of Bath now rides
upon a donkey, and gasoline has replaced the pilgrim's staff.
There was an interval of honking horns and again Glastonbury's streets were quiet.

It was on the hint of this pilgrimage, before dinner when
a dirty little drizzle had turned to sunlight, that we set out to
climb the Tor. At the edge of town a steep path leads upwards through a meadow and climbs a narrow stile that must
have broken for a moment the processional hymn of an hour
before. There were sheep and cattle on the hill, ignorant
that they were grazing near the Holy Thorn.

The top of Avalon, so lately crowded with trippers, was
now bare of any pilgrims but ourselves. Before us lay a
comprehensive map of all this district—its towns and roads
and drainage ditches, its meadows and distant hills. It

seemed strange, we reasoned, that here on this lofty footing man has stood in worship since Egypt's oldest pyramid was new. Druid rites called this a place of blessed spirits. And the wind today seemed humming to itself in far-off contentment the Valkyries' call.

We were back at the George for dinner.

We have commented on the appetite of the English essayists. And now to support our assertion we have pulled down a few volumes—but just at random. Addison described the London coffee-houses too succulently for a man of abstemious stomach, and his friend Steele did some of his mightiest work with his head in ice. At the Cheshire Cheese there is a Johnson's chair, with legends of milk punch and meat pies. Charles Lamb immortalized roast pig. Thackeray wrote "The Ballad of Bouillabaisse." For *The Edinburgh Review* Sydney Smith suggested a Latin motto—We cultivate literature on a little oatmeal—and these pathetic words from a Scottish attic prove a love for heavy meat. Hilaire Belloc seems to be forever eating cheese at country inns. Chesterton, as a monstrous fat man, is certainly not averse to any second helping. And this general obeisance to the platter is not entirely wrong. If it be natural that we love ourselves, then it is right that we be not indifferent to these stuffings of the plate that are to be annexed presently *in corpore* to advance from the stomach to the soul. As an old writer has expressed the thought—What the lion eats is lion.

The Vicars' Close
Bath

LI. WELLS AND THE CHEDDAR GORGE

SUNDAY, May 31st. This is the last of our travels, for today we are to see Wells and then thread the Cheddar Gorge to Bath, where our journey will end at the Pump Hotel. We shall divide a week between the eighteenth century and the years of Imperial Rome, then proceed to our steamer at Southampton.

We left our bags with the porter of the Swan Hotel at Wells and started out afoot. Other cathedrals are more to our taste than Wells, whose thirteenth-century façade seems too crowded with saints in bad repair—a façade, however,

that is praised by critics. But it is certain that no other
cathedral in all the British Isles is set in such a lovely garden. A stream from the Chilterns on the north has been
tutored into pools and peaceful runways. In the midst of
it sits the Bishop's Palace on an island whose wide-circling
walls hedge a lawn and a tuft of trees. A drawbridge crosses
running water.

The Palace and its garden on this Sunday morning were
closed to the public; but it was enough to stand beside the
moat and see the trees waving their branches above the
wall. It was a gay gesture—almost of invitation—as if the
trees might presently unlock the gate, when the old bishop
had trotted off to service. Swans were floating on the water,
rippling the glassy outlines of the Palace.

We decline to describe the interior of Wells Cathedral.
It is enough that we went to service, not crowding ourselves
into the choir among the city's best black cloth, but con-
tenting our tweeds with a stone bench at the western door.
We heard the organ searching for God in the shadowed
vaults.

We walked in the Vicars' Close—a long narrow yard of
fifty attached cottages beyond a gate-house. Here lived the
fifty vicars of the cathedral before the Dissolution, each vicar
with a tiny square of grass and flowers inside his gate. I do
not know the duties of a vicar in the fourteenth century
when the close was built, except that he "was a canon's
substitute." Wells, evidently, has no such armament now,
for the close is today occupied by theological students.
Among many exquisite vistas at Wells none is lovelier than
these rows of stone cottages. Any one of these houses would
be a charming home for a man of quiet ecclesiastical tastes
who sought shelter for his declining years. On the easy terms
of fancy, we bought a cottage but will sublet it until we
have come to crutches and soft food.

Only persons of chilly thought will fail to like Wells—

its walls rising from mirroring pools, its waters of drifting leaves, its trees and grass, and a mighty cathedral in the midst. Edward Hutton, our cicerone, has quite a spasm over Wells. "As you . . . gaze upon the city in the meadows at your feet, you might think it still a city of that divine and joyful kind, uplifting the heart, which was once common in England, and . . . it remains in its beauty and completeness perhaps the best example of all that we have been compelled to sacrifice to that Moloch of Industrialism which has risen to enslave us upon the ruins of the Protestant heresy." Hutton is getting a bit hot again under the collar, so we skip.

Sanctus, sanctus, sanctus, Dominus Deus Sabaoth, rang the bells. *Pleni sunt coeli et terra majestatis gloriae tuae.* We said amen, and went to the Swan Hotel for lunch.

It was towards the end of the afternoon that we set out for Bath by the way of the Cheddar Caves. These caves are a babel of shrill advertisement. There are several of them, each with its separate proprietor and its hawker at the gate to cry it up. Everywhere are huge signboards with monstrous pictures of the wonders to be seen inside—great halls inside the cliff, stalactites and stalagmites, blankets of glistening corruscated lime that are the drippings of a thousand years. If Barnum had ever heard of Cheddar Gorge, he would have bought the place, taken it apart, and set it up again on Coney Island.

Motors were quarreling for a place to park. Old ladies and children were scrambling out from under wheels and counting noses against a loss. Waiters with raw voices were bawling offers of tea and clotted cream. Tables were huddled at every cottage window and inside the enclosure of every fence. A hundred little rackets were soiling the air. It would seem as if all the noise of Somerset had met here in convention and were electing a king of discord—as if quiet Wells had banished all sounds from the garden of the Bishop's Palace, and that these malcontents were protesting here in exile. There is a legend that a church bell purges the air of devils; and, if this be true, noisy Cheddar is their refuge. Dunstan's red-hot tongs would be needed to restore a Sabbath here.

We selected a cave by the flipping of a coin and were huddled to a group of trippers who were waiting for a guide. No guide is really needed, for all of the paths are marked by ropes and the caverns would be less tiresome without his chatter. Nor is there room at Cheddar for any one to wander by himself and be lost in darkness. One can't go astray when there are two elbows in his ribs. Our cave was crowded even now in the month of May. In August, when holidays are at their height, the caves must moil with trippers. We outwitted our guide. We had walked in his crowd for a hundred yards, when another returning throng came pressing down the runway on the other side of the rope. Watching our chance, we ducked under and escaped to daylight. We missed the corruscating blanket of limestone, NATURE'S MOST MAJESTIC SIGHT, PATRONIZED BY H.R.H., and for this we are thankful.

We now motored through a great slash between cliffs and only when we had passed out of this defile did we leave the crowd of motors that were parked along the road. This defile was once another cavern until its roof fell and was carted off. It is the custom of travelers to describe Cheddar with uncontrolled ecstasy, but they must have come this way before gasoline was king.

We now entered a valley of the Chilterns and saw before us city towers and a scattered suburb.

"Bath," said our driver.

"The Pump Hotel," we answered.

We came through broad streets of modern houses, then entered the eighteenth century with its more sober fronts and stopped opposite the Roman Baths.

*The Abbey
Bath*

LII. ROMAN BATH

SAMUEL McCHORD CROTHERS laments the confusion of Rome. "It economizes space," he writes, "to have the vegetable market and the martyrdom of Giordano Bruno and the assassination of Julius Caesar all close together. But they are too close. The imagination hasn't room to turn around. Especially as the market-women are very much alive and cannot conceive that any one would come into the Piazza unless he intended to buy vegetables. Somehow the great events you have read about don't seem to have im-

pressed themselves on the neighborhood. . . . You are the
only person in the Piazza Campo de' Fiori who is thinking
about Giordano Bruno or Julius Caesar; while the price
of vegetables is as intensely interesting as it was in the year
1600 A.D. or in 44 B.C."

Bath isn't like that. It is quite conscious of its antiquities.
It is a decayed city, rather than a modern metropolis like
Rome, and it broods, therefore, of its youth. It is a repeti-
tious old lady in a rocking-chair. A street of excellent shops,
it is true, displays current London fashions; but we are sure
that every one of its broad windows would prefer to show
Roman togas or the frippery of Queen Anne's reign. Bath,
however, in some respects resembles Rome. It has so huddled its relics to a common heap that a tourist must go
ducking back and forth between the ancient and the modern
world. There are three Baths at least—a Roman city, a Bath
that was crowded with the convalescents of the eighteenth
century, and a Bath that stands today and beckons to its
healing waters. Our diary must untangle these three cities
and keep them separate.

Bath, says legend, was founded by King Bladud. If any
meticulous reader ask for a date of this origin, we reply
that Bladud was the eleventh in line from Venus, that his
son was King Lear, and that his contemporaries were the
prophet Elijah and King Solomon. One has only to run his
thumb down the margin of a family Bible, therefore, to get
almost the exact year of Bath's foundation.

"Bladud," says Geoffrey of Monmouth, "builded the city
of Kaerbadon, that is now called Bath, and fashioned hot
baths therein, meet for the needs of men, the which he
placed under the guardianship of the deity Minerva, in
whose temple he set fires that could not be quenched"—
with that consequent odor of warm flatirons, we might add,
that was lately observed by Samuel Weller during the sojourn here of Mr. Pickwick, P.P.C. Bladud was a magician.

He could fly like a bird. He tried, indeed, "to go upon the top of the air," says Geoffrey, and, when breasting a gale, he fell on a tile roof of Bath and was killed.

Another legend affirms that Bladud, while still a prince, became a leper and was banished from his father's royal court to become a swineherd. He had already given his leprosy to his pigs when he observed them one day running down a slope to wallow in thick mud. Whereon he jumped into the ooze himself and was cleansed of his foul disease, for it was beneath this mud that Bath's healing waters were already bubbling up. The legend, therefore, suggests that these hot springs were known to the ancient Britons before the Romans landed. Prince Bladud rushed home, inherited his crown and became the father of King Lear. On the table that held his bride's gifts there were cut-glass pieces from the prophet Elijah and King Solomon.

Bath's credible history starts with Rome. There is no record of the legions' discovery of these waters; but Barbeau, who is Bath's popular historian, finds a latest probable date to be 50 A.D. "The new masters of Britain," he writes, "attracted by the hot springs they esteemed so highly, founded a city around them, constructed baths, temples and buildings of all sorts, and settled there in large numbers, protected from attack by the ramparts which afterwards served as a base for the mediaeval walls." The rise of this provincial city, therefore, antedates by more than one hundred and fifty years the Baths of Caracalla in Rome itself; and the Baths of Diocletian by more than two hundred and fifty years. To find a contemporary for this healthful valley of the Avon, we must seek Nero's Golden House, now unearthed near by the Coliseum.

That Bath became an important center of provincial life, there is ample proof in the relics that the tourist sees today— fragments of carvings, pavements, lead conduits, columns with decorated capitals, remnants of heating systems, statues,

coins, all the precious litter of antiquity that is still shown
on the payment of an entrance fee. Excavation, moreover,
is confined to only a small district of the city, although
each decade reaches out in a wider circle of fresh discovery.
That the circle is still too narrow to reveal the whole of
ancient Bath seems evident enough; for its shovels have
come against the foundation walls of the city's modern buildings.

The Rome that has been found is many feet below the
surface of present Bath. The ancient city was the victim of
the slow silting of wind-blown dust that was never swept
away. Pavements here in the north are of late invention;
and it is only when a city lays down cobbles in its streets
that its proper level stays fixed against the dust that seeks
to smother it. Or shall we say, rather, that dust is the great
preserver—that it was the dust of volcanic ash that saved
Pompeii and made it our clearest document of ancient life?
Its destruction became its immortality—a text for a funeral
sermon. An antiquarian's best assistants are wind and dust.

In Rome, we might add, it is not always careless dust that
buries the ancient footings. When an emperor wished to
build himself a palace, he sometimes filled in solid the palace
walls of a predecessor with broken stones and set his new
construction on the roof. This gave no extravagant height
as these palaces were of one story. The work was accomplished by opening a hole in the vaulting of each room and
pouring in this rubble until the apartment was stuffed from
floor to vault. As one wanders today in the now-excavated
rooms of Nero's Golden House, he is told by his guide that
two later palaces are above him and that a Renaissance
church is perched on the top of the whole composite building. A tourist is told, moreover, that the Palatine Hill is
not a hill, as he was taught in school, but a succession of
palaces each one set on the roof of the one below—each
palace, when its day was done, filled in tight with rubble

as an added layer to the base of rock that serves as foundation to the latest palace to be built. If trees are growing far above, it is only nature's mite to crown the work of man.

But we must suppose that Bath was covered by careless dust, blown on the wind until it leveled up each cranny of the ancient world.

Because of the richness of its discovered treasures, however, we must not suppose that Bath was ever a mighty city and the rival of York or Lincoln, Chester or London. The argument of recovered relics, as far as it applies at all, runs to an opposite conclusion. Great cities have been too busy to find leisure for preserving their origins. Dust is not permitted, moreover, to smother a building that stands on valuable land. Where traffic is thick, narrow lanes must be widened and old structures demolished. It is usually a small town, therefore, somewhat off the track of progress, that can best afford to save its ancient footings. York was a stronghold on the north; and it saved, chiefly, its encircling wall. Chester guarded the empire against the unruly west; and only its shape is Roman. London became a great market at an early day; and its extreme antiquities are all below the Strand. Bath was none of these things. It was not even a military post, although the town was walled. Bath was remote and small, untouched by progress for more than twelve hundred years after Rome's legions left. It is in consequence of this that its ancient treasures exceed those of York or Lincoln, or Chester or London.

We must assume that the Bath of those Roman centuries was what it is today--a health resort, first for the occasional travelers who needed mending, then later for those who settled here for a longer convalescence. The Fosse Way made travel easy to this valley of the Avon from Exeter and Cirencester and points beyond. It was written in the third century that "in Britain are hot springs furnished luxuriously for human use." The patrons of the springs we may learn from tombstones—soldiers largely from the legions, with now and then a visitor from Gaul, "from so far as Metz and Chartres, but not from south of the Alps." Roman Bath endured for three hundred and fifty years, and it fell only when Rome withdrew its British legions to protect its capital from northern conquest. Dust then settled on the pavements and kept them safe for our recent discovery.

One wonders what kind of city this old Bath was. On the finding and use of the waters a temple of a Latin goddess was erected, and with it were houses for her priests. A great pool was built, with all of its usual accessories—tepidarium, frigidarium, calidarium, central heating, colonnaded pavements for exercise and gossip. Whatever you would have found at the Baths of Caracalla, you would have discovered in miniature at Bath. To attract and hold travelers, buildings for their accommodation must have been erected. Most of this has been swept away, but the pool remains with confused apartments around it and a litter of fallen ornaments. Water still trickles through lead conduits as it did when Rome's great emperors were alive.

One wonders how this Anglo-Roman Bath differed from those of Rome. It was far smaller, of course. Bath had, at most, only a few thousand inhabitants. Rome had more than a million. Twelve hundred thousand is Gibbon's estimate for the year 400 A.D. Nor could England's cold and wet climate produce the easy way of living that was common beside the Tiber. During Rome's hot summer her great baths were popular clubs for all citizens above the status of a slave. Rome resorted to them for exercise, for pleasure, for idleness and company. Rome's baths were cousins to the Coliseum and to the Circus Maximus. Diocletian and Caracalla built baths with the same idea and purpose that are now employed in modern municipalities in the erection of stadiums—councilmanic monuments on easy taxation—mighty pleasure grounds to entertain the masses and win their support. These baths of the Roman emperors absorbed the activity of idleness and made their thrones secure. A good bull-fight or a massacre of Christians made Caesar a hero. It is obvious, therefore, that all comparison between Rome and Bath breaks down in the wet fog and sparse population of the River Avon.

Roman Bath was a walled town of about twenty-three acres, with its center near the site of the present abbey. No remnant of the walls is left, nor any gate. There exist no foundations of the houses on the streets of the Roman city. That there were ancient baths under the modern city seems always to have been known, but it was not until the year 1727, when pulling down a building, that Rome's great bathing pool was found. It was after 1880 that the first extensive excavation was made that laid bare the bulk of what we see today. My own three visits to Bath have been made at intervals of several years, and each of the last two have shown considerable progress in discovery.

The Royal Crescent Bath -

LIII. BATH IN THE EIGHTEENTH CENTURY

BATH'S Roman history ends in the year 411 with the departure of the legions. For the next three hundred years, while conflicting peoples are seizing the spoils left behind by Rome, all records are obscure. Of England's black centuries history furnishes scarcely more than shadowy battles. If London went into grey twilight, it is to be expected that Bath would be submerged in darkness. We know that Bath's old name of Aquae Sulis was lost and that a new name of Akemanceaster was being used. And inch by inch the temple of a Latin goddess was sinking under dust.

In the eighth century a ray of light fell on these dark hill-

sides of the Avon. In the year 775 King Offa founded a Benedictine monastery at Bath. The ancient city of the Romans,
therefore, that had died when convalescent fashion turned
its back, came to life again with religious meditation. A
ritual of masses had replaced a softer round of pleasure. A
Nunc Dimittis was celebrated instead of the practice of
Epicurus. In the Saxon Abbey, erected when Christianity
had swept through England, Edgar was crowned king. This
coronation was a great event in Bath, and it so impressed
itself on the town's imagination that in the seventeenth century the election of a fictitious king became a custom. Beau
Nash, the monarch of Bath's fashion in the early eighteenth
century, was thus a shadowy cousin of the Saxon Edgar.

Although we must suppose that when the darkness lifted
the Roman temples and the remnant of ancient walls had
long since sunk beneath the dust, there existed more than
a mere suspicion that there were healing waters buried there.
In the twelfth century certain Latin verses praised their
power, and in the year 1138 a little hospital was built for
lepers. In the fifteenth century a decree was published to
keep order and decency in bathing. As we can hardly think
of lepers indulging in happy riot, we must suppose that by
this time the baths were used for general cure and convalescence. Leland in the sixteenth century wrote of Bath
"as very much frequented."

In the year 1616, Anne of Denmark, the wife of James I,
came to Bath to be cured. And the result of this visit was a
trickle of fashion westward out of London—old gentlemen
with gout or ladies possessed of whatever diseases were then
in vogue. One can hardly think, however, that they really
enjoyed their holidays in the crude accommodation that
was offered them. "All kinds of disorders," we read, "were
grown to their highest pitch in Bath, insomuch as the streets
and public ways of the city were become like so many dung-
hills, slaughter-houses and pig-styes. . . . The baths were

like so many beargardens, and modesty was entirely shut out of them . . . and dogs [and] cats . . . were hurled over the rails into the water, while people were bathing in it." There is no mention, as yet, of nosegays and sedan chairs, and we may be sure that life at Bath was crude.

It was in the year 1663 that Charles II and Queen Catherine came to Bath, and their visit somewhat mended Bath's discomfort, and prepared the way for the prosperity to come. Fashion was returning—a fashion hardly different from that Roman vogue that had left Bath more than twelve hundred years before. Wherever Charles II went his merry sycophants were sure to follow, and now they came rushing in a stream from London. A hedonism corrupted from Epicurus was revived. "Bath was on the way," writes Barbeau, our mentor in these facts, "to become a sort of general casino for the whole kingdom, a periodical rendezvous for polite society, and a holiday resort common to all sorts and conditions of men."

It would be an interesting study to find the origins of the modern health resort. For Roman use there had been such towns as Puteoli and Baeae, where emperors went for air and relaxing pleasure. When Tiberius built his palace at Capri, a colony of idlers must have followed him and got up games and dissipation to amuse their empty days. Other throngs pursued Diocletian to his retirement at Spalato, and Hadrian to his country villa at the foot of the Sabine Hills. The castles of the Loire were nothing but vast hotels for the lodging of the French kings' friends. Our first resorts were probably of royal contrivance and were for a selected few. If these caravansaries resembled our present hotels de luxe of the French Riviera and Palm Beach, there was a vast difference—guests had no bills to pay. Their entertainment was supported by a general tax and the sweat of peasants.

But we are thinking particularly of more recent times.

In his life of Beau Nash, Goldsmith mentions Aix, Spa and The Hague as flourishing resorts, together with a lament that Englishmen were obliged to cross the Channel for their fun. To the continent, therefore, we must look for our original resort for health and pleasure. It was possible, of course, in England to bathe in healing waters or drink sulphur and strong salts, but that was all. No gayety went as yet with convalescence. But if Bath is not the original resort of our modern world, it was quick to imitate the continental spa.

Our fancy might hint that in this dawn of fashion Roman ghosts were haunting Bath—that they were rising from the pavements of the buried city with tales of Puteoli and Baeae that had once entertained the emperors—that it was on information from the tomb that Bath revived a custom dead in England for more than twelve hundred years.

However this may be, Charles II, returning from the continent at the Restoration, had brought with him a Gallic zest for pleasure. Once an outcast, he had a palace now—a handsome allowance for pin-money—an eagerness to enjoy his crown. He was accompanied by ladies of doubtful virtue and gentlemen of no virtue whatever—an assortment that fitted the habits of a merry monarch. Under a continuance of Puritan rule, Bath would have stayed smothered under the dust of centuries. But with the Stuarts in Whitehall, all of fashion was on tiptoe for excitement and new ways to waste time. Nothing can be more fitting than that the Stuarts should invent for their country the modern health resort. At any *Hotel d'Argent et Louis d'Or,* either in Europe or America, we are the inheritors of their lazy attitude towards life. All this was happening at a time when France had not

"At this time," writes Goldsmith, "London was the only yet discovered a use for its beaches, when the Riviera had not erected its first pavilion, and when the Swiss mountains were as yet uncaptured by cog railroads.

theatre in England for pleasure and intrigue. A spirit of gaming had been introduced in the licentious age of Charles II., and had by this time thriven surprisingly. Yet all its devastations were confined to London alone. . . . Bath, Tunbridge, Scarborough, and other places of the same kind here, were then frequented only by such as really went for relief; the pleasures they afforded were merely rural, the company splenetic, rustic and vulgar. In this situation of things people of fashion had no agreeable summer retreat from the town, and usually spent that season amidst a solitude of country squires, parsons' wives and visiting tenants, or farmers; they wanted some place where they might have each other's company and win each other's money, as they had done during the winter in town." A new Bath of modern pattern was evidently needed if that phenomena of history known as the Restoration was fully to express itself.

In this development Bath was not alone, for Epsom and Tunbridge Wells were also coming into fashion. "The watering-places," writes Barbeau, "offered themselves for the purpose under the most propitious conditions. In the first place, necessity brought a certain number of sufferers together in them, who were not so ill as to be obliged to resign every kind of pleasure, and who naturally sought to enliven their enforced retirement and inactivity by all possible means. . . . With such advantages as are proper to cities, Tunbridge, Epsom and Bath, villages or little towns, combine the pleasure of the country; they are half urban, half rustic; in them the citizen finds the degree of change that he enjoys when he goes to the fields, the charm of fashionable amusement and of country surroundings; this combination drew an ever-increasing crowd of strangers, bathers, and mere idlers, to the springs."

To this list we might add social upstarts. For it was possible for persons on the edge of society and debarred from the inelastic coteries of London to cut a pretty figure here by a lavish spread of money—to buy an equality denied in Mayfair—to force and hold a position during a month of expensive holidays which they could not support throughout the year at home. There is nothing surprising in this. It is the same today. It is possible to strut in new clothes at Pasadena or along the Riviera for a reckless fortnight, and then restore the balance of the ledger by tight living at home where our neighbors know the thinness of our purse and pretense is useless.

It was in the year 1702 that Queen Anne paid her celebrated visit to Bath—a royal progress to healing waters that would henceforth mark the town with enduring fashion. Several hundred young men and women dressed in special uniform waited for the queen at the border of Somerset and fetched her to Bath along the wooded valley of the Avon on a road that was built new to serve this great occasion. There were songs, brass music, shouts and excitement. Every inn was crowded. The pumps of warm flatiron water pumped as they had never pumped before. Bath from this time onward for a hundred years was to be England's chief center of fashionable escape in the summer season from pain and boredom.

This brings us to Richard Nash and to the narration of his life that was written by Oliver Goldsmith; for Nash was the instrument by which Bath came to its highest fame.

He was born in the year 1674 and came from a family of modest competence. For several years he idled at Oxford, ogling pretty ladies instead of studying, until he was at last rusticated for intrigue. He bought an ensign's commission, thinking that a red coat would further increase his charms, and he served briefly in the army. Then between bouts at the gaming table and heavy drinking he studied law. He was conspicuous, even in poverty, for lavish dress—"the very summit of second-rate luxury," wrote Goldsmith, who himself liked plum-colored jackets. "Though very poor he was

The Roman Baths –

very fine; he spread the little gold he had in the most osten-
tatious manner, and though the gilding was but thin, he
laid it on as far as it would go. They, who know the town,"
continues Goldsmith, "cannot be unacquainted with such a
character as I describe; one who, though he may have dined
in private upon a banquet served cold from a cook's shop,
shall dress at six for the side box; one of those, whose wants
are only known to their laundress and tradesmen, and their
fine clothes to half of the nobility; who spend more in chair
hire than housekeeping, and prefer a bow from a lord to a
dinner from a commoner."

By assiduous devotion to men of wealth and station, Richard Nash became a marked man; and presently, when the
Middle Temple wished to honor King William at his coronation, it was Nash who was chosen to conduct the Temple's
pageant. For his success in this a knighthood was offered
him. Nash hinted to his monarch that an annuity should be
added to support the expense of the honor, and this suggestion failing, declined the title as impossible with his slender
purse. Nash was now a pretty fellow, as the saying went, the
kind that would "drink no wine but what was strained
through his mistress's smock." This exploit passed for wit
and as a proof of fidelity in love. If a lady did not accept the
proof, a lover went a step farther and ate "a pair of her
shoes tossed up in a fricassee." And Nash in all such ritual
was at the top of fashion, although his landlady stayed un-
paid and his door was beset by creditors who waited for his
streak of luck at the gaming table. At about this time he
won a wager by riding a cow through a village. In short, he
was the epitome of the follies that ended the seventeenth
century. The betting-book of a London club contempora-
neous with him has been published; and it includes such
things as a wager whether my Lord X— will be able to furnish proof within six months that he has seduced the Count-
ess Z—.

Nash was thirty years old when Bath was coming to be a resort of fashion; and it was, therefore, to Bath he went, like a hundred other busy idlers. The lodgings, as yet, were crude. The floors of public rooms were brown "with soot and small beer." The city was mean and contemptible, without elegant buildings or open streets or squares. Pleasure was in disorder. There was no ritual of manners.

Nash was the man that Bath needed. It needed a master of ceremonies, and had not this fop from London just achieved fame for his successful production of King William's pageant at the Temple? Under the old tradition of Saxon Edgar, Nash was elected king. It was a title unsupported by any salary or public budget—a mere fiction without police power—but it offered its holder emolument in the opportunities of profitable gambling. To Nash's credit, Goldsmith affirms that he did not cheat.

The next few years were to see great changes in the appearance of Bath and in the conduct of its pleasures. A subscription was raised for a band of music. A row of new houses was erected for more comfortable lodgings. A pavement was laid for fashion's morning promenade. The streets were surfaced, cleaned and lighted. An assembly-room was built, for chalybeate in the morning, for tea in the afternoon, for balls at night and gossip at all hours. The meadow by the river was laid out to be a garden where fashion might hear the chirping of birds and think they were nature's children. Book-shops were opened in which current publications could be bought or thumbed through on the payment of a fee. For a fee one could rent a table in a coffee-house and use its monogrammed note-paper for a letter home. There were shops of fripperies. Modistes came to town to reënforce a lady's stock of dresses. Men could buy new wigs and boots from London.

In public entertainment, Nash's will was absolute. He ordered the balls to begin at six o'clock and to end at eleven, "lest invalids might commit irregularities to counteract the benefit of the waters." Each ball opened with a minuet danced by the "two persons of the highest distinction present." At eight o'clock the country dances began, "ladies of quality, according to their rank, standing up first." Sharp at eleven, Nash held up his finger, and now the ladies cooled and "were handed to their chairs."

Rules were posted for every one's guidance at these balls. It was ordered that chair-men be quiet as they wait at the door and abstain from quarreling with their fellows. No gentleman was allowed to give away his ticket to any but gentlewomen, "unless," adds Nash with irony, "he have none of his acquaintance." Elder ladies and children were asked to "be content with a second bench at the ball, as being past or not yet come to perfection." And ladies were instructed in patience if their time to dance was delayed and they were kept waiting at the wall. It was ordered "that all whisperers of lies and scandal be taken for their authors." Nash permitted no lapses from formal dress. On one occasion the Duchess of X— appeared in what is described as a "white apron." Nash stripped it from her and threw it behind the benches, remarking that "none but abigails" wore such costumes. A great gentleman once entering the ballroom in his boots, Nash advanced with a bow and asked him if he had forgotten to bring his horse.

When a stranger arrived at Bath, he was welcomed by a peal of the Abbey's bells; and for this attention he paid the ringers a half-guinea or more in proportion to his "fortune, generosity or ostentation." At the first sounding of the chime all Bath sent out its footmen to inquire the names and titles of the new arrivals. It was now a stranger's duty to subscribe two guineas at the assembly-room for music and ballroom tickets. He laid down another guinea for the privilege of walking in the garden by the river. He gave a fee to the bookseller for the use of books. There was another fee at the coffee-house to cover the pen, ink and paper for such letters as he might write. The master of ceremonies called upon him to instruct him in the town's entertainment—the hours of parade, of tea and healing waters, the nights of minuets and country dancing, the appearance of a London actress in the theatre just constructed. He informed a stranger where boots could be made, where wigs could be combed and where flowering waistcoats were fitted to a perfect cut. Or a newcomer was acquainted with the names of the personages already come to town, with gossip that my Lord X— was being mended from the gout, that the celebrated Mr. Y— was being seen abroad with the pretty mistress Z—. Such tales as we find in the "School for Scandal" were unofficial, we must hope, and were not scattered by Nash himself.

"In the morning," writes Goldsmith, "the lady is brought in a close chair, dressed in her bathing clothes, to the bath, and, being in the water, the woman who attends her presents her with a little floating dish like a basin, into which the lady puts a handkerchief, a snuff-box and a nose-gay. She then traverses the bath . . . calls for her chair and returns to her lodgings." She is soon back in the pump-house for three glasses of chalybeate, with intervals of music and general conversation.

"Thus," continues Goldsmith, "we have the tedious morning fairly over. When noon approaches and church (if any please to go there) is done, some of the company appear upon the parade and other public walks, where they continue to chat and amuse each other till they have formed parties for the play, cards or dancing for the evening. Another part of the company divert themselves with reading in the book-sellers' shops, or are generally seen tasting the air and exercise, some on horseback, some in coaches. Some walk in the meadows round the town, winding along the side of the river Avon and the neighboring canal, while others are seen scaling some of those romantic precipices that overhang the city. . . . Every Tuesday and Friday evening is concluded with a public ball. . . . Thus Bath," concludes Goldsmith, "yields a continued rotation of diversions, and people of all ways of thinking, even from the libertine to the Methodist, have it in their power to complete the day with employments suited to their inclinations."

During the time when Beau Nash was Bath's social dictator, another man was using equal talents to convert a muddy village into a city of enduring beauty. Ralph Allen, as deputy postmaster of Bath, had observed that London was England's only clearing-house in the exchange of letters; and he therefore devised in 1720 a carriage of mail cross-country to his private profit. For a period of rather more than forty years this service netted him an average return of ten thousand pounds. This huge amount, together with an income from the quarrying of stone, made him the wealthiest man of Bath. He planned for his own use a great house several miles from town, and called in John Wood for architect. Prior Park "remains one of the finest eighteenth-century palaces in the country." Allen's greatest task, however, lay in the streets of Bath. The North and South Parades were designed and erected by Wood under his patronage and cost. Queen's Square, Gay Street, the Circus, the old Assembly-rooms were built. Later, on the designs of another John Wood, his son, there were added the Royal Crescent, the Upper Assembly-rooms, the Hot Bath, the Royal Private Bath and many streets and other buildings.

The two Woods were more than the architects of many buildings here and there. They were the builders of a city, of which each structure was adapted to a general whole. Vistas were provided. Low ground and hillsides were utilized with a regard to their natural advantages. The site of the parades was chosen for its outlook on the river. The

Pumphouse completed the Abbey's open square. A paved bankside commanded the towers of this lantern of the west. It was a task such as Paris imposed on Haussmann in the nineteenth century—such as designed the city of Washington in the early days of our republic. "The peculiar merit of the Woods," writes Barbeau, "in proposing and accomplishing this task was they were architects and not mere builders, that they had the beauty of the city they were transforming always before their eyes, that they conceived and carried out a vast and harmonic whole."

Bath, as left by Allen and the Woods, was the city we see today, except for its recent sprawling suburbs—a town of an Augustan model that suggests not only the eighteenth century in its most urban mood, but gives some slight hint also of the ancient Rome that lies beneath its pavements. Landor, who knew the Latin districts below the Alps, thought that Bath looked like Florence as one sees it from the hills above the Arno, and he found a general resemblance to Italian cities. We feel something of this ourselves, although the most concrete evidence that we can muster lies in the position of the Abbey. Unlike the majority of English churches, it possesses no lawn or garden but rises directly from the pavements of a crowded district. A typical English church is reared softly behind a convent wall. In Italy, on the contrary, the churches are cheek by jowl with shops and tenements at the center of densest living. In England a church is usually a somewhat haughty aristocrat that does not mingle in the crowd. In Italy it is a boon companion of the poor; and, more convenient in location, its steps are worn to a deeper rut. In this contrast we may discover a reason why few heresies break out southward of the Alps.

A hint of Italy—of Tuscany, perhaps—lies also in the streets of Bath; but it is Tuscany in its noblest mood. Compare these streets with those of other English cathedral towns and you will catch our meaning. The streets of Canterbury, for instance, are in a huddle, with a wiggle of lanes between them, as if every path of traffic had been squeezed by the city's mediaeval walls. Canterbury is a town of gargoyles and grotesque beauty, of disordered growth rising out of freedom. Its streets are picturesque ragamuffins that seem gathered for a circus or a fire; and, in their eagerness to push in close, they have shoved the buildings out of line. But while Bath's streets are also conscious of a lack of room, they haughtily decline to be crowded or to rub shoulders with their inferiors. Bath shows the control of a despot, rather than free growth, and Allen was its Lorenzo. Every square and crescent of Bath possesses the perfect manners of the court. Even its narrow lanes can curtsy and take snuff.

A list of the personages who visited Bath in the century of its prosperity would be as dull as the catalogue of ships that fought at Troy. Every one of any note came here at least for a single season. No one prominent in the world of politics, of fashion or of letters confesses in his diary that he neglected Bath entirely. The bronze plates on the houses of the squares and crescents are chapters from Imperial history—footnotes, as it were, that here its heroes rested for a bit between their discoveries, their battles and their adventures. To walk through the streets of Bath and read these plates is like thumbing an encyclopaedia and turning up familiar names. Each district is a hard assignment to a schoolboy—what did Fielding write, and who was Pepys? Any one who could have lived in Bath continuously for these last two hundred years would have seen the complete procession of England's national biography. Delete Bath from the chronicles of England's worthies and many chapters would be missing—strange lapses like the lost years of Shakespeare.

There is an ample record of this in the novels and prose of the eighteenth century. We know Bath from Smollett, Jane Austen, Fielding, Sheridan, Goldsmith, Pepys, Burney,

Steele, Boswell, Anstey. Make the list as long as you will, many names will be omitted. For ourselves we shall always see Bath through the eyes of Mr. Pickwick and Sam Weller, through the letters of Humphrey Clinker and the adventures of Bob Acres, who fought his cowardly duel in the meadows by the river. But each reader will have his favorite cicerone.

England's greatest provincial theatre was once in Bath. And fame here meant equal fame in London, for its good report was carried home by fashion's birds of passage. Elizabethan companies and the strollers of the seventeenth centuries had acted in stables. It is probable, but unproved, that Shakespeare appeared on the stage at Bath in the summer of 1593 when plague had closed the London theatres; for it is known that his company—Lord Strange's Company of Actors—came to Bath "where the infection was not." Whether Shakespeare was with them on this trip is not entirely sure, although learned articles have been written to prove it so. There is a supposed reference to Bath in two of his later sonnets—mentioning "a dateless lively heat . . . a seething bath, which yet men prove against strange maladies a sovereign cure." That he visited Bath seems likely from a couplet of this sonnet:

> I, sick withal, the help of bath desired,
> And thither hied, a sad distemper'd guest.

This reference, of course, might have been to the hot springs of Tunbridge Wells; but the reference is interesting, for it shows that Shakespeare, on one occasion at least, took waters to be cured.

It was not until the year 1705 that the first real theatre was built at Bath. In 1747 a building of monumental proportions followed, and it was here that Bath's great dramatic tradition was born and prospered. Henderson, second only to Garrick in fame, played here. Siddons, still young and dismissed from Drury Lane, made her first success at Bath, to reign thenceforth as England's foremost tragic actress. "Hard labour indeed it was," she wrote, "for, after the rehearsal at Bath, and on a Monday morning, I had to go and act at Bristol on the evening of the same day, and reaching Bath again, after a drive of twelve miles, I was obliged to represent some fatiguing part on the Tuesday evening."

Macready and Edmund Kean, John Philip Kemble and Charles Mathews, played at Bath. Every one played here—names still famous like those of Elliston and Mrs. Jordan, Munden and Grimaldi, the clown, and a hundred others whose once bright fame time has tarnished. Bath's Theatre Royal, all through the eighteenth century and in the first years of the nineteenth, stood next in fame to Drury Lane and Covent Garden, and was a cradle of England's dramatic genius. In the corridors today, outside the Assembly Rooms, we can see the portraits and the playbills of those mighty years.

The Saxon Church
Bradford -

LIV. WE SPEND A WEEK IN BATH

WE FOUND the Pump Hotel entirely to our liking. Although the building is not old—a mere upstart, hardly ready for a crutch—it fits antiquity, just as now and then a younger person can sit among his ancients without the raw betrayal of his youth. We were given an excellent room that looked out upon the great bath—a view that was of Rome, of the northern renaissance and of the eighteenth century, punctuated here and there upon the pavement by a tourist's modern golf-pants. Yet all were blended to a single delightful pattern that pleased the eye.

If our diary were not already too long, we would indulge ourselves with a full description of the ancient ladies and gentlemen who sat evenings in the lounge of the Pump Hotel. There were heavy ladies in lavender and old lace who employed their lorgnettes upon a stranger. Gentlemen of hardened arteries and bulging waistcoats relied on wrinkled servants to get them deposited in an easy-chair. Yo ho, now altogether! Bump! And there was a sprinkling

of youth, just turned sixty, who merely suffered from gout
and took the waters for a cure.

I fancy that our hotel's clientele was both aristocratic and
rich; and that their grandsires' grandsires had gathered here
when Richard Nash was living and ruled the ballroom.
These lace fans surely, on this draughty night, could not
have been fetched in merely to create a breeze. They were
used rather, as I choose to think, for sly glances above their
tops at wealthy old Diabetes writing letters in the corner.
When our small orchestra began its initial tune, I thought
I detected a wiggling of these ancient toes. As for those letters in the corner, I have no doubt they were concluded
"your obliged obedient servant" as was the fashion years
ago.

On the tables of the dining-room, in addition to tall boxes
of Bath biscuits, there were special diets such as anaemia or
kidney trouble demanded—little messes of health food,
things concocted out of bran, stewed fruit on a doctor's
order, sweets that were tempered to a shorn digestion. Old
ladies, too modestly delicate for real chewing, lodged a bite
behind their teeth, looked all around the room for a private
moment, and gurgled the morsel down. There were thickly
powdered widows and salty-tempered bachelors who guarded
their remaining freedom against loose smiles.

England's youthful wealth and fashion depart, I believe,
for continental pleasures at St. Sebastian and the Italian
Lido. We must suppose, therefore, that our Pump Room
clientele once, many years ago, had endured the mistral and
spaghetti and that they did not like them. Now certainly
they despised a Channel crossing and were British to the
core. They were a silken refuse, as we might say, that declined to float southwards with fashion's tides, and lay
stranded here like a rim of ancient seaweed on the dry
edges of pleasure's beach.

These old ladies and gentlemen should have dealt out

hands at basset or at omber or at some such game as Pope mentions in his poems. The ladies should have suffered from the vapors, like the pretty women of Joseph Addison. In actual fact, I have no doubt but that each old lady moved among the shops all morning, with a servant to hand her to her motor, that she took the warm chalybeate at eleven o'clock in the Pump Room, retired to a beauty sleep after lunch, and emerged in lavender for tea. Another change, and she was still in lavender for dinner and the evening. There was no lack of petticoats at our hotel. Each lady was wopsed in them. It was Roger de Coverley who always wore the style of dress that had been in fashion when a certain widow had repulsed him; and perhaps these old ladies of the Pump Hotel kept to the vogue of their youthful conquests.

Only once did a youthful breeze blow across the lounge. This wind sprang up at the coming of the Australian polo players. On that night, while their bags were being piled about the porter's door, there was a sudden racket of fresh voices that drove old gentlemen to bury themselves in the *Morning Post*. It was in vain that stiff lorgnettes strove to stare the newcomers down. On this night our ancient seaweed was much ruffled and tossed about, but it clung like a limpet to its easy-chairs until the orchestra had sawed its final tune and had gone to bed.

We went to the theatre in Bath. But our thoughts were set on Kean and Siddons, and the tawdry ill-acted farce was beneath contempt. We had hoped, at least, that the building would be of an ancient grandeur; and in that too we were disappointed, for it was of flimsy material and cheap decoration. It was the kind of theatre that advertises on its curtain all the merchants of the town—one in which a visiting Hamlet would be mingled between the acts when the asbestos was down with beauty parlors and a local chemist's cures for chilblains and a sour digestion. Lear's tragedy must have concluded with "*Bevo* for fatigue." We saw a *talkie* out of

Hollywood; nor did this match the solemn Augustan house-fronts.

We took the waters for the taste of warm flatirons that Sam Weller so disliked. We were served by a pretty girl in uniform, and Mary made a sketch of her. We explored the Great Bath and its litter left by Rome. We looked at the theatrical pictures in the hallways of the Pump House and read the old playbills. We walked in the Circus in search of the door from which the valorous Mr. Dowler chased the night-shirted Mr. Pickwick. We stood in Queen's Square and tried to remember which heroine of Jane Austen's disliked it as being out of fashion. We strolled on the North Parade and looked for Sir Lucius O'Trigger. We saw a variety show in the fields where once Bob Acres fought his duel. We spent time in old book-shops. We read bronze plates. We climbed the hills and looked down on Bath; and from these hills we saw the same city, except for its suburbs, that Smollett saw and Goldsmith and Beau Nash. We shopped, finally, for English wool; and I was almost persuaded to buy a pair of flannel trousers that wrapped themselves around my chest to the complete confusion of my belt and what the English call my braces.

Our chief excursion out of town was by a public bus to Bradford to see its ancient bridge and Saxon church. This church is said to be the oldest church made completely of stone to be now standing in England. Certain authorities put its construction as early as the year 700 and others as of the tenth century. It is a small building, rather lofty for its horizontal dimensions, and is disfigured by two modern buttresses. A best view is, therefore, from the north. The church now stands out prominently on a hillside; but it was once so crowded by stables and houses, so overgrown with ivy, that the original use of the building was forgotten. A deed of the year 1715 called it "a skull-house" and it was then used for the storage of bones that were disturbed by new burials in the graveyard. It was only in 1871 that this despised building was discovered to be one of England's most priceless treasures. Mary made a sketch of it from a friendly neighbor's garden.

We saw Bradford's famous tithe barn, its parish church and its bridge across the Avon, a dog swimming in the river

Taking the Waters,
Bath –

that engaged us for an hour, with our lazy elbows on the stone coping of the bridge. On this bridge there is a small stone structure, and one would like to think it an ancient chapel. It proves to be, however, the town lock-up of the seventeenth century. "John Wesley," says our guidebook, "was forced to spend a night in this uncomfortable lodging." Good Methodists, at least, will know that he was not drunk.

Here at Bradford, while Mary was sketching, I talked

with the attendant of a small reading-room whose sign had caught my eye. The room was supported by a society formed for spreading the gospel that all the Saxon peoples are descended from the tribe of Juda, and that all Hebraic prophecies of paradise referred to England. The lady in attendance loaded me with a dozen pamphlets to support this assertion and a chart from King David to King George V. She was a friendly soul and she asked me to help spread her gospel to America. Fifteen minutes later I was standing on the old bridge, when this woman's son came on a trot with a copy of another pamphlet, "The True Purpose of the Great Pyramid." It was a long document filled with measurements inside and out, to prove again that George and David were distant cousins.

It was almost twilight when we jounced back to Bath—at first above the wide valley of the Avon, then at the side of a wooded gorge, until the old city lay below at the bending of the stream.

And now, on June 6th, our journey starts towards our ship at Southampton.

-Salisbury Cathedral-

LV. WE SEE THE DISTANT LIGHTS
OF CHERBOURG

LIGHT thickens in the dusk of winter as I finish this record of an English spring. The bare poplar at my window
echoes faintly Boscastle's noisy tide, the wind that stirred
the grass of Devon moorland. Memories of snug firesides
dance in the fall of snowflakes. One chapter more and we
shall finish.

A glimpse of Winchester and its cathedral close, its ancient
college hallways vibrant with young life—a hasty day at
Salisbury in search of Trollope's warden. Then came Southampton last of all.

It had been our intention to spend a final week on the
Isle of Wight; and as a preliminary to our visit, we em-
barked on a boat down Southampton Water. We met a

Scotswoman standing at the rail. She had been living on the Isle of Wight ten months, having taken the word of her physician that it was filled with sunshine.

"Indeed, yes," I said bitterly, turning up my collar and unreefing my umbrella, "that is its great charm."

"Indeed, no," she answered. "I've been in a cold fog most of the time. I'm just waiting for the end of my lease to escape home to Edinburgh." She shivered. "And I hope that I shall last that long."

We found Cowes, the chief city of the island, cold and wet and empty. We walked up the beach and then ate lunch in a desolate pavilion beside the water. Sir Thomas Lipton's yacht was lying in the inner harbor, and the giant *Bremen* of the German Line was anchored outside. They both looked chilly in the fog. We hired a motor and drove to Carisbrooke. We walked around the castle's rampart. It was somewhere hereabouts that Keats once wrote a poem, but he must have worn his tall galoshes. On our return to Cowes we saw something through the mist that our driver told us was Osborne House—"A residence of the old queen," he said.

On entering the docks of Southampton, we saw the steamship *Majestic* lying in her berth.

"When does she sail?" I asked the hotel porter.

"Tomorrow," he answered.

The morrow dawned cold, with rain on the windows in a monotonous patter. After breakfast I walked to the White Star Line's office and bought tickets for the *Majestic*. Before lunch we lifted our old umbrella for a last time and climbed aboard. There was a fog hanging on Southampton Water, and it dripped upon our decks as if the ship were weeping for a change of weather. But down in our cabin the umbrella rested from its labor.

And now night settled on the Channel, while far ahead were the lights of Cherbourg.

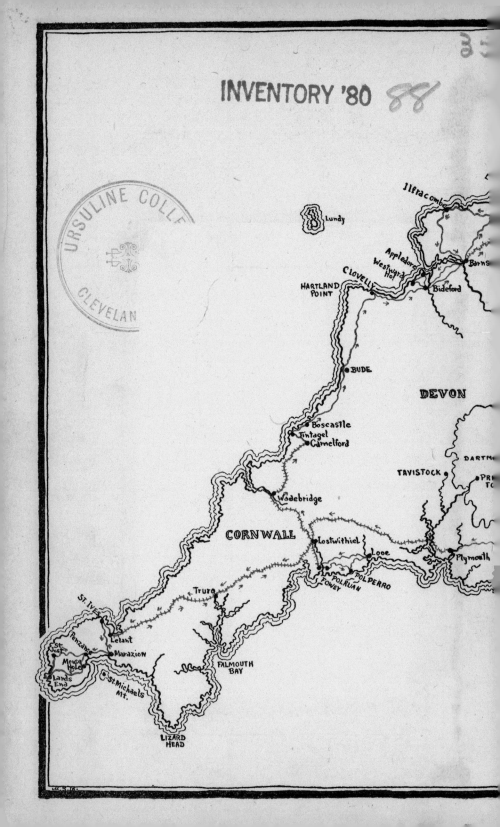